SURPASSING WIT:
Oliver St John Gogarty, his Poetry and his Prose

ERRATA

P. 28, l. 9, read Gargantua'.)

P. 62, l. 12, read Like speech that breaks in a laugh . . .

P. 63, l. 22, read pays tribute

P. 65, ll. 3, 6; p. 89, l. 36, read *Hyperthuleana*

P. 73, l. 32, read effects for efforts

P. 77, l. 19, read rooted blossomer

P. 82, l. 24, read leads for lends

P. 83. l. 4, read Merging the Seeker and the Quest?

P. 136, l. 3, for by 'A.K.' etc., read 'A.K.,' who did the review, was clearly all at sea.

P. 138, l. 24, read supernaturalistic naturalist

P. 144, l. 23, read Patrick's aristocratic qualities

P. 171, l. 6, read four works

P. 216, ll. 12–13, read And in the fields beyond / The ducks upon the pond

James F. Carens

SURPASSING WIT

Oliver St John Gogarty, his Poetry and his Prose

I gaze until my mind is naught
But wonderful and wordless thought!
Till, suddenly, surpassing wit,
Spontaneous meadows spring in it . . .

Fresh Fields

COLUMBIA UNIVERSITY PRESS
NEW YORK   1979

Library of Congress Cataloging in Publication Data

Carens, James Francis, 1927–
  Surpassing wit.

  Bibliography: p.253
  Includes index.
  1. Gogarty, Oliver St. John, 1878–1957—Criticism
and interpretation.   I. Title.
PR6013.028Z58 1979   821'.9'12   78-12644
ISBN 0-231-04642-1

318499

For Oliver Duane Gogarty

in appreciation for his generous encouragement
and because in his speech
I have heard the living accent of the Gogarty wit

Contents

Acknowledgments

I wish to express my appreciation to all those who have assisted me in gathering essential information for this book, to those who have given me access to unpublished letters and manuscripts, and to those who have granted me and my publishers permission to use copyright matter. My sincere thanks are therefore due to the Ellen Clark Bertrand Library, Bucknell University; the Lockwood Memorial Library, State University of New York at Buffalo; the Colby College Library; the Olin Library, Cornell University; the Devin-Adair Company; Faber and Faber Ltd; Mr Grattan Freyer; Mr Richard Gregory and the Gregory Estate; Harcourt, Brace, Jovanovich; the Houghton Library, Harvard University; the Morris Library, Southern Illinois University at Carbondale; the Macmillan Company of London and Basingstoke; the Macmillan Co. Inc., New York; the Otto G. Richter Library, University of Miami; the National Library of Ireland; the Henry W. and Albert A. Berg Collection, New York Public Library; the Oxford University Press; the Stanford University Libraries; the George Arents Research Library, Syracuse University; the Humanities Research Center, University of Texas at Austin; Trinity College Library, Dublin; the Viking Press, New York; and Anne and Michael Yeats.

To Dr J. B. Lyons my thanks for numerous collegial exchanges. To P. L. Travers my great appreciation for her responsive and illuminating correspondence. I should like also to express my particular gratitude to Senator Michael Yeats; and to Mr Oliver D. Gogarty, S. C., son of Oliver St John, who has really made this study possible, my profound gratitude.

Introduction

BUCK MULLIGAN, THE WITTY DOCTOR, SENATOR GOGARTY, AND OLIVER ST JOHN GOGARTY, POET

GIVEN his unusual versatility and the nature of his literary associations, it might be expected that the place of Oliver St John Gogarty among early modern writers would be an established fact of literary criticism and literary history. Given too the vividness of his personality and the intensity of his impact on other writers and artists, one might assume that it would be relatively easy to characterise Gogarty. After all, he puts in an appearance in a dazzling number of reminiscences, memoirs, autobiographies, biographies, notebooks, and letters; and when he appears, Gogarty is never dull, always provocative—loquacious, opinionated, sometimes cruelly satirical but just as often more engagingly witty, frequently kind, generous, and gracious. Ulick O'Connor's biography of Gogarty, written with zest and admiration, filled with amusing stories of the Gogarty wit that still circulate in Dublin, surely suggests something of the crowded life and imaginative range of its subject, though there are such *lacunae* even in O'Connor's crowded book, the only 'life' we have, that Gogarty seems to elude us even as we gain a sense of his many-sidedness.

In his youth, journalist, medical student, classical scholar, cyclist, and swimmer; then, Sinn Feiner, associate of Free State leaders Arthur Griffith and Michael Collins; nose and throat specialist and surgeon in Dublin for twenty years or more and in London, too, towards the end of his practice; archer, horseman, and aviator; a Senator for more than a decade and the most outspoken and flamboyant critic of de Valera, during the thirties, when sheer drabness seemed to have settled permanently on Ireland; at the age of sixty-one, an expatriate who became a lecturer, a journalist once more, a New Yorker, and an American citizen: Oliver Gogarty crammed a dozen lives into one.

He was, moreover, a very talented and very complex man. That so many exceptional people should give us fascinating and contradictory interpretations of his character attests to that complexity. In an early notebook, James Joyce ticked off an extensive list of what he regarded as Gogarty's shortcomings and vices. Among Joyce's most devastating indictments were the following, the second of which seems to identify Gogarty with Mephistopheles, the eternal spirit of negation: 'His coarseness of speech is the mask of his cowardice of spirit. . . . Heaven and earth shall pass away but his false spirit shall not pass away.'[1] Yet James Starkey (or Seumas O'Sullivan as he called himself) who visited the famous Martello Tower both before and after Joyce's outraged departure from it, addressed the following lines to Gogarty:

> Gogarty when I think that you and I
> On these same rocks, under the self-same sky
> Lay all day naked while the mirrored sun
> Beat on us from the blue, till we grew one
> With all that cloudless world of sea and land;
> Now there is no blue anywhere
> And Gogarty thus I have come to know
> There is no way henceforth that we must go
> There is no path whatever we must tread
> But each will find the other by his side
> Within the call of silence . . .

And Starkey continued:

> I know I will remember even as now
> The courage of the heart I knew, the brow
> Bright still with some unrisen sun of hope
> I will remember these and I will grope
> Even in the darkness, I will stretch my hand
> And find you there; . . .[2]

Other observers offer perceptions of Gogarty that further complicate our sense of him. 'To sit at dinner with Oliver Gogarty', wrote Lord Dunsany, 'is to be entertained by the many personalities which he will assume in the course of the evening.'[3] Lady Dunsany described Gogarty as a 'charming flibbertigibbet'.[4] Sir William Rothenstein saw him as 'an intellectual aristocrat . . . glorying in the Aristophanic spirit of which . . . he has a noble portion'.[5] Of him, James Stephens once said, 'Joyce made him out a terrific snob. Of course he is, but a brilliant mind.'[6] Another gifted poet, W. R. Rodgers, attributed to Gogarty, 'The kindest heart in Dublin and the dirtiest tongue'; and Rodgers believed him to be 'the most generous man' he ever met.[7] In Monk Gibbon's petulant book on Yeats, Gogarty is the bawdy-talking, calculating villain; in *The Jerome Connection*, a book of memoirs by Winston Churchill's cousin, Seymour Leslie, Gogarty is a waggish, high-spirited practical joker. In Lady Gregory's *Journal,* this man (who later had some sharp things to say about Lady Gregory's plays) is 'kind Gogarty'.[8] In the painter Augustus John's *Chiaroscura*, he is, like the artist himself, a Renaissance man *manqué*. In one of Yeats's letters to Olivia Shakespear (10 July 1917), Gogarty is 'the witty doctor' in whose company there is 'a whirl of excellent talk'.[9] Years later, in a number of the letters written to Dorothy Wellesley during the last years of his life, it is apparent that Yeats's sense of Gogarty has deepened. The latter has become for him a heroic adventurer.[10]

It would be the easiest thing in the world to say that such a man was a chameleon, taking colour from his surroundings; it might be tempting to say that he was so volatile that he must remain forever as elusive as quicksilver. To be true to the substance of the evidence, however, I think one has to recognise that Gogarty's nature was as multifarious as his interests, and as paradoxical as much of what he wrote.

In the opening chapter of *Ulysses*, where James Joyce depicted Gogarty as the character Malachi Roland (Buck) Mulligan, we hear Mulligan, quoting Walt Whitman and alluding to Graeco-Roman mythology, exclaim, 'Do I contradict myself? Very well then, I contradict myself. Mercurial Malachi.'[11] Quite possibly that quotation from Whitman is one Joyce actually heard from Gogarty, many of whose words, notions, and inventions appear in the novel. The lines from 'Song of Myself', together with the allusion to the flashing messenger of the gods, suggest Mulligan's volatility and Joyce's sense of inconstancy in the nature of the former friend upon whom he based the character. But Whitman follows the line Mulligan quotes with an aside, one of the utmost importance in the poem—'(I am large, I contain multitudes.)'— which suggests that oppositions and contradictions may be reconciled within the individual being, as Joyce himself implied in both

Ulysses and *Finnegans Wake*. Actually there *were* conflicting forces in Gogarty, or conflicts that he experienced. By 1905, for instance, he could describe himself as one who worshipped nature and yet also evoke Platonist notions: 'One becomes many, God becomes man, Being becomes appearance, the Root puts into leaf. . . . This is the mystery of the world: The Soul makes the Body.'[12] On the basis of this paradox, he was able to claim both the natural order and a supernature. Looked at from a variety of perspectives, Gogarty embraces as many contradictions or oppositions, but surely his aim was to reconcile them.

Born in 1878, the son of Dr Henry Gogarty, a County Meath man with a practice in Dublin, and of Margaret Oliver of Galway, Ireland's western port, he was of the Catholic majority of Ireland but of its small professional class.[13] Prepared for the university at Catholic schools, he first attended the National University, a Catholic institution, and then abandoned its medical school for additional study at Trinity College, bastion of the Protestant ascendancy. Following a year at Oxford, he returned to Trinity to undertake medical training, and then chafed under the requirements of medical study. He would rather have devoted himself to poetry. Indulging in a fantasy of escape, he wrote to a friend in 1906, 'On the first opportunity that offers I shall precipitately depart to and remain in some southern watering place on the chance of a livelihood from visiting invalids who come without a doctor held in fee. Life is so short and Art so long there is no time to lose.'[14] Yet though he despised 'money making as an end in itself',[15] he knew that he could not dismiss it as a means, that he needed it to live as he wished; and then he proceeded to qualify for medicine in as leisurely—and, at times, as riotous—a fashion as possible.

Fascinated by the low life of Dublin, which he came to observe at first hand during his years of medical study, he was equally at home in the company of the Trinity classical scholars and wits, J. P. Mahaffy and R. Y. Tyrrell, who introduced him to the language and literature of Greece and revealed to him the pleasures of Latin poetry, very nearly destroyed by public school drill in grammar. If he alienated Joyce—and was alienated by him—he was able to be on terms of close friendship with such leading figures of the Literary Renaissance as Yeats, George Moore, and AE (George Russell), and that despite the rivalries among them.

Influenced and instructed by Yeats and developing over the years an irreverent but profound admiration for 'the Archpoet', Gogarty nevertheless dismissed, from the turn of the century on, what he regarded as the 'folk-smoke' of Synge and despised the 'peasant' aspect of the Abbey Theatre, which seemed to him a celebration of the lowest common denominator.[16] He would be Irish, he seemed to insist, and classical too, just as he would enjoy his associations with Yeats, Moore, Russell and others such as James Stephens and Seumas O'Sullivan and, at the same time, exchange poems, jokes, and gossip with literary men from the Anglo-Irish aristocracy like Lord Dunsany and Sir Shane Leslie. In effect, Gogarty was discovering that he could embrace all of Dublin, from the kips to the literary salons, from the pubs frequented by the city's intelligentsia and eccentrics to the operating arena—and play a role, too, in his country's very different literary sets.

Dionysian in spirit, early in his career he could urge a sedate friend like G. K. A. Bell to 'binge'[17] and he was suspected by Stanislaus Joyce of leading his brother, James, to drink.[18] He would urge the painter, Augustus John, Dionysian himself, and idealised by Gogarty into a principle of male energy, on visits to Ireland to 'Float your intellect!'[19] In 1941, Gogarty told Horace Reynolds, whose notes do not reveal to what period the former referred, that 'For two years I drank three bottles of Jameson a day.'[20] Whether one is to credit so stupendous a feat to an extraordinary constitution or an extraordinary imagination, it would appear from the testimony of his friends that Gogarty could hold what he took better than other men could. Padraic Colum tells us, 'Joyce had a physical weakness that needed it, whereas Gogarty was a hundred per cent fit, he didn't need drink, and he was rather contemptuous of the way Joyce took his liquor.'[21] Whatever Gogarty's drinking feats may have been in his heyday, in his late sixties, according to a friend, he could, reminded of a gift he wanted to present, sprint down the street, up into his Manhattan apartment, and then return, still sprinting and yet unwinded, to the astonishment of his companions.[22]

A close associate of Arthur Griffith, a contributor to his newspaper *Sinn Fein*, a supporter of Sinn Fein policies, once Ireland had its independence Gogarty became a foe of the narrow and puritanical nationalism that ensued. At the height of that reaction, as a member of the Irish Senate, he continued to disdain, publicly and volubly, as he had at the turn of the century, the revival of Gaelic as a bogus effort and to insist upon the importance of the English literary tradition and of Ireland's relation to Europe. A doctor with no disdain for matter or material being, he held progressive views on preventive medicine and on the relationship between disease and social conditions. But throughout his later life he heaped ridicule on such modern figures as Freud and Einstein, for offering what seemed to him schematic, rigid, and abstract versions of reality. The modern myths of science he repudiated for the myths of the imagination and spirit.

And then there is the oddest paradox of all: it is that for a man who lived so public a life, played so many roles, and contributed so enthusiastically to the legend he became, Gogarty very firmly drew lines in what he wrote beyond which he would not permit the public or his readers to pass. His poetry, even when occasional and however deeply felt, is the furthest thing one can imagine from the confessional mode that has emerged in the United States during the past decade and a half; and much of his own most personal and private experience never even entered into his 'autobiographical' works. 'Beyond Reynold's Introduction to my book of verse," he wrote in 1941, 'there are hardly any facts of my life which would be of interest—hardly to myself even now that they are parcels and portions of the survived past.'[23] And it was altogether characteristic of him that in the very year he published his autobiography, indicating, *en passant*, no great enthusiasm for an unnamed English Jesuit school to which he was sent as a boy, he should have written to an American editor: 'My only regret is that you give my school, Stonyhurst, the publicity that your publication[s] commands. That school was the scene of such unhappiness that I accepted unhappiness as the norm! I have never mentioned it to anyone. It is amusing that you heard of it! Stonyhurst the Accursed.'[24]

Had this paradoxical man not turned to poetry and various forms of fiction, it seems likely that he would have left his mark upon his time—in journalism, in medicine, in politics, to each of which he devoted part of his life. But he lived in Dublin during the height of the scarcely believable efflorescence of genius that we speak of as the Irish Literary Renaissance. Perceptive and receptive; sensitive, ambitious, bold to recklessness at times; in love with words, colourful people, and natural scenery; he could not but respond to the cultural atmosphere that produced in a brief time span Oscar Wilde, George Moore, J. M. Synge, G. B. Shaw, W. B. Yeats, Augusta Gregory, James Stephens, James Joyce, Sean O'Casey, Liam O'Flaherty, Frank O'Connor, Sean O'Faolain, Flann O'Brien, Samuel Beckett, and many lesser talents.

With the exception of Wilde (whose wit and social elegance he admired and imitated) Gogarty knew most of these figures well. Indeed, several of them with whom he was closely associated made substantial contributions to the 'myth' of Oliver Gogarty. George Moore first appropriated his name and essential aspects of his character in a masterly short novel *The Lake* (1905), in which the hero experiences a conflict between emotional impulse and social convention—as did Gogarty, though he opted for the respectability of a career in medicine. Going even further in *Salve*, the second volume of the trilogy he eventually termed *Hail and Farewell* (1911), Moore further contributed to the legend of the doctor. In his brilliant characterisation, he depicted the younger man as 'the arch-mocker, the author of all the jokes that enable us to live in Dublin . . . author of the Limericks of the Golden Age' and he emphasised the joyous Rabelaisian qualities of his friend.[25] Decades later, William Butler Yeats was to heighten the mythicisation of Oliver Gogarty, in his Introduction to the *Oxford Book of Modern Verse* (wherein he makes Gogarty a symbol of freedom, ease, and power in art), in his BBC address on Modern Poetry, and in one of his last poems. Both in the Oxford 'Introduction' and in the lyric 'High Talk', Yeats sees Gogarty's gaiety and wit as the comic and defiant gestures of a contemporary artist. In 'High Talk', Gogarty, dubbed Malachi Stilt-Jack in a reference to Joyce's Malachi Mulligan and a verbal play on St John, is conscious of a heroic past and at war with a banal present to which he will not submit. An early version of Gogarty's poem 'Colophon' which Yeats surely saw—'While the Tragedy's afoot / Let us stalk in the high boot'—contributed a key word 'stalk' and the image of height to the poem.[26] 'Colophon' also contributed to Yeats's contrast between a tragic and a comic view:

Processions that lack high stilts have nothing that catches the
eye.
What if my great-granddad had a pair that were twenty foot
high,

And mine but fifteen foot, no modern stalks upon higher,
Some rogue of the world stole them to patch up a fence or a fire.
Because piebald ponies, led bears, caged lions, make but poor
shows,
Because children demand Daddy-long-legs upon his timber toes;
Because women in the upper storeys demand a face at the pane,
That patching old heels they may shriek, I take to chisel and
plane.

Malachi Stilt-Jack am I, whatever I learned has run wild,
From collar to collar, from stilt to stilt, from father to child.
All metaphor, Malachi, stilts and all. A barnacle goose
Far up in the stretches of the night; night splits and the dawn
breaks loose;
I, through the terrible novelty of light, stalk on, stalk on,
Those great sea horses bare their teeth and laugh at the dawn.[27]

It is not surprising that Yeats should have seen Gogarty in so
symbolic a way, as the comic counterpart of the tragic rebels of the
1890s, for the two men shared many attitudes and feelings about
modern Ireland and the levelling, vulgarising tendencies of the
modern world.

Indeed, Yeats was present on an important occasion when
Gogarty cast himself in a symbolic role. In 1923, in the midst of
the civil strife that followed the end of British rule in Ireland,
Gogarty, a prominent Senatorial supporter of the Free State
Government, was abducted by Republican gunmen, who threatened
to kill him. Whether his captors intended to murder him (as other
Senators were assassinated at the time) or merely to intimidate
him, we do not know, for Gogarty managed to escape, leaping
into the Liffey and swimming to safety. Later, in a public
ceremony, attended by Yeats and President Cosgrave, he presented
two swans to Dublin's tidal river in gratitude, and gave the title
An Offering of Swans to his first published volume of poetry,
issued by the Yeats Cuala Press in 1923.[28] This gesture of his, like
the dedicatory verses he composed, was no mere expression of subjective egotism. It was a ritual gesture by which he exorcised the
violence of the period; it was a symbolic action by which he
associated Celtic with Greek mythology, identified himself with a
cultural tradition, and projected the self into a timeless realm of

beauty. His allusion in these stanzas of the poem is to the meta-morphosis of the children of Lir:

Keep you these calm and lovely things,
    And float them on your clearest water;
For one would not disgrace a King's
    Transformed, beloved and buoyant daughter.
And with her goes this sprightly swan,
    A bird of more than royal feather
With alban beauty clothed upon:
    O keep them fair and well together.

The capacity of the early modern Irish imagination to transform personal and public experience into myth was further illustrated when Senator Gogarty, whose own efforts and those of his fellow Dubliners had already turned many of his stories, actions, and quips into legend, became the subject of a roistering ballad, based on his adventure. This is the conclusion of the ballad:

The rain came down like bullets, and the bullets came down like
                                                                rain,
As Oliver St John Gogarty the river bank did gain;
He plunged into the raging tide and swam with courage bold
Like brave Horatius long ago in the fabled days of old.

He landed and proceeded through the famous Phoenix Park;
The night was bitter cold, and what was more, extremely dark;
But Oliver St John Gogarty to this paid no regard,
Till he found himself a target for our gallant civic guard.

Cried Oliver St John Gogarty, 'A Senator am I!
The rebels I've tricked, the river I've swum, an sorra' the words
                                                                a lie.'
As they clad and fed the hero bold said the seargent with a
                                                                wink:
'Faith, thin, Oliver St John Gogarty, ye've too much bounce to
                                                                sink.'[29]

Rowdy and mock-heroic though it is, that ballad sums up essential elements in the legend that Gogarty himself helped to create and that Moore and Yeats expressed in different ways: his indestruct-ible zest for life, his aspiration towards classical and heroic values.

It happens, however, that the mythic role Gogarty devised (with some help from imaginative townsmen and from artists like Moore and Yeats) was an intensification and simplification of his actual complex being. It was consequently subject to distortion by the envious or the hostile. Moreover, the symbolic identity, by its apparent emphasis upon personal flamboyance, tended to obscure what the artist Gogarty produced in poetry and prose. Yet it is to Joyce's *Ulysses* probably more than anything else that we must attribute the fact that, even today, decades after his death, Gogarty is known more as a 'character' than as a gifted writer. And it is to *Ulysses*—initially—that one must ascribe lingering misconceptions of his nature and talent.

Soon after Joyce left Dublin in 1904, it was pretty well known in the circle of his Dublin acquaintances that he intended an unflattering portrait of his former friend in the novel he was writing.[30] Though Joyce decided not to use Gogarty in *A Portrait of the Artist as a Young Man*, it was Gogarty's fate to provide the basic ingredients (and many of the words) for one of the great comic creations of our literature. Gogarty's very words, his songs, his jokes, his parodies, even certain comic characters he invented, pervade our century's greatest novel. Though he came to loathe his identification with Buck Mulligan, Gogarty was never really to escape Joyce's characterisation of him, an interpretation of his personality significantly different from that of Yeats. It was not merely that *Ulysses* embarrassed Gogarty in a Dublin never indifferent to gossip nor that it contained buried insults many readers have never sensed, nor even that it appeared at a critical stage of Gogarty's professional and political career, but that, from 1922 on, he was to be beset by those who were unable to distinguish between the fictional and unchanging Mulligan of the novel and the real, developing, far more authentic Oliver St John Gogarty. Reflecting privately and perspicaciously, in 1933, on the difficulty of portraying Gogarty's character, Horace Reynolds wrote: 'Gogarty has been ruined as a character by too much publicity. All the publicity about stately plump Dr Gogarty will have to fade from the public memory before he becomes a fit subject for a character portrait.'[31] Modest, even diffident, about his own poetry, startlingly so for a man who exhibited so much boldness and assurance in his conduct, Gogarty had to contend throughout his mature life with the offensive notion that his talents were only those of a ribald, a mocker, and a clown. It would be inappropriate at this point to explore in detail the Daedalian maze of *Ulysses* or the more bewildering maze of Joyce criticism. Suffice it to say that while Buck Mulligan's witty sallies are a necessary relief from the sullenness of Stephen Dedalus, that while they are true in what they reveal about the sterility of Stephen and Dublin, and that while Mulligan is by no means as unattractive a figure as he is often mistaken to be, he is the closest thing to a villain in the novel and he is surely no artist. Moreover, Oliver St John Gogarty has become a villain, a gross materialist, and, necessarily, an insignificant talent for some who regard Joyce as a culture hero and who seem unable either to distinguish life from fiction or to recognise that Joyce might have been a very great writer and a desperately neurotic man, or that Gogarty, as generous as he was reckless in his youth, in his maturity was a poet and writer of substantial merit.

Richard Ellmann's massive and distinguished biography of Joyce (1959) and his later pamphlet on the Tower at Sandycove (1969) are fundamentally biased against Gogarty, the former work assuming that Buck Mulligan and Oliver St John Gogarty are indistinguishable. Even when Richard Ellmann reviewed Ulick O'Connor's biography of Gogarty in 1964, he scoffed at O'Connor's suggestion that there was compassion in Gogarty's nature. 'While Gogarty could go out of his way to explore slum conditions,' he asserted, 'his attitude was more clinical than humanitarian.'[32] If Ellmann is right, one wonders why Gogarty ever troubled to go out of his way to explore slum conditions. Why did he not, like a good clinician, simply enter the laboratory? One wonders, too, why no less than W. B. Yeats and Lady Gregory sponsored Gogarty's dramatic attack on slum conditions for performance at the Abbey—scarcely the proper stage for a clinician.

Sometimes it does no harm to look at a writer's work. At the conclusion of Gogarty's slum play, *Blight*, Dr Tumulty (the author's spokesman) and Foley, a veteran of the first World War whose family has been evicted from a tenement so as to permit the expansion of the Townsend Thanatorium and two of whose children have died in his absence—victims of the slum—confront the hospital board and what Tumulty terms the 'system that has betrayed' the returning veteran. What, it seems fair to ask, are the emotions implicit in the passage of dialogue that follows?

Norris and Tisdall: Now, a little patience—a little patience, my good man, just a little patience and you'll be heard.

Soldier: I've had enough of your patience.

Norris: Hush, hush, you are overwrought; we must make allowances for you.

Tisdall: Assuredly we will make allowances for one that fought for liberty, faced the barbarian and all—that sort of thing.

Soldier: Liberty be damned, what do I get from liberty? I haven't a house over my head! Where's my wife? Where's my poor girl? Where's my son and the baby that was born when I was away?

Norris: Dear, dear, did you lose a second child. This is unusually sad.

Tisdall: Added to the list of infantile mortality I suppose.

Soldier: The baby's dead, and that fellow there that I kept before ever he had a job, wouldn't put a hand out to save them.

Tully: It was summer diarrhea killed the baby, if ye want to know . . .

Soldier: All I know is that a curse is on you for your treatment of human beings. Ye'll be all wiped out and not one of ye left. The strong races that look after their own and that have homes to fight for will overwhelm ye. Yes! the men that's not starved into fightin' will beat hell out of ye for ye don't deserve to live the way ye treat mankind. How can ye win when you're killing your own. The curse of God is on ye all and ye'll feel it—for ye have neither sense nor pity—the curse of God is on ye all—for ye don't care. (Exit.)

Chairman: Dear, dear, not a word of gratitude, not a sign of recognition either for the kindness of the nurses or the surgical staff!

Tumulty: The tragedy is that you are all so well meaning. Can there be no reform without revolution?

Tisdall: Reform? Surely you do not mean that we are to be reformed? How are we to blame?

Tumulty: As usual where the system is rotten no one is to blame; but you are all to blame, for you are all part of charity's ineffectual farce. The only people who benefit from charity are the charitable people themselves . . . .[33]

Foley's indictment, the Board members' fatuous indifference, Tumulty's ironic reflection upon both, can have no other meaning than that social institutions are failing to meet human needs; and the dramatist's handling of the materials, unsentimental, to be sure, but surely angry, could not be further from the clinical aloofness that Ellmann ascribes to Gogarty. Our emotions are engaged for those who have suffered; our anger is directed against the failures of men and institutions.

Going further in his indictment of Gogarty on the occasion of this review, Ellmann charged that, 'His wit was heartless, and always in danger of involving him in libel suits as on one occasion it did.'[34] To be sure, Gogarty was sued for libel on the publication of *Sackville Street* and found guilty, the occasion for the suit being some lines of poetry (actually written by his friend George Redding) and a passage of prose that ridiculed members of a Dublin mercantile family. A curious feature of the case was that all of the witnesses for the plaintiff were relatives, employees, or close associates, all of whom had been urged to read the book by him. Even Samuel Beckett, who might have been taken as a representative of the wider reading public, appeared as a witness for his uncle by marriage![35] It does not seem to follow, however, either as a matter of logic or of fact that Gogarty's wit was 'always' on the edge of libel or that he was constantly threatened by lawsuits, though once a man *has* been sued for libel, there is every likelihood that others will be tempted to sue, if given the chance.[36]

In point of fact, Gogarty's wit operated on many levels on only one of which was it the punishing instrument of satire. From the time of Aristophanes to the present, satire has surely had a strong lacing of cruelty in it—indeed, often of savagery. Gogarty, like most members of the Dublin intelligentsia, was entirely capable of malice. As Conor Cruise O'Brien has written, 'Dublin's malice . . . is a constant presence, electric and reductive. It is a style, a way of going on . . . usually present as a general corrosive irreverence.'[37] It should also be said, that what distinguishes the malice of Dublin from that of most other cities is that it is so well aimed and so well expressed. Gogarty lacked neither a good eye nor a sharp tongue. Frank O'Connor tells us in *My Father's Son* that 'I couldn't help liking Gogarty, though he did make a vicious attack on me later at an Academy dinner describing me as "a country boy with hair in his nose and hair in his ears and a brief-case in his

hand." ' That description, however wounding (and however in-
appropriately reported to O'Connor), has the deadly ring of a
sharp satiric observation. It is worth noting, moreover, that
O'Connor's anecdote follows a passage in which he describes the
kindness of Gogarty in rescuing him from an unnecessary operation for malignancy of the throat: ' "Jesus Christ!" I heard him
muttering. "There are doctors in this town that don't know the
difference between cancer and a sore toe." ' And there, too, one
recognises the satirist's thrust. Even more interesting is it that
O'Connor's passage on Gogarty opens with his own report of a
sword thrust by W. B. Yeats at a Committee of his Academy of
Letters composed of himself, AE, F. R. Higgins, Lennox Robinson,
Seumas O'Sullivan, and Gogarty: 'two of whom . . . make themselves drunk and a third who came drunk from his mother's
womb.' 'The two who made themselves drunk,' O'Connor adds,
'were O'Sullivan and Robinson. . . . The one who came drunk
from his mother's womb was Oliver Gogarty.'³⁸ And there one has
the brilliant malice of Dublin—in Yeats, if one credits O'Connor's
story, and certainly in O'Connor—a part of the essential ethos of
the city and no unique Gogartian vice! Only those unsophisticated
in Dublin's ways could regard Yeats as passing an ultimate judgment on Gogarty's effervescent high spirits or even on Robinson's
drunkenness.

Make no mistake about it: Gogarty himself could indulge an
inspired capacity for invective and insult. In his personal correspondence, during his American years, as no doubt in his conversation, he pursued Mary (Molly) Colum, who was as consistently hostile to him in her criticism as in her social strategies,
with a gleeful and exhilarating malice, dubbing her 'Mollie
Coddle'³⁹ and describing her in one letter as 'one of those rancid
women who shake one's belief in the juniper berry.'⁴⁰ Gogarty's
epistolary invective against a noted political figure of the century
scarcely ever abated over the decades from the peak of 'that dago
cross between a cormorant and a corpse';⁴¹ nor did he hesitate in
public to describe the same figure as 'this Mussolini of Miseries'.⁴²
As the art historian Professor Thomas Bodkin once observed,
whatever Gogarty said of anyone he was prepared to say to their
faces, and, as Lady Hanson added, 'he encouraged a reciprocal
tongue'.⁴³ But neither invective nor sarcasm were the only instru-
ments of his satire; and just as often as he could be said to have

been purely personal in his attacks he also exercised his talent for good reasons—and these rested upon positive values that He esteemed.

Richard Ellmann's onslaught on Gogarty's character reached its climax in his review of Ulick O'Connor's biography, when he declared, 'Gogarty's inner coolness is perhaps also suggested by his embalming the bodies of his close friends Griffith and Collins, an act exceeding friendship or the calls of surgical duty.'[44] Just as one wonders how Yeats and Lady Gregory could have been so foolish as to sponsor a play on slum conditions by one who was merely clinical in his observations and lacked humanity, one wonders how two men such as Arthur Griffith and Michael Collins, both unusually gifted and each extraordinarily different from the other, could have given their friendship to one who in his inner being was so cold as Ellmann accuses Gogarty of having been. Following the death of Griffith and the assassination of Collins, the English journalist J. M. N. Jeffries wrote what was, in effect, a letter of condolence to Gogarty. In the course of that letter, he exclaimed, 'I can't get that scene altogether out of my mind—a day or so before I left Dublin—when both Collins and Griffith were in your room, Collins fondling little Brenda.'[45] Would a journalist of some professional skills have deemed such a letter appropriate, unless he felt Gogarty had been profoundly shaken by the deaths of two men he admired? And would he have evoked such an image of family intimacy as he did—to remind Gogarty of the atmosphere in his Ely Place house when the two leaders visited there—had he not sensed Gogarty's emotional commitment to his friends?

Indeed, to get at the heart of Richard Ellmann's indictment, should one not ask whether it is really true that if a doctor who has been on terms of intimate friendship with two of his nation's foremost leaders, both tragically dead at a moment of national crisis, prepares the bodies of those friends for burial, his action demonstrates heartlessness and coldness? Would it not even be possible to argue that no man *other* than Oliver Gogarty could more appropriately have prepared those bodies for entombment; that his was, in fact, an act of honour, friendship, and personal responsibility? It was to Gogarty that William Cosgrave, Griffith's successor as leader of the pro-Treaty party and shortly to be Prime Minister of the Free State, wrote, in October 1922, to determine the whereabouts of deathmasks of Collins and Griffith and to make certain that the masks were retained in Ireland.[46] Why were those masks taken and why did Cosgrave wish to preserve them? In the interests of some vulgar curiosity, some heartless coldness? Surely not. Those masks were cast, President Cosgrave sought to preserve them, for the same reason that Gogarty embalmed the bodies of his friends: two national figures had to be memorialised and honoured. If the composed skill of a medical man was needed for the task of embalming, the imagination of a stoic paying a last tribute of respect and admiration was also demanded by the occasion. Fortunately Gogarty recorded his observation of the dead Collins in a letter written to Shane Leslie after the event. And sometimes it is worth looking at the real facts of a writer's experience. Gogarty begins, certainly speaking as a scientist and making 'clinical' observations, 'I saw the wound for I embalmed him, over his right ear—a stellate fracture. There was no exit wound.' But the apparent detachment soon gives way to another tone, as the doctor reaches back imaginatively to Rome and Greece, in order to suggest the force of Collins even in death: 'There was not a blemish on his body. He was too young to be fat. We have a death mask like Caligula or that maligned aesthete, the young Nero. To see the like of it one would have to search the Greek busts in the British museum. This gives rise to the thought that those calm full round-chinned faces must have possessed great mental energy and abilities as well as athletic prowess.'[47] Taken in its entirety that passage is neither clinical nor sentimental, but it does reveal Gogarty's sense of the many talents of Collins and his immediate impulse to apotheosise him by classical and heroic association. When he wrote to the sculptor Theodore Spicer-Simson, to suggest that a bust of Collins might be appropriate, Gogarty's description of the death mask emphasised its aesthetic strengths and, once again, its classical associations: 'I have had a death mask of Collins taken, it goes back to the ears and it has turned out rather successfully. Seen with the light behind the head the full chin rolls out like a Greek face of the best period. The planes of the forehead are straight and smooth. . . . The eyes could be opened and filled as full of life and the lids half raised as if they were falling slowly during his peculiar gaze.'[48]

Of Gogarty's attitude towards Arthur Griffith, I believe that some tangible evidence and the reports of his friends and contemporaries have more to tell than does Richard Ellmann. **President** Cosgrave once observed, 'I've never known a man to idolise another as much as Gogarty idolised Griffith. He was almost mortally wounded when Griffith died, he was so very, very much attached to him.'[49] Without question when embalming Griffith's body, Gogarty approached the task with professional skill. But he had another concern too. Writing to Shane Leslie, Gogarty assured his correspondent that 'Griffith was not poisoned. I suspected it but reassured myself. It was a lesion of some vessel which flooded a ventricle of his brain.'[50] The careful medical observation of that passage is not separable from an understandable personal anxiety that motivated it. Further evidence enabling us to understand Gogarty's response to Griffith's death has been offered by Kevin O'Shiel. In fact, O'Shiel has given us a description of Gogarty that is essential to any understanding of him. In a crowd on the night of Griffith's death, O'Shiel found Gogarty, 'hard, cynical as ever, laughing . . . ten times more bitter against Griffith's enemies and opponents than ever. . . . And many people said "Extraordinary that man, a man like that was so close, he does seem to be quite unmoved." '[51] Yet O'Shiel happened also to have been present when Gogarty arrived to examine Griffith and has recorded for us the moment: 'When he was absolutely certain he was dead, Gogarty burst into tears and he walked to the window saying, "My poor Arthur, my poor Arthur." ' O'Shiel's conclusion gets at something that is essential if one is to understand Oliver Gogarty either as a man or as a writer: 'That night he had pulled the thing round to cynicism, which I called his mask, his armour.'[52] Like Wilde, like Yeats, Oliver Gogarty knew the value of a mask— for the living as well as the dead. And throughout his life, he disciplined his deepest emotions, impulses, and intuitions by assuming visages of satire, persiflage, ironic mockery, and stoic comedy.

The world of literary criticism and scholarship is one in which once a view, even an error, has been enunciated, it goes echoing down the corridors of all the literary commentaries that follow it. In his life of Joyce, Richard Ellmann seems to assume that the character Buck Mulligan (static, aesthetically speaking, however kinetic in behaviour) and the living man, Oliver Gogarty, were indistinguishable, 'Stephen's charge against Mulligan is that Mulligan is brutal and cruel,' he asserts, then adding in a note,

'Joyce completed in this character his analysis of Gogarty.'[53] In Hélène Cixous' *L'Exil de James Joyce* (1968), a tome as substantial as Ellmann's biography and substantially indebted to it, though more critical of its subject, Mme Cixous argues that Joyce was able to obtain psychological power over his associates, his 'victims', by suggesting to them that he would use them in his novels. Mme Cixous then writes 'Gogarty en particulier se sent menacé et se livre tour à tour à la flatterie et à la brutalité grincante.'[54] I think the use of the word 'brutalité' may be ascribed to the influence of Ellmann. But how do we explain what happened to the French text when translated into English? By 'brutalité' Mme Cixous may have understood and intended something like our 'crudity'. The adjective 'grincante' that she uses is, to be sure, translated only with difficulty; its sense might be something like 'setting one's teeth on edge' or 'nerve-grating'. Yet the English language text, published in 1972, reads, 'Gogarty in particular felt himself threatened and alternated between flattery and threats of violence.'[55] Now that statement is incredible. Yet how very easily we have moved from 'brutal' to 'brutalité grincante' to 'threats of violence.' The error will persist, we may be sure, and generations of naïve graduate students may be expected to describe how Gogarty—or was it Buck Mulligan?—constantly threatened Joyce with monstrous acts of violence.

But Richard Ellmann's work on Joyce rests on years of devotion to his subject, on an impressive labour of documentation, on an assured grasp of the Joycean canon. His treatment of Gogarty, though I regard it as regrettable, has to be seen in the context of his accomplishment and his commitment to Joyce. Of the work of other writers who have transmitted stereotypical notions of Gogarty or believed that as good Joyceans they must deny Shaun and commend Shem, such a defence cannot easily be entered. Recently even a relative of the Samuel Chenevix Trench who served as a basis for Haines in *Ulysses* has entered the lists to reiterate a stereotype and inform us that 'Making people look ridiculous was a well-known pastime of Gogarty's, as I learnt in my youth when I spent a few days with him at Renvyle as his guest for Christmas 1928.'[56] Proof itself of an endemic cultural malice, that statement is possibly also a useful piece of literary gossip. Still it is disconcerting to have C. E. F. Trench bluntly admit that he actually enjoyed Gogarty's ridicule as he 'spent some very entertaining hours walking up and down the strand with him'. Even more disconcerting, however, is it to have C. E. F. Trench, who is somewhat confused not only about Joyce's attitude towards Haines but about Gogarty's attitude towards Trench, tell us that 'Gogarty would have us believe that it was [his relative S. C.] Trench's eccentric behaviour that drove Joyce from the Tower.'[57] Yet in the two works by Gogarty from which he draws his muddled conclusion, C. E. F. Trench manages to ignore Gogarty's perfectly explicit description of how he fired his revolver at the pans over Joyce's head, following Trench's second nightmare, and thus caused Joyce's departure. He ignores, too, Gogarty's admission in 'James Joyce: A Portrait of the Artist' that 'To this day I am sorry for the thoughtless horseplay on such a hypersensitive and difficult friend,'[58] and his entirely frank statements in *It Isn't This Time of Year at All!* that he does not 'wish to pose as a blameless observer of my contrary friend Joyce', that he was perhaps 'wrong to try to make him genial', that Joyce must have regarded his efforts as those of 'one who wanted to master him and shape him' and that Joyce's 'constant air of reprobation and his reserves and silences annoyed me.'[59] But so fixated is C. E. F. Trench on the stereotype of Gogarty as incessant and cruel mocker and so insensitive to language that he takes Gogarty's light-hearted reference to George Russell, AE, as Sir Horace Plunkett's 'pet editor' to be an instance of Gogarty's 'evident scorn'[60] for the former, despite the innumerable passages in which Gogarty paid emotional tribute to AE. However it is worth attending to the words of an intimate of both men who knew at first hand the nature of Gogarty's friendship with AE. After AE's death Pamela Travers—wise enough to distinguish man from mask—wrote the following to Oliver Gogarty of the event she witnessed:

> You were the last person he spoke to. You will always proudly
> remember that and I shall always proudly remember how you
> came to him. I never felt more your friend than then, though
> I have often secretly praised you for your steady love of him
> that I recognised and for letting me perceive, under the galli-
> maufry, the true man in you.[61]

Even among far more critically sophisticated writers than C. E. F. Trench, and decades after Gogarty's death, one encounters a hostility to him that is very nearly personal in nature. Thus, to cite one instance, as late as 1971, one finds a Jesuit whose knowledge of Joyce's work is extensive praising an essay by the pretentious Mary Colum (who surely exploited her minimal acquaintance with Joyce for all it was worth) for its 'noble attempt to show up Gogarty's slick incompetence and jealousy'.[62] Difficult as it is to understand how Gogarty could have been at once slick and incompetent, it is more difficult to understand why Joyce (who surely knew the emotion of jealousy as intensely as any man ever did) would have been drawn to Gogarty to the extent that he was had the latter been no more than slick and incompetent.

But to pursue any further these lingering confusions, distortions, and prejudices would be fruitless. At this point, however, the words of Sean O'Faolain are so striking and cogent that they must be placed in evidence. Other tributes, both public and private, have been paid to Gogarty, but the words of a gifted writer of the generation following his seem uniquely pertinent:

> I would like to pay tribute to Oliver Gogarty. Joyce did him an immense and cruel injustice in *Ulysses* in presenting him to posterity as something approaching the nature of an insensitive lout whose only function in life was to offset the exquisite sensitivity and delicacy of Stephen Dedalus. Gogarty was a kind and sensitive man, full of verve and zest. . . . His essential nature, which nobody could ever possibly gather from *Ulysses*, was his nature as a poet—he was a fine poet—and it must have hurt him deeply that from the time *Ulysses* appeared everybody knew him as the original of Malachi Mulligan and only a very few as a poet.[63]

It would seem that it must now be possible to admire the genius of James Joyce but also to respond to the real accomplishment of Oliver Gogarty, to recognise that Gogarty was nothing like the stereotype detractors have imagined him to be, and to admit that Buck Mulligan is only a version of one of his masks, at a particular moment in his life. The man Oliver Gogarty devised a series of self-concealing masks; he was perhaps over-protective of his inner feelings. P. L. Travers has written of him recently (in a letter to me, of 3 August 1978): 'He did good by stealth and blushed to find it fame, would even vilify anybody who might say such a thing of him.' Often as Gogarty the writer introduced the admired AE into his books, never once did he depict the particulars of his final visit to his dying friend. With all the intensity of art, P. L. Travers has given a brilliant insight into the man behind the mask in that particular moment. As a young writer, welcomed by AE and his circle, she had come to know Gogarty,

> the Comus, the clown. . . . He was wonderful to talk with; to be driven by him to Glenn na Smol, Glendalough and all the homes of Hecate he took me to, was to be educated—not only in the scandal of Dublin—if there was nothing going on at the moment he would invent it, making it more hilarious and more horrendous than any fact—but also in the classics.

It was her privilege and her perception, however, to see beyond these masks. In attendance on AE in his last hours, she responded to Gogarty's wire, Tell me if I shall be in time to see my old friend? with Come quickly! She continues:

> And he was there in a few hours. He kissed my hands. 'Be ever blessed for this!' he said. Then straightened himself, already weeping, and went in. Before the door closed I saw him—the Feste, the Touchstone, the Autolycus—on his knees beside the bed, his cheek on the hand of the man who, I think, he revered more than any other.

The writer Oliver Gogarty always closed the door.

Surely now it must be possible to enjoy the dash with which Gogarty created his legend and the imaginativeness with which others enlarged and extended it, but also to turn to the poems and books Gogarty left us, recognising their paramount claim on our attention. Whatever the range of Gogarty's interests and activities, he was, above all, a poet and a maker of books. Buck Mulligan was not Oliver Gogarty; Oliver Gogarty was not Buck Mulligan. The witty doctor, the outrageous and outraged personal satirist, the flamboyant Senator, however entertaining, are now only 'parcels and portions of the survived past'. In his works, the quintessential Oliver St John Gogarty survives.

I

The Play of Wit

OLIVER St John Gogarty's first significant published poems appeared in 1904 in *Dana*, a short-lived journal edited by John Eglinton, and in *The Venture*, 1905, an annual published in London. The best of the four *Dana* poems was a short lyric 'To Stella' that opened 'Stars by the light they shed / Only are known, / Songs by the verse they wed / Time have outgrown.'[1] Like Joyce's 'Song'—opening 'My love is in a light atire / Among the apple trees / Where the gay winds do most desire / To run in companies'—which appeared about the same time in *Dana*, Gogarty's verses revealed some influence of the Elizabethan songs the two young men admired and discussed, and very little influence of the Celtic Twilight. When Gogarty, in the first issue of *Dana*, reviewed *New Songs*, a collection made by AE from poems by his young disciples—Padraic Colum, Seumas O'Sullivan, and others—he indicated, in fact, that he wanted none of what Joyce would eventually dub the 'cultic twalette'. Though he praised the skill of the versification in the small collection, he noted 'a want of full-ness of matter, of inspiration' and a 'perfection which belongs to the conservatory, an artificial perfection'.[2] His own aim, by im-plication, was not the mistiness and hush of the twilight but sub-stantial feeling and clarity of lyric form.

Less fragile than the poems Gogarty contributed to *Dana* and perhaps therefore more nearly approximating his ideal were the songs he contributed to *The Venture*. Still, Gogarty's 'My love is dark, but she is fair; / As dark as damask roses are,' is scarcely distinguishable stylistically from Joyce's contributions to *The Venture*, 'What counsel has the hooded moon' or 'Thou leanest to the shell of night'. Joyce's songs we know as parts of the *Chamber Music* suite; but of all his early songs, Gogarty preserved only his other *Venture* poem, 'Gaze on Me', which he included later in his

Collected Poems.[3] Slight though it is, 'Gaze on Me' avoids not only the melancholy of the Twilight poets but the romantic lushness of Joyce's and his own other earliest lyrics. A lacing of metaphysical wit, a suggestion of the Cavaliers, provide the first indication of the direction Gogarty's talent would eventually take:

> As gloaming brings the bending dew,
> That flowers may faint not in the sun,
> So, Lady, now your looks renew
> My heart, although it droops adown;
> And thus it may unwithered be,
> When you shall deign to smile on me.

Most of the other 'serious' verse that Gogarty produced at this point in his career was occasional in nature: poems written for the Vice-Chancellor's Prize at Trinity College, Dublin (which he won three times), the poem he submitted for the Newdigate Prize while at Oxford in 1904 (for which he was given a *proxime accessit*),[4] even some pieces produced for *Ireland*, a Dublin society magazine, in the manner of Swinburne.[5]

He obviously enjoyed doing these poems on set subjects and wanted the pocket money they provided for student revels, yet only two of the Trinity Prize Poems, 'In Memoriam: Robert Louis Stevenson' and 'Cervantes: Tercentenary of *Don Quixote*'— found at the National Library of Ireland and the British Museum respectively—and the magazine pieces have survived. The most one can say for these poems is that they gave a restive medical student a grounding in nineteenth-century poetic styles. Neither a new enthusiasm for Swinburne (chiefly important as a culture hero for Gogarty) nor a penchant for elevated public themes contributed much to the development of his style. Though he would later produce an 'Ode on the Bicentenary of the Medical School, Trinity College' (1912) and an 'Ode, Written at the Request of the Irish Government on the Revival of the Tailltean Games' (1924), the latter of which came as near to succeeding as the subject permitted, the formal public ode was not his—nor our age's—form. Late in his life he himself would observe 'I fear that the Tailltean Ode is rather tripe.'[6]

When Gogarty turned to parody of inherited forms, he was much more successful, for in parody he could exercise that play-

B

fulness of spirit from which his more enduring work would grow.
His 'Threnody on the Death of Diogenes, the Doctor's Dog',
which appeared first in a Trinity magazine and then in Arthur
Griffith's *United Irishman*, is too much an in-group joke of the
period to interest most readers now, but it amusingly parodies
Swinburne and the lisping voice of John Pentland Mahaffy, one
of Trinity's great classical scholars and a very great snob: 'When
I wambled awound / In the gwound that was Greece / I was
given that hound / By the King's little niece.'[7] 'In Haven', a
'serious' parody that appeared in *The Oxford Magazine* (March,
1906), indicated that Gogarty was learning the manner of Keats.
However, a few years later, his stay in Vienna and his discovery
of Kraft-Ebbing occasioned a funny and much better parody of
Keats: 'Much have I travelled in those realms of old / Where
many a whore in hall-doors could be seen / Of many a bonny
brothel and shebeen.' The sestet, under the influence of Kraft-
Ebbing's case histories, raises an alarming question: 'Was I quite
normal when my life began / With love that leans towards rural
sympathies, / Potent behind a cart with Mary Ann?'[8]

By the time George Moore wrote of Gogarty in *Salve*, the
doctor was famed in Dublin and elsewhere for his limericks.
Whereas Gogarty in his later works quoted Joyce limericks that
dated from the days of their friendship, with the exception of a
later and particularly brilliant limerick inspired by the elevation—
in every sense of the word—of his friend G. K. A. Bell to the
Bishopric of Chichester, he made no serious effort to preserve his
own verbal games in this form. The Bell limerick was a tour de
force of tri-syllabic rhyme:

> There was a young lady of Chichester,
> Whose curves made the Saints in their niches stir;
> Each morning at matins
> The swish of her satins
> Made the Bishop of Chichester's breeches stir.[9]

Given the way limericks travel and the elegant variations to which
they are subject, it is difficult to ascribe them with certainty; and
doubtless Gogarty forgot many of his own composition. It was
James Joyce's brother, Stanislaus, who ascribed to Gogarty the
following limerick, which captured something of the paradoxical
nature of Joyce:

There is a young fellow named Joyce,
Who possesses a sweet tenor voice.
He goes down to the kips
With a psalm on his lips
And biddeth the harlots rejoice.[10]

Facetiae such as this depend for their effect on a sharp sense of incongruity and on an equally sharp sense of phrasing. Although George Moore claimed for him the famous limerick of the dons and the swans of St John and may have been right in ascribing it to him, in a letter to Horace Reynolds of 20 September 1952, Gogarty denied that he had composed it.[11] Still, it is reassuring that he was willing to have ascribed to him such undatable and dateless classics as those mathematical lines about 'A Professor of Trinity Hall' who 'Possessed an octagonal ball' and these:

A lesbian maid of Khartoum
Took a nancy boy up to her room;
    As they turned off the light,
    She said let's get this right:
Who does what and with which and to whom?[12]

Perhaps by chance, perhaps by poetic justice in view of Gogarty's resentment of *Ulysses*, in the United States these lines were popularly transformed to open, 'There was a young fairy named Bloom.'

Probably not only the most but the best of Gogarty's earliest poetry was randy and parodic or ribald. Joyce's *Ulysses* is a storehouse of allusions to it: 'Medical Student's Song' ('So here's to copulation'), 'A Soldier Sings' ('Staboo, stabella'), 'Alfred Lawn Tennyson Sings', 'Song' ('The first was Medical Dick / The second was Medical Davy'), 'Sinbad', and 'The Song of the Cheerful (but slightly sarcastic) Jesus'.[13] Some of these songs and ribald poems, most of which survive only in bits and pieces, provide more details and motifs in Joyce's novel than has yet been fully recognised; obscene, rowdy, and wonderfully funny to all but prudes, a personally therapeutic response to medical study, a comic exorcism of the crudest facts of life, they vibrate with Gogarty's sense of the grotesque. Regrettably, he did not regard them as worth preserving, so that what has survived, has done so mostly by accident. 'Sinbad', begun as a student's mnemonic device, developed into an elaborate account of the adventures of a poxy sailor who has been so pumped full of Mercury that he is knocked unconscious by the rising and volatile liquid if he so much as stands too close to a source of heat. It survives only as a few passages quoted in *Tumbling in the Hay* and in a few additional fragments. AE once described Gogarty's 'brilliant grotesques in verse, sometimes as intricate in pattern as the ornament on the Book of Kells'. The available fragments of 'Sinbad' do suggest just such intricacy of design, as for instance :

> Oh what a wondrous paradox!
>   A sailor who escaped the rocks
> Was wrecked by going down the docks
>   When safe ashore
> And brought to light a hidden pox
>   And Hunter's sore.[14]

Known by Joyce, portions of Sinbad's 'epic' may have stimulated the imagination and retentive memory of that intricate designer, for in *Ulysses* a one-legged sailor and allusions to Sinbad figure thematically and significantly. Fortunately Gogarty's 'Cheerful Jesus' ballad, which even more than the 'Sinbad' contributed to Ulysses—to the rock-bread, substantiality-transubstantiality leit-motifs, for instance—has survived. When Horace Reynolds asked him about this poem, Gogarty—rather generously, under the circumstances—replied, 'Yes I am guilty; but it shows Joyce's mastery that no one attributed the verses to me though he quotes them almost accurately.'[15] Curiously enough, given the reputation to which *Ulysses* contributed, in a later letter, he observed, 'I am opposed to introducing blasphemy and skepticism into the world of bawdy.'[16]

Indeed, it is puzzling that Gogarty never sought to set right the way Joyce distorted his point of view by selective quotation from the 'Cheerful Jesus' ballad so that it seems, in *Ulysses*, to be only flagrantly blasphemous. The series of letters Gogarty sent to his friend G. K. A. Bell in 1904–5 reveal that he had then worked out a complex world-view far different from the scientific material-ism *Ulysses* ascribes to him and derived from diverse sources in Greek philosophy and literature, the Transcendentalism of Emer-son, Thoreau, and Whitman, the 'paganism' of Swinburne and Wilde, the more recent thought of Nietzsche and Santayana, among others. Gogarty could worship the natural order because he could regard it as the visible manifestation of the Divine Idea, or God. As early as 1903, in a signed review of Colum's *Broken Soil*, Gogarty had made perfectly explicit the grounds for his criticism of orthodox Christianity. Irish peasants, he argued, need to be taught 'hate for holiness—hate for all that tends to enslave, emasculate'.[17] As far from a crude materialism as a man could be, Gogarty was in rebellion against puritanism, against the ascetic, life-denying strain in Christianity, against institutionalised hypocrisy, against all the 'rules' devised by narrow dogmatism to prevent the fullest expression of man's being. Satire rather than bawdry, his 'Cheerful Jesus' ballad was, at heart, an attack on the Hebraic as it contrasted in his imagination with the Hellenic; an attack on the Church and the anthropomorphic (not on the divine); on the priesthood (not on priests) as emasculating, enslaving, and above all, socially reactionary:

> My methods are new and are causing surprise:
> To make the blind see I throw dust in their eyes
> To signify merely there must be a cod
> If the Commons will enter the Kingdom of God
>
> . . . .
> Whenever I enter in triumph and pass
> You will find that my triumph is due to an ass
> (And public support is a grand sinecure
> When you once get the public to pity the poor.)
>
> Then give up your cabin and ask them for bread
> And they'll give you a stone habitation instead
> With fine grounds to walk in and raincoat to wear
> And the sheep will be naked before you'll go bare.
>
> The more men are wretched the more you will rule
> But thunder out 'Sinner' to each bloody fool;
> For the Kingdom of God (that's within you) begins
> When you once make a fellow acknowledge he sins.
>
> Rebellion anticipate timely by 'Hope',
> And stories of Judas and Peter the Pope
> And you'll find that you'll never be left in the lurch
> By Children of Sorrows and Mother the Church.[18]

Audiences, even today and even Irish audiences, would not laugh at those lines, as they do, unless they recognised the string of effective and very funny satire in the doggerel beat. Gogarty's 'Cheerful Jesus' was no piece of unfocused blasphemy; it was an incisive attack on commercial Christianity.

Throughout his years in Dublin, Gogarty continued, on occasion, to produce Rabelaisian verses, and these circulated among his friends. (At some point, indeed, he produced a particularly earthy elaboration on Rabelais, 'The Getting of Gargantua'. Between the clearing of the Kips—the razing of the red light district—in 1924 and 1933, he probably wrote 'The Hay Hotel', a celebration of one hostel that survived the clearance and of the legendary kip bullies and whores once known there.[19] Two stanzas of the poem are quoted in *Tumbling in the Hay*, one of which does not even appear in two reliable typescripts, though in one of these there is an envoi and both have an added stanza and an 'apocryphal' one. Probably there was never anything like a definitive text for such poems: stanzas might be added or deleted to suit particular occasions.[20] Villonesque in spirit and form, 'The Hay Hotel' was inspired by 'A Ballad of Dead Ladies' and echoes its 'où sont les neiges d'antan':

> May Oblong's gone and Mrs Mack,
> Fresh Nellie's gone and Number Five
> Where you could get so good a back
> And drinks were so superlative.
> Of all their nights, oh man alive!
> There is not left an oyster shell.
> When greens are gone the grays will thrive;
> There's only left the Hay Hotel.

According to Gogarty, Yeats once proposed to add this *ballade* to his Cuala broadsheets, and though 'The Hay Hotel' was never produced by the Cuala Press, one can understand Yeats's interest in it as a piece of popular poetry.[21] What is appealing about 'The Hay Hotel' is the quality it shares with Villon—an awareness of the squalid that is balanced by an unsentimental acceptance of what is human. There is both nostalgia and zest in the concluding stanza of the version Horace Reynolds preserved:

Where is Piano Mary, say,
Who dwelt where Hell's gates leave the street
And all the tunes she used to play
Along your spine beneath the sheet?
She was a morsel passing sweet
And warmer than the gates of Hell.
Who tunes her now between the feet?
Go ask there at the Hay Hotel.

In *Tumbling in the Hay* Gogarty gave his fullest and most particularised account of the bizarre world of Mrs Mack and her ladies that he discovered as a medical student. There is also, in manuscript, a wildly comic account of a rumoured visit of the Prince of Wales to the house of Mrs Mack, probably written in the same period as 'The Hay Hotel', with which it shares stanza and measure. Bawdy as can be and filled with grotesque detail, 'The Old Piano Player' is a narrative of the *persona's* memories. Mrs Mack's former piano player tells how the madam, stunned by a royal visit, is transformed by the honour done her establishment: 'She grew so lady-like and stately, / and had herself so bowdler-ised / She lost her grip on things completely.' Not one to lose her grip, Fresh Nellie makes the Prince—who really only came to visit—so lively an offer that he finds he cannot refuse. Mrs Mack's sense of decorum is outraged! 'Excuse me gloves!' Said Mrs Mack; / Then whispered 'Christ, when I get after / That mouldy whure, I'll break her back.' The final words of the *ballade* are those of the old piano player himself, who reveals how true and unbowdlerised a Dubliner he is:

> . . . Good night, sweet Prince,
> Has Nellie put your back in splints;
> And will you tell the Jersey lily
> That Dublin can, at all events,
> Take London on and fuck it silly?[22]

A rowdy indecorous set of verses, 'The Old Piano Player' happens to be one of the few pieces that has survived intact to give a sense of Gogarty at his most ribald—of the Gogarty whose comic imagination entertained Joyce, Moore, and Yeats. Inasmuch as his bawdry did show a special kind of genius and he has been criticised for dismissing it, the argument he advanced to Horace Reynolds (who was permitted to gather some of the early pieces together for an unpublished selection) deserves attention. 'It would never do', he wrote, 'to have the volume cast up before his daughter for instance, in later years when they both were gathered etc.'[23] There, certainly, we have one of the important reasons why Gogarty was content to leave most of his comic poems 'underground'. If his decision was not founded on any kind of universal principle, it was not grounded in hypocrisy either, but in feelings that were entirely human and understandable. Simply stated, he did not want to embarrass his family. Before that concern is dismissed, one must reflect that the Dublin of 1908, 1918, 1928 and 1938 was not the Dublin of 1978. (Indeed Gogarty's bawdry entertained in its day precisely because it expressed what was publicly unutterable.) Furthermore, Gogarty was conscious very early in his career that the ease with which he could turn an arresting phrase, devise a ribald limerick, or dash off some scatological verses might result in his being taken, as he put it in 1904 'as a "smutster and funster" only'.[24] Aside from any familial, social, or professional concern he might have felt, there was in him always a desire that his real talents and overriding interests not be misconceived.

For though he might enjoy amusing his friends and shocking the *bourgeoisie* of the spirit, Gogarty was never satisfied with the production of *facetiae* any more than he wanted to be identified exclusively with them. For many years, therefore, because of the demands of professional training and practice, he was to be a frustrated poet. Writing to his friend Bell in 1905, about his failure to complete 'significant' projects, he exploded: 'If I could get 6 months like Colum clear for my "Beside the Ford"; if I could get a month for "Iseult in Ireland" : a week or two, for my political pantomime "The Cows", or a day for a sonnet with consecutive thinking I might do a little but not much. Meanwhile I magnify the importance of wretched scrannel things, and for wilfulness impute to them intentioned and deliberate parodies that they may never have held.'[25] A few years later, when he was about to begin practice, he described himself as one 'about to return to the distasteful occupation of a Dublin surgeon amongst Dublin surgeons' and promised to 'kick hard for the last 3 weeks of liberty left before a life-time of respectability'.[26]

Indeed, only in 1916, after a decade of medical practice, did Gogarty gather a volume of poetry. *Hyperthuleana* ('Beyond the

Beyond . . . leaving Ultima Thule in the penultimate place') is a bibliophile's treasure, for no more than twenty-five copies were printed: of these, four of the first five copies were presented to George Moore, to the painter Augustus John, and to two minor poets, Seumas O'Sullivan and Dermot Freyer.[27] Throughout much of Gogarty's life, poetry was something to be shared, a social act. During his most productive years, he was constantly jotting down verses, frequently purely occasional and topical, generally not intended for publication or regarded as finished. His correspondence with some acclaimed in their own time, with others scarcely known—with Joyce, G. K. A. Bell, Dermot Freyer, George Moore, Augustus John, Seumas O'Sullivan, James Stephens, Lord Dunsany George Redding, Hugh McDiarmid, Shane Leslie—indicates that verses were the natural and spontaneous medium of wit, satire, feelings, and friendship. Of the thirty-one poems in *Hyperthuleana* (only five of which were carried over to the *Collected Poems*) one-third were either addressed to, or dedicated to, friends.

Hyperthuleana, like *Secret Springs of Dublin Song*, which followed it in 1918, is a *jeu d'esprit*. Oliver Gogarty was not yet writing the poetry for which he will be remembered, but he was beginning to find a voice of his own and to explore compelling themes. The Muse he invokes ('To the Muse') at the beginning of this curious little book is a 'typical daughter' of 'Dublin and Dublin's lanes', which is to say that the lady is not *quite* proper:

> Flushed is your bonnie face
> Cambered your belly
> Muse, like the straying Grace
> In Botticelli.

When Gogarty addresses Seumas O'Sullivan ('To his Friend the Apothecary Poet'), he does not hesitate to prescribe the kind of verse he wishes returned, proscribing, to start with what he will not have:

> Nothing like Herbert's send me home
> (Or with it send some laudanum),
> No thought of Newman's send me back
> (Or send an aphrodisiac),
> Nor brusque and Browningesque offence
> Of poetry and commonsense.

Those rhymes are rowdy, but, in his own way, Gogarty is making a point similar to that T. S. Eliot was to make later in a series of influential essays on English poetry:

> Send me the brew that Shakespeare knew
> And Ben, and all the Mermaid crew,
> That made both soul and body well
> Ere these grew incompatible.

Beat and rime sound may be comic, but Gogarty was articulating the notion that a dissociation of poetic sensibility followed the English Renaissance and that poetry must seek a new unity of being. In requesting a remedy that would be 'translucent, not too strong' and 'have body, yet be light' he was, moreover, approaching his mature conception of poetry.

In addition to that group of addresses to friends, there is, in *Hyperthuleana*, another group of addresses—but certainly not to friends. Suggestive of Yeats's 'On Those that Hated "The Playboy of the Western World", 1907', but directed at particular characters, these satires are economical and deadly. 'To an Art Critic' is a single quatrain:

> With your regrets don't move my mirth
> That Beauty walks no more on Earth,
> For you would be revealed at once
> In your true colours as her ponce.

'To an Amphisbaenic Friend', on the other hand, does not allow a single devastating word like 'ponce' to pin its wriggling victim to the page, but builds its indictment through an amplitude of cruel and precise physical details. One passage reads:

> Long faced, squat backed, the shoulders high,
> The lashes gone from wet blue eye,
> The lip protrudes, the chin does not,
> The huddled teeth are undershot,
> Scant chestnut hair, King Billy's nose,
> Long legs and silken underclothes.
>
> You would be thought though sick with lust,
> Clean, and though undersized, robust;
> And brave! You who have puked with fear;
> And yet, though whiskey-soaked austere.

In attaching the tag 'Buck' to Mulligan-Gogarty, Joyce apparently meant to suggest his kinship with such swaggering eighteenth-century men-about-town as Buck Whalley; lines like the above suggest that Gogarty might also have found kinship with an Alexander Pope.

Like Yeats and other early modern writers, Gogarty had a vision of heroic action, a vision that began to manifest itself in certain poems of *Hyperthuleana* and was to be a central concern in his career as poet and writer. Compelled by the notion of flight—and by a fall that is not Icarian—he envisions flight in sexual terms in 'To an Aviator' :

> White-lipped confronting God,
> Pallid with insistence
> Falling, you rise again
> Raping the distance.

And in a sonnet addressed to Kasimir Dunin Markiewicz, the Polish aristocrat who married Constance Gore-Booth, he sees the Count as a Nietzschian 'centaur' and 'stallion' in conflict with the petty world around him : 'We whinge in art and ethics, you're above / Our best in painting, poetry and love.' Too conscious himself, as the letters to Bell written between 1904 and 1907 reveal, of the conflict between convention and freedom and between his profession and his literary interests, Gogarty could not evade the reality of the conflict between heroic ideality and the quotidian. The sonnet was not really his form despite the interest of the one to Markiewicz. Another in *Hyperthuleana*, 'Spirat Adhuc Amor', is clumsy until Gogarty reaches the concluding couplet. The 'problem' of the sonnet is the distance "twixt Troy and Stephen's Green'—a distance that Yeats resolved through his vision of history. As Gogarty reaches his comic conclusion, this poem comes alive :

> Yet who shall say our housemaid's evenings out
> Hold less of the romantic though she hear
> Nor stricken steeds nor armed Ajax shout,
> Nor see the tranced forest dimly lit?
> The cabmen and the soldiers still are here—
> She's twenty-one, and that makes up for it!

In 'To a Cock' Gogarty can be seen coming into his strength as a poet. Within this work, which may be found in *The Collected Poems*, tone, diction, form, and theme are so controlled as to achieve the ease he sought. The trimeter line, the eight-line stanza, the apparently casual structure of the whole, all permit him to range from Troy to the barnyard. And in the mock-heroics of the poem he finds the comic attitude he needs to suspend an ideal world in the midst of our squalid reality :

Why do you strut and crow,
And thus all gaudy go
Through squalor, with a show
That tempts derision?
. . . .
Colours of dawn and joy
That with delight destroy :
Your body all a Troy
To house desire,
. . . .
Strange that a small brown hen
Should charm you thus !

Doubtless 'The Nun's Priest's Tale' lies behind the poem, but Gogarty could no longer berate himself for any parodic dependency : whatever Chaucerian influence there may have been has been so fully assimilated that it is scarcely apparent. The poles of Gogarty's imagination move easily between classical mythology and the Ireland he knew, between the comedy of the barnyard and the torment of sexual desire :

To Semele none came,
None to each Sabine dame,
Not Hercules aflame—
Not dawn to heaven,
Came with as great a fright
As you do burning bright,
Not—for the poor hen's plight—
To Kathleen Kevin;

Further she cannot go,
She falters and lies low
Brought down by love, a throe
That throws us all;

Soon to be scaled and hacked
And, like a city, sacked
With nothing left intact
Within the wall.

In those lines Gogarty's friend William Butler Yeats found a
suggestion—indeed 'the burning roof and tower'—that worked
upon his imagination as he composed his great sonnet 'Leda and
the Swan'. But even were it not for this distinction, 'To a Cock'
shows how Gogarty's imagination could juxtapose the ordinary
and the heroic through fantasy and wit. Writing to him decades
later about another collection of poems, L. A. G. Strong sensed
this quality of Gogarty's verse: 'Somehow, in a very real sense,
though the secret is hard to define, you bring the spirit of Horace
to the good talk of a Dublin dinner without straining either.'[28]

Secret Springs of Dublin Song, less rare than *Hyperthuleana*
but still a bibliophile's find, was published anonymously. Though
it was a group effort by Gogarty, Seumas O'Sullivan, AE, Robert
Y. Tyrrell, George Redding, Susan Mitchell, and Lord Dunsany,
Gogarty's verse predominated; he was the moving force behind
the collection. Almost pure intellectual play and private entertainment, this volume of comic and satiric verses gives us a real insight into the atmosphere of Dublin at the time—its fascination
with personality, its elevation of gossip into art. If the collection
could be said to have a main satiric object, it would be George
Moore, who is everywhere. Indeed, Gogarty provided the finest
censored ballade in the language, 'To George Moore on the
Occasion of His Wedding': three stanzas and an envoi composed
entirely of asterisks for the man whose sexual frankness could
always shock Yeats.[29] The uncensored poems in the collection do
not all reveal such comic inventiveness, and *Secret Springs* has its
longueurs but there are enough verbal gymnastics to make it
memorable—as when, for instance, Gogarty follows a polished
Latin quatrain version of 'Little Jack Horner' by one of his Trinity
masters, Tyrrell, with an ironic translation into a laboured English
octave, or when Tyrrell himself translates a triumph of Dublin
cynicism, 'Johnny I Hardly Knew Ye' from Dublinese into Swin-
burnese and Miltonese.

Dublin itself comes in for a share of satire, particularly in
Gogarty's contributions. But the 'city unclean with a paid Lord

Mayor / . . . . Bawdy and faithful, squalid and fair,' is well-celebrated by this gathering of her songs. 'Spring in Dublin', not carried over to the *Collected Poems* but deserving to have been, evokes the eternal return in the midst of sheer grubbiness:

> When East winds roll of ruin blows,
> And tenements hang out more clothes,
> And old men go on frozen feet,
> And spits lie spattered on the street,
> . . . .
> Then she comes tripping down the street,
> And not a Bobbie on his beat
> Can hold her up, or stop the Spring
> From shamelessly soliciting—
> Even the Vigilance Committee
> Can't keep the Spring from Dublin City.
> . . . .
> She strews fresh sawdust in the pubs,
> Fresh laurels in the area tubs,
> Rathfarnham's lanes with song she fills
> And lover's monosyllables.

Even the echoes of Swift's tetrameter couplets and of the catalogue of satiric details he amasses in such a poem as 'Description of a City Shower' seem right for this poem of an eighteenth-century city. Yet its success depends primarily on Gogarty's ability to catch up all the dirtiness of the city he loved and to include it in his joyous sense of rebirth.

Among Gogarty's poems in *Secret Springs* only 'To The Maids Not to Walk in The Wind' was carried over to the *Collected Poems*. It is a poem that, given the fashion in dress and manners that have prevailed for many decades, may communicate nothing to the young—who today never can quite understand why Leopold Bloom is frustrated when he fails to catch a glimpse of an elegant lady's ankle. To a young reader, its implicit reference to a cultural context may now seem almost as remote as the vexing conceits of a Donne. 'To the Maids' serves as a reminder that Gogarty was an Edwardian. Its engaging combination of naughtiness and wit would only have been possible in an age when woman had not fully emerged from the swathings of skirts but when it was finally possible—though a touch impertinent—to refer to her doing so.

Something of the same bantering naughtiness had been there in *Hyperthuleana's* 'To a Mushroom' : 'Of all growing things the oddest; / Only of a sudden seen / Unexpected and immodest / As above a stocking, skin!' But nothing in Gogarty's early poetry equals the perfect blending of song, eroticism, classical allusion, and wit in the conclusion of 'To the Maids' :

> But when your clothes reveal your thighs
> And surge around your knees,
> Until from foam you seem to rise,
> As Venus from the seas . . .
>
> Though ye are fair, it is not fair!
> Unless you will be kind,
> Till I am dead and changed to AIR
> O walk not in the wind!

The Ship and Other Poems (1918) is another bibliophilic rarity and curiosity. A small volume, bound in paper and with illustrations and cover by Jack B. Yeats, it contains only five poems; it may be seen as an approach to a first volume of lyrics, a trial effort by a poet now gaining, less hesitantly, a sense of his own voice and characteristic subject matter. Of the five poems, four are, in one way or another, concerned with the relation—in conflict or resolution—of the real and the imagined. All five celebrate energy. Three of the group were to be carried over to the *Collected Poems*. In its theme 'The Ship' ('For I believed when I was young / That somehow life in time would show / All that was ever said or sung.') and even in its style ('over the golden pools of sleep') is reminiscent of A. E. Housman's romanticised elaboration of classical motif and epithet. But its concluding line, 'By God, I half believe it yet!' has a gustiness that is more characteristic of Gogarty. 'The Old Goose', a far better poem, has the leisurely structure of a Horatian 'address', though it is not grouped among 'Odes and Addresses' in the *Collected Poems*. Contemporaneous with Yeats's 'The Wild Swans at Coole', it is far from symbolist in manner. And yet, as in Yeats's poem, the theme, the implicit rather than the explicit situation of the speaker himself, emerges from the poem's rendering of the bird's situation. That situation—the bird afloat, its imagined flight—closely parallels Yeats's poem as does the subject, the encroachment of age.

There are, furthermore, verbal correspondences too numerous to be an accident of the material: Gogarty's 'cold', 'stream', 'lover', 'all is changed', 'paths', 'tide', all having parallels in one of the finest lyrics of our age. The influence of the master? Most probably, since 'The Wild Swans at Coole' as originally published was dated October 1916 and since Gogarty only introduced another verbal parallel, 'mirrors', as a revision in 1924. While the composition of 'The Old Goose' cannot be exactly dated, Yeats might have seen it well before its publication in *The Ship*. Still, as I have indicated, Gogarty's 'To a Cock' helped to shape Yeats's 'Leda and the Swan' (as did also two later Gogarty poems 'To the Liffey with the Swans' and 'Tell me Now'). So it is at least possible that the thematic and verbal parallels between 'The Old Goose' and 'The Wild Swans at Coole' reveal another instance of a Gogarty poem, one incidentally that also links a bird to the age of myth, providing stimulation to Yeats's imagination. At this point in the friendship of the two poets, the initiating impulse might have gone from Gogarty to Yeats as easily as from Yeats to Gogarty. Comic details in 'The Old Goose' might have stimulated Yeats's visionary imagination; Yeats's tantalising meditation might have nudged the mock-heroic inventiveness of Gogarty. If there is not now sufficient evidence in the case of these poems to demonstrate in which direction the 'influence' travelled, I am inclined to feel that Gogarty must have responded to Yeats—not to imitate but to transform utterly. However the verbal correspondences may be explained, it would be critically meaningless to judge the two poems by a comparison of one with the other in which Yeats's lines would inevitably triumph. It is more critically pertinent to note that by comparison to Yeats, whose imagination is of the highest intensity, Gogarty is a poet of fancy who yet makes a claim on our attention as he did on Yeats's.

It is 'The Image Maker' that, of all five poems in *The Ship*, most deserves analysis. Gogarty's enthusiasm for Swinburne, which eventually emerged as parody and was at its height in the period around 1904, depicted by Joyce in *Ulysses*, left no discernible imprint on his style; the pure lyric quality of the Elizabethan song, the wit of the sons of Ben, the terseness of the Greek anthology, the direct appeal of the traditional ballad, the urbanity and ease of Horace: all these were more significant influences, and they were, in fact, more assimilable to modern idiom than were the mannerisms of late Romanticism or the *fin de siècle*. Thus by the time of *The Ship*, Gogarty's lyric 'classicism' had few traces of derivativeness about it, and little that was falsely archaic in it. 'The Image Maker' is at once in the classical tradition and modern; its language is chiselled, firm, in keeping with its theme:

> Hard is the stone, but harder still
> The delicate performing will
> That, guided by a dream alone,
> Subdues and moulds the hardest stone,
> Making the stubborn jade release
> The emblem of eternal peace.

In this stanza, as in the second which completes it, paradox releases paradox; indeed, each couplet of the six that compose the poem is a paradox. It is not that these lines manifest an irony of tension or conflict but that each advances, through wit, to an apprehension of the artist's aim, 'To clothe in perdurable pride / Beauty his transient eyes descried.'

Behind the lines lies a whole series of philosophical and aesthetic assumptions about the nature of mind and of reality. Yet the poem is not one of cerebration, even less of rumination. In 'The Image Maker' wit is perception, and perception is fleshed in the chiselled language and measure of the poem. Between the turn of the century and the middle of the second decade, the wit of play had led Gogarty to the play of wit.

Some Plays for the Abbey Theatre

BY March, 1905, when he published 'The Irish Literary Revival: Present Poetry and Drama in Dublin' in the Dublin *Evening Mail*, Gogarty had developed an interest in the Abbey Theatre. Yet just as his masters at Trinity, R. Y. Tyrrell and J. P. Mahaffy, aroused in him an enthusiasm for classical poetry, they also disposed him to revere classical standards in the theatre and to disparage both the folk drama of Synge and the mythic, Celtic element in Yeats. Thus while he could admire 'the redeeming and extraordinary brilliance' of Synge's dialogue in *The Well of the Saints* and praise Yeats's *Shadowy Waters* as 'a lyric staged, a dream and not a drama,' he clearly indicated that he did not regard these works as successful dramatic actions and that he believed 'experiments like "Baile's Strand" [would] liliputianise our legends'.[1] Decades later, Gogarty would write to Ernest Boyd, 'I alone resisted Deirdre in Ireland and survived the epidemic of the disinterred.'[2] Still, Gogarty's interest in the Abbey persisted, as did his interest in subject matter for the stage. When he finally did write a play, however, it was no more to Aristophanes or Menander than to Yeats that he turned for a model. Though his poetic values, insofar as they were formulated, reveal a marked preference for pure song, Gogarty had the urgent impulse of the social reformer in him, an impulse that would in time lead him to turn from poetry to prose. It was the reforming impulse of the satirist to which he gave expression when he wrote for the theatre.

Performed for the first time at the Abbey on 11 December 1917, before an audience that 'was abuzz with excitement', *Blight: The Tragedy of Dublin*, manifests, in particular, the social concerns of a doctor.[3] Joyce had sensed the relation between Gogarty's medical and social concerns, even if he tended to cast them in the worst possible light; and it is probable that Mulligan's speech at the opening of *Ulysses* is an accurate report of Gogarty's words in 1904: 'If we could only live on good food like that . . . we wouldn't have the country full of rotten teeth and rotten guts. Living in a bogswamp, eating cheap food and the streets paved with dust, horsedung and consumptive spits.'⁴ Firmly committed to preventive medicine and purposeful social action by 1910, Gogarty was convinced of 'the need for medical inspection of school children in Ireland' by the time he joined the staff of the Meath Hospital in 1911; two years later he delivered a public address on the subject, slashing away at society's failure to confront the needs of slum children.⁵

A letter of October 15, 1913, communicates Gogarty's sense of outrage at the conditions of slum life in Dublin:

> Does a tenement only cease to be a tenement, when it becomes a tomb? The houses in Church Street, as elsewhere, have the saving attribute of killing only one generation or part of a generation . . . but what of the houses of Church Street, the houses of six and seven feet high, that cannot fall, but can only go on reeking forever. The houses in Kean's Court—what of those? And what of those structures in Thunder's Court, where the one common privy bemerded beyond use, stands beside the one common water supply which a corporation notice guards from waste.

Convinced that venality and irresponsibility on the part of members of the Dublin Corporation were at the root of the problem, he argued that 'a list should be published of the names of those who hold property' in the slums, and he insisted that 'we are dealing with a form of property that is so injurious to public health and public morals, that it should be made accordingly publicly responsible.'⁶ Thus by the time he composed *Blight*, Gogarty had developed a bold analysis of the social causes of pestilence and he had come to see that institutionalised charity works hand in hand with political corruption to perpetuate conditions under which the poor are exploited and disease flourishes. A play with both a thesis and a purpose, *Blight* was the first Irish drama to deal explicitly with the subject of venereal disease and to advance the notion that the slum, like disease itself, might be eradicated if false pieties were abandoned and effective preventive rather than remedial action taken. As Joseph Holloway observed, the play was 'quite interesting to Dubliners as it discussed a problem sincerely that eats into the heart of our city'. Though he was not entirely sympathetic to the author of the play (whose reputation for bawdry shocked him), Holloway had to admit that, despite the crude realism of the play, it 'nevertheless brought home its lesson—that the evil of slums can never be checked by charity, nor extension of hospitals, but at its own roots alone'.[7] Possessed by an ideal vision of the City (a vision, incidentally, that was not to leave him), Gogarty brought this play to its climax in the speech of his *persona* Tumulty: 'Until the citizens realise that their children should be brought up in the most beautiful and favourable surroundings the city can afford, and not in the most squalid, until this floundering Moloch of a Government realise that they must spend more money on education than on police, this city will continue to be the breeding ground of disease, vice, hypocrisy, and discontent.'

As a drama, *Blight* suffers from the limitations of its kind. Its purpose is just as explicit as Tumulty's concluding lines. In fairness, it should be mentioned, though, that when Andrew Malone considered *Blight* in relation to other social dramas of the time, he found it to be 'without any propaganda content' and 'an objective study presenting a problem for the audience rather than describing a remedy'. The play, he argued, 'is marked by a critically ironic insight into social conditions.'[8]

When Lady Gregory received the first two acts of the play, she indicated that she found it 'stirring', was eager to see the last act, and sure the Abbey could do it.[9] Later she commended revisions of the third act: 'It is just what it wanted—a closer connection with the others. I think it will be a great success and will do real good in stirring up public indignation. Some may fall on us: but we shall suffer in a good cause.'[10]

But considered merely as a dramatic form, *Blight* still suffers from a structural flaw. The first two acts, which take place in a dilapidated tenement room, focus on the situation of the impoverished Foleys and recount the rise to political eminence of their uncle Stanislaus Tully. The third act, which is needed to demonstrate Gogarty's thesis that political and financial skulduggery are abetted by charitable enterprises, shifts its location to the Boardroom of the Townsend Thanatorium; though Tully figures prominently in the Act, the Board members and George Foley, a discharged soldier, appear for the first time, and Tumulty, the last of these to arrive, seizes the centre of the stage to state the 'thesis'. Apparently Yeats, to judge from a letter of 16 December 1917 to Lady Gregory, advised Gogarty about the improvement of the last act; and, in fact, by itself, the act has considerable stage interest.[11] Gogarty has a lot of fun with the garrulous and saucy charwoman Mrs Larrissey: 'Evidently you are a believer in prophylaxis, Mrs Larrissey. / *Mrs Larrissey*: Is it any business of yours what religion I am?' He sports also with the foibles of the Board members, two of whom manifest the affectations of his Ely Place neighbours, George Moore and Sir Thornley Stoker. Even today, Gogarty's broad mockery of Irish sectarian differences and of public monuments to the dead is amusing: after a clash between Nonconformism, Church of Ireland, and 'Popery', the Board decides to spend a recent bequest on a 'tripartite mortuary building shaped like a shamrock'. It is startling too, and anything but funny more than sixty years later, to discover lines contemporary enough to have been written yesterday, like Tumulty's wryly ironic, 'As usual where the system is rotten no one is to blame.'

Topical and structurally flawed though it be, *Blight* has retained its interest and vitality. In his history of the Irish drama, Andrew Malone also observed of the play that it 'is undoubtedly the best play yet produced by an Irish dramatist dealing with a specifically Irish social problem'.[12] But it was in the first two acts of the play that Gogarty made his most original contribution to the Irish theatre. The Abbey audience had already seen successful problem dramas—for instance Seamus O'Kelly's *The Bribe*, 1913, and even one play, Edward McNulty's *The Lord Mayor*, 1914, which dealt with political corruption and the slum—even if these could not be termed 'specifically Irish'. Indeed, the latter exercised a considerable influence on *Blight*, providing analogues for the speech from the window, for the sale of old tenement houses at exorbitant profit, and for the bawdy singing of the charwoman. It was *Blight*, however, that first took an Abbey audience into the slum itself and exploited, for the first time, the lively *patois* of the slum world. Impressed by a series of articles on slum life published by Joseph O'Connor in the *Evening Mail*,[13] Gogarty apparently saw the possibility of combining a serious theme with the comic vitality he had, as a medical student, himself observed in the city's tenements; and he saw too that it was possible not merely to talk about the slum but to render it on the stage. *Blight* is at its best in the first two Acts, when the earthy language of the characters is given free play, when, in fact, their vitality is so evident that we are more absorbed in them than in the solution of their problems:

> (Enter Lily in fur coat. Looks boldly at Miss M-K and draws quilt hanging on clothes-line to screen her bed. Powders her face and whistles while arranging her hair. Miss M-K, seeing her, looks her up and down critically with lorgnette.)
>
> *Miss M-K:* The wages of sin is death.
>
> *Lily* (Singing 'Hi tiddy li-i-ti. Carry me back to Blighty,' makes a gesture at Miss M-K, with her fingers and thumb.)
>
> *Miss M-K:* The wages of sin *is* death.
>
> *Lily:* The wages of sin is a month in the Locke. (Attempts to go out but is opposed by Miss M-K.)
>
> *Miss M-K:* Why are you not at the laundry doing *honest* work?
>
> *Lily:* Because I didn't get *honest* wages—if ye want to know.
>
> *Mary:* Lily is in a restaurant, Miss. Don't mind her, she'll be going out shortly.
>
> *Lily:* I am. I'm in a restaurant and I get seven and six a week and two rounds of bread and margarine and a cup of tay, and free temptation, which is more than comes in other people's way. (Making a face aside.)
>
> *Miss M-K:* May I inquire where you are going?
>
> *Lily:* Will ye go look and ax?
>
> *Miss M-K:* If I were you my poor girl, I would not go on the streets.
>
> *Lily* (Surveying her): Sure I'd know by the old beak of ye, ye wouldn't.

Lily, one can see, is hurrying towards a fate worse than death; and she does, we eventually learn, contract syphilis. Still her insolence, in the face of Miss Maxwell-Knox's stupid official virtue, is a living thing, as are her language and her gestures. Even more richly comic is the speech of her incorrigible uncle. Here, for instance, he recounts the pre-trial details of his lawsuit:

> Out comes my solicitor—a bald, big-headed, innocent-looking baby of a fellow, but as cute as six ould min. 'Have you any sensation in the legs?' sez he, in a whisper. 'Awful!' sez I.

'Nonsense,' sez he, 'ye don't feel them at all!' 'In the name of heaven! . . . is it after me three weeks' suffering . . . ?' 'That'll do ye' sez he. 'Remember now, not even if they stick you with a pin!' 'Is all me agony to go for nothing?' sez I. 'Which of us is conducting the case?' sez he. 'On which of us did the bag fall,' sez I.

And this is Tully's irrefutable defence of the social efficacy of alcohol: 'Did it ever strike you that nothing good was ever done by preaching in this town? What built Findlater's Church? Was it preaching or drink? Drink. And the new hostel in Hatch Street? Drink. What renovated St Patrick's and cleared Bull Alley? Drink. What gave us Stephen's Green—Drink—and the ducks swimming in it!'

According to Joseph Holloway, the first night audience of *Blight* was a dazzling one; at some time during the course of its run, however, there was in the audience a yet unrecognised talent upon whom the play was to have its greatest impact: Sean O'Casey. No frequenter of the Abbey, an admirer of Boucicault, Shakespeare, and the variety stage, O'Casey found in *Blight* a precedent for what he would later do in this same theatre.[14] In fact, it is startling to notice the parallels between Gogarty's play and *Juno and the Paycock*. It is not merely that the tenement settings are comparable or that both plays mingle serious concerns with comic dialogue and characterisations. O'Casey's Boylans bear some striking resemblances to Tully and the Foley clan: in each work we find a crippled brother, a fallen sister, a Mother desperately trying to hold the family together, a braggadocio male who is also a malingerer. In short, it is necessary to see *Blight* and the Abbey plays to which it is indebted as the missing link between the melodrama of Boucicault and that of O'Casey.

Gogarty wrote three additional plays for the Abbey, though only two of these were performed there. *Blight* had been presented pseudonymously as the work of Alpha and Omega, though Gogarty's sole claim to authorship has now been established.[15] *A Serious Thing* and *The Enchanted Trousers* were both produced in 1919 as the work of Gideon Ouseley, a name Gogarty also used in his prose work *Tumbling in the Hay*. The real Ouseley was a Protestant controversialist whose works John Ellwood, Joyce's 'Temple', had pounced upon at the National Library, as a source of comic references.[16] (A printer's error in the title page of *A Serious Thing* has occasioned some confusion in histories of the Abbey as to the spelling of the last name.) These two one-acters, slighter works than *Blight*, even if better constructed, are both topical in nature. Oliver D. Gogarty has told me that Yeats praised *A Serious Thing*; and Yeats himself was later to employ a situation remarkably like that in this farce—a 'rebirth' rendered through the conversation of two contrasting observers, who are joined by a third at the climax—in one of his most intense, brilliant, and troubling plays, *The Resurrection* (1931). Yet of the two farces, it is *The Enchanted Trousers* that is the more successful.

According to one Dublin reviewer, *A Serious Thing* 'kept the house in shrieks of laughter'[17] and one can imagine that in the political context of the day, its satire would have gone over well with an Irish audience. Employing a favourite regeneration myth of modern Irish writers and a favourite historical parallel of his time, Gogarty depicts the summoning of Lazarus from the tomb—to the total consternation of a Centurion and two Roman soldiers, all of whom wear the khaki, which, as a programme note wryly comments, 'is well known and widely distributed.' The satiric butts of this one-acter are, for one, the Englishman's total inability to understand Ireland's rebirth and, for another, the fatuous jargon of military authority. And there are one or two private jokes. The verbal mannerisms of the Centurion (Looky here now!) were modelled on those of Gogarty's millionaire neighbour in the West, Talbot Clifton; and allusions to the dream of Potiphar's wife, to spirit-rapping, to spiritualism and seances indicate that Gogarty was having a bit of fun with the esoteric activities of W. B. and Mrs Yeats. Still distinctly minor among Gogarty's works, *A Serious Thing* attests more to the Doctor's continued interest in the theatre as a medium for public statement than to his real comic and lyric talents. Another reminder that the myth of death and transfiguration pervades modern Irish literature, its importance is really historical. Even the unsympathetic Joseph Holloway had to admit that 'the moment the dead Lazarus awoke from his tomb to join those who wished their country free was the cream of a very [brutal?] joke!'[18]

By contrast, *The Enchanted Trousers*, a satire, according to Holloway, 'on the Department (as the Plunkett House crowd is usually called)' has better survived the passage of time, despite its

topical nature and despite the fact that Gogarty accepted none of
the many revisions Lady Gregory suggested.[19] Satirising the tendency of Sir Horace Plunkett's agency for Irish agricultural reform
to offer its best positions to Englishmen, Gogarty managed to
sustain a farce that develops an amusing contrast between the Irish
and English character, and between various illusions and the reality
beyond them. If the topical elements within the play mean even
less than the private jokes of *A Serious Thing*, the situation—that
of the bogus Englishman in Ireland—and the satire on bureaucrats
and officials continue to entertain. Lady Gregory was bothered by
the number of allusions to spitting and the reviewer for the
Freeman was concerned that the play seemed to ridicule not only
British rule but the Irish.[20] Yet the spitting of Humphrey Heavey
(an unemployed Irish actor who is adapting a novel in which a
Duke spits into the fire) really works, inasmuch as it is a sharp
reminder of the discrepancy between the illusory and the actual;
and the action, in which Humphrey dupes a visiting committee
into believing him an Englishman and appointing him a Minister
of Potato Spraying but then leaves his mother and brother in the
lurch, continues to amuse us for the very reason that the *Freeman*'s
reviewer feared: it gets at something characteristic of Irish experience—and, for that matter, at something silly in human
nature.

In effect, Gogarty's career in the theatre ended with the performance of these two curtain-raisers at the Abbey. He was to
write another one-act play intended for the Abbey years later:
Incurables, which was never performed but published in the
posthumous collection *A Week End in the Middle of the Week*
(1958). A macabre little farce in which stage Irish dialogue con-
tributes to the grotesqueness of the situation, *Incurables* was provoked by a post-war visit to Ireland and by Gogarty's realisation
that an aspect of the theme of *Blight* needed restatement. His
implication in this farce is that charitable institutions, in particular
hospitals for the aged, are less a matter of necessity than of wish-
fulfilment; and the 'conceit' on which the play is based is the sup-
pression of a restorative elixir by the hospital Governor who argues
that the country is not ready to do without charitable institutions
for the poor and decrepit. The comic energy of the piece is exactly
that of every good Pat and Mike joke involving physical decay and
death. Its whimsy is the characteristic mood of the ageing and

American Gogarty, looking back upon his youth. As his Pat says, 'Them was the days.' But according to Gogarty, in a letter of April 1951, Ernest Blythe (who represented the government as Director of the Abbey) rejected this genial satire as 'too cruel'. Gogarty's response was a postcard bearing the words 'Bird thou never wert.'[21]

There exists in typescript an act of two scenes for *Caerleon* or *The Camp of the Legions*, possibly a dramatisation of some of the themes developed in *I Follow Saint Patrick* (1938).[22] But to judge from a tantalising fragment that has survived, perhaps the most interesting Gogarty play after *Blight* was a work of at least two acts, *Wave Lengths*, of which we know only that, in Gogarty's words, 'unaccountably it is lost'.[23] Some manuscript pages with the author's revisions did manage to survive and these are interesting enough to make one regret the loss of the play and wonder at its disappearance. Apparently a work of the later thirties, *Wave Lengths* (which was reworked in America, without much success, as a possible television script) concerns an invention—theoretically possible, in fact—by means of which living voices might be taken from the ether. Unscrupulous advertising men seize on this remarkable invention as a means of blackmail. The dialogue of the manuscript fragment is lively and the notion is a compelling one, for it raises essential moral issues about the uses to which science has been put in the modern world. Even more compelling, however, are clear pointers to Joyce's *Ulysses*, and to the problems created by an imaginative work that has so complex a relation to reality as Joyce's great book. The presence in one fragment of *Wave Lengths* of an advertising man named Leopold and of allusions to transvestism unmistakably evoke Leopold Bloom and an important psychological motif in *Ulysses*. Furthermore, when the inventor of the 'voice machine' protests that he will not allow the unscrupulous promoters to intimidate or make 'a show of some poor silly mortal whose youth or whose tongue ran away with him' one cannot help but reflect that in quoting Gogarty extensively and verbatim, Joyce had indeed lifted his erstwhile friend's voice from the ether. In considering Gogarty's later apparently irrational attacks on Joyce, therefore, it is worth reflecting that even if *Ulysses* is the greatest novel of our century, it may have been difficult for Gogarty to view it objectively. *Ulysses* had not only given to the world what he had intended for a somewhat smaller audience, but it attached to him—almost with the magic force of a bardic curse—an identity that he came to loathe.

Seen in relation to the rest of his work, Gogarty's plays, with the exception of *Blight* and the promise of the *Wave Lengths* fragment, are of minor importance. After the intense period of productivity between 1917 and 1919, his interest in the drama was incidental. 'I want none of my stuff which was written to serve in the Abbey of the moment resurrected,' he wrote Seumas O'Sullivan, probably in the mid-twenties.[24] Topical and satirical— indeed, farcical in the case of the three short pieces—his plays indicate that in him the dramatic impulse was closely allied to the impulse to change or reform the ways of man in society: to that part of his nature that also responded to the practice of medicine. Yeats had certainly encouraged him, even though Gogarty's dramatic work was anything but what Yeats wanted in his theatre. Lady Gregory, though profoundly interested in the production of the plays and enthusiastic about *Blight*, probably had seemed less responsive to the farces. Having once said something that needed saying and having contributed, in *Blight*, to the development of modern Irish drama, Gogarty was satisfied to make a few brief returns to the dramatic form. Throughout the twenties and well into the thirties, it was the lyric that held him. Only when the political pressures engendered by Irish independence from England and by the political currents of the thirties compelled him to seek other than lyric expression was his interest deflected from poetry, and then with far more substantial consequences.

3

The Rhythm of Herrick

IT WAS during the twenties and thirties, in the troubled years of the Treaty negotiations, the establishment of the Irish Free State, the Cosgrave government, the Civil War, the coming to power of De Valera, the abolition of the Senate, that Oliver Gogarty produced his best poetry. His medical practice, well-established by 1920, was disastrously affected by the 'Troubles' and the notoriety he gained in the Senate. Immediately following his kidnapping and escape in 1923, when he was under government protection, it became difficult for him either to write or to practise medicine. As he wrote Lady Leslie in March, 1923:

> With the best intentions I couldn't write here for at least 3 or 4 months. The guard is still necessary and to them tobacco and cards. Patients cannot be invited to undergo strict scrutiny and as I have to give a description of whom I expect before they are admitted, it is perfectly obvious that my practice here could not *grow*.[1]

Later in the spring, he indicated that while he was beginning to make a London name, his income in Dublin had been 'interrupted' for five months.[2] By February 1924, he was able to close down his London office, though he continued to operate in England; yet Gogarty was not thereafter to know so flourishing a practice as had been his. Increasingly he was distracted from his medical career by his interest in writing; and a considerable amount of his energy was expended in Senatorial activities and in social ones. Then, too, Gogarty was not immune from the economic depression of the late twenties and the thirties: in 1931 he wrote to Shane Leslie that he did 'not expect to see such affluence as I once enjoyed again.'[3] Nevertheless, to an American friend who had expressed concern about the multiple demands that were being made upon him and the consequences to his creative work, Gogarty wrote, in 1929, 'It is a mistake to think that ease or a decent income would improve my writing. All I do depends on the "tension" at which I live, and a modicum of worry, work and want of wealth helps. The Muses distract rich men who might keep other mistresses.'[4] And to be sure, in these years of conflict, stress, and intense activity, Gogarty published the collections—*An Offering of Swans* (1923), *An Offering of Swans and other Poems* (1924), the three *Wild Apples* (1928, 1929, 1930), *Selected Poems* (1933), *Others to Adorn* (1938) and *Elbow Room* (1939)—on which his reputation as a poet will largely rest.

The least theoretical of men and the least doctrinaire—not to say that he was not opinionated—Gogarty can scarcely be said to have formulated a poetic or to have articulated a defence of his practice, any more than he can be said to belong to a particular movement or group of poets. To say this is not to say that he did not have a definite conception of poetry and of the poet's role, a firm view of technical matters, or a relation to important developments in modern poetry. Of course he did. But he was in no sense programmatic; and, though he may even be said to have had a historical view of the development of English poetry and lectured and wrote about his poetic preferences late in his life, he had made no effort to formulate anything like a theory. A number of letters he wrote to Bell in 1905, in particular the letter of April 7, reveal that his fundamental conception of poetry and of the poet's role rested on metaphysical assumptions. 'The imagination is the bridge between subject and simile; it is that which makes symbols possible and just; it is the one which remains. . . . Imagination is the mirror of God. He who has most is the greatest poet.'[5] In an unpublished essay, occasioned by the performance of Yeats's *The King's Threshold* in 1903, he made his transcendental point even more aphoristically : 'Religion is the World's Memory of its Creator and art the labour of the Memory, Mother of Muses, to express the divine Idea in beautiful form and sounds.' From that initial assumption, Gogarty never wavered. 'Beauty' he never equated with morality despite his work in the theatre; both mystic and poet he regarded as moving 'in a region beyond ethics where poetry and religion are one. . . . [I]t is he who would have art teach that is immoral.'[6]

Gogarty's initial response to the *fin de siècle* Yeats was most enthusiastic. To both *The Shadowy Waters* and *The King's Threshold* he paid high tribute, observing of the latter, 'Looking on Seanchan as he chanted with the hero light around him I realised that a great soul was indeed standing awaiting incarnation in Ireland.'[7] However, it was to the heroic element in these plays that he responded; to the arcane, the esoteric, and the legendary in Yeats he was generally unsympathetic, and, for him, Yeats's plays were always secondary to the poetry. Under the influence of his Trinity mentors, the anti-folk Joyce of 'The Day of the Rabblement', and the Sinn Fein politics of Arthur Griffith, Gogarty was simply hostile to the early peasant enthusiasm of Yeats and the Abbey, and he did not respond to the theatre of Synge, Lady Gregory, and Colum.[8] However, much as he might admire the lyric Yeats, he was not in the least attracted by the mistiness of the Celtic Twilight (which Yeats himself was actually rejecting during the first decade of the century). As we have seen, when Gogarty reviewed *New Songs* (1903) he praised the craftsmanship but indicated that he found the poetry rather thin stuff. Quoting Yeats, he complained, 'Here is not the "bursting pod." ' Curiously enough, given his invocation of Yeats, he also objected that 'Many of the poems are definitely "symbolist", and abound in graven images alien . . . to the true god of song.'[9] This last criticism has to be seen not as a rejection of imagery but of the vagueness and preciosity of the imitators of Yeats and AE.

Though Gogarty has never been associated with the term 'Imagism' or the Imagist movement, he was strongly influenced by certain of the tenets of the Imagist movement in its pre-Pound phase. Before 1905, when their correspondence began, Gogarty had become acquainted with Dermot Freyer, another medical student with a strong interest in poetry. His friendship with Freyer resulted in the frequent exchange of letters, poems, books, and visits; and it was Freyer who introduced Gogarty to F. S. Tancred and T. E. Hulme himself. Neither Freyer nor Tancred ever really developed as poets, but both men were members of the Poets Club formed in 1908 by Hulme, and both published verses in the volume published by the Club in 1909. Tancred, with whom Gogarty was to exchange poems, for a number of years, was also a member of the second and more loosely organised association of poets which gathered around Hulme in Soho in 1909.[10] By 1910, Gogarty was on such terms with this circle that he could promise

Freyer he would pick up an automobile in England and 'tool Hulme and Tancred down & pass through Cambridge on my Western way.'[11] In Gogarty's poetic exchanges with the genial Freyer and the eccentric Tancred, the emphasis was usually upon the craft and precision of verse. None of these three men were interested in the free verse with which Hulme was experimenting, but they all shared Hulme's appreciation of hard, precise, 'classical' effects in the line and of clear, sharp, visual images. Without having consciously repudiated the qualities of Romantic imagin- ation upon which Hulme was launching an attack, Gogarty was naturally inclined to the poetry of wit and fancy that Hulme was demanding for the new age. Whether influenced by the Hulme group or simply responding to what was in the air, he dismissed the poetry of rumination. 'I think that all English poetry after the blitheness of Chaucer became damned' he wrote in 1934, 'and this reached its deepest in a Wordsworth. What nation on earth made poetry a subject for the pulpit?' The answer he found to English didacticism was not 'to distort the grammar or the idiom of the tongue'. On the contrary, he suggested Irish poets could shape their own tradition by paganising English. 'All we can do is to invigorate it in terms of its own pulsations.'[12]

From the Yeats who had set about remaking himself and his style, Gogarty, in 1905, learned the most important lesson of his poetic career:

> I received a long lecture on modern literary languages. He forgave William Morris for his archaism for it was both original and scholarly. An archaism was [was] only admissible when one discovered it for oneself: there was no defence for the continuance of mere metrical conventions: 'Hast', 'Shalt', 'thou', 'thee', 'wert', 'art', etc. They were part of a language highly artificial and conscious, a language that would pass for poetry if one were to find it at a future date in a single instance. . . . He calls all inversions in verse & 'thee' & 'thou' convention labour-saving devices and assures me [me] that he could im- provise verse by the hour if he permitted himself the use of inversions and the conventional language of poetry. . . . I have retreated and am now studying Yeats' work with interest and respect.[13]

Given the shaping influences of classical forms and measures, given his early training in imitation and parody, given his brief enthusiasm for Swinburne, and given his Renaissance and Caroline models, had Gogarty not learned this lesson from Yeats and had Yeats not read and criticised his poetry during the twenties and thirties, it is possible that Gogarty might never have been more than what detractors have called him, a trader in classical clichés, despite the intensity of his perceptions and sensuous responses. But because he did take Yeats's advice and practice to heart, he became, in his most successful poems, at once a classical and a contemporary poet. Despite the early influence of Hulmian Imagism, Gogarty was (like the other Irish poets, including Yeats) entirely unresponsive to the modernism of Pound and Eliot which was to dominate English and American poetry throughout the period of his greatest productivity; he was, nevertheless, through his friendship with Yeats, directly influenced by the notion that poetry might be both traditional and contemporary, and by Yeats's sense of the natural idiom, syntax, and cadence of poetry.

The danger for a poet such as Gogarty, who began to write poetry as a form of witty play and for whom the poem always remained a kind of gesture to be shared with close friends, was that he would overindulge his propensity for prosodic gamesmanship. Thus, for instance, struck by the astonishing changes in women's clothing and by what newspaper photographs now revealed, he addressed some lines to his good friend George Redding (2 July 1927) in another friend's newspaper, the *Irish Statesman* of AE. These are the concluding stanzas of four:

> Say in what time, in what city has there been a
> Beauty to compare—oh, not in Rome or Paris—
> With Helen Wills or with the lovely Senorita Alvarez?

> Why can't we sing as the men of old? The simple
> Reason is this that our cup of joy too full is:
> Countess Bezzi Scali had but with a dimple
>   Silenced Catullus.[14]

It tells us something about the social and literary culture of Dublin in the twenties that George Redding (who held a managerial post in the Guinness brewery) replied in the same poetic measure, a fortnight later, and that a third correspondent then responded to both Gogarty and Redding.[15] If such prosodic exchanges between a doctor-Senator and a brewery manager contributed to the charm and liveliness of a distinctive epoch in Dublin's history, they did not *always* elicit from Gogarty his best work. Clever his lines are, but they are strained by the arbitrary nature of the form. He himself later insisted that the lines to Redding are 'An awful mixture of quantitative verse and rhymed; two things that cannot blend successfully.'[16]

Inasmuch as Gogarty's talent flowered as the product of social exchange and correspondence with men of broad and generous culture such as Bell, Seumas O'Sullivan, James Stephens, AE, George Redding, Lord Dunsany, Hugh MacDiarmid and others, it was his good fortune that during his most productive years he should also have been in constant touch with Yeats and subject to the latter's criticism, as he prepared his poems for publication. Why, Yeats asked himself, in the Preface he wrote for *Wild Apples* (1930), was he willing to go through 'so much careless verse for what is excellent?' Admitting that he was *not* disinterested, Yeats concluded that it was because Gogarty gave him something he needed. 'The great Romantics had a sense of duty and could hymn upon occasion, but little sense of a hardship borne and chosen out of pride and joy. . . . I find it in every poem of Oliver Gogarty that delights me, in the whole poem, or in some astringent adjective.'[17] The relationship of Yeats and Gogarty was thus one from which each benefited. 'My brother, Willie, was your father's friend,' the painter Jack Yeats was to say to Gogarty's son.[18] Yeats's imagination was stirred by particular Gogarty poems upon which he drew and by the unique quality of Gogarty's work. The critical interest of Yeats was the very standard of excellence the doctor-Senator most required: his hardship borne and chosen out of pride and joy. To have learned from the century's greatest poet and to have remained so uniquely himself that he had something to give in return was no small accomplishment.

In the Preface he contributed to *An Offering of Swans* (1923), Yeats wondered aloud if Oliver Gogarty's return to England, his visits to old English country houses, had brought to his friend 'a new sense of English lyric tradition and changed a wit into a poet.'[19] Indeed, among the poems in this small Cuala Press volume there is one richly evocative address to Lady Ottoline Morrell, which describes her 'gables . . . by Oxford on their watery hill' and a stroll she took there with Yeats:

C

Under the elms—and all the air was Spring's,
A leaven of silence in the misty dew
Leavening the light, the shadow leavening,
Your cloak and that tall feather, white under blue—
Walking beside a poet in the evening.

Of course, several of the lyrics in this volume were written much earlier than 'To A Lady'; and, in truth, Gogarty had been drawing imaginative sustenance from the English lyric tradition as from the classical tradition since the turn of the century. (As a practising surgeon, he carried a small edition of Horace in his pocket.) And the transformation of a wit into a poet had been going on long before Gogarty's great season in England. Still Yeats was right in sensing that among these lyrics were poems demonstrating that something new had been released in Gogarty. (The 1924 *An Offering of Swans and Other Poems* gave even more striking evidence of enhanced poetic energy and discipline.) Probably, though, there were other causes for the outburst of poetic activity between 1923 and 1939. It seems likely that the acute political tensions of the period had released creative energies, even that they provided the doctor with an opportunity, a distraction, he had long subconsciously sought, to turn from medicine to literature. It may well be that the glimpses Gogarty now had of a way of life seemingly formed by esthetic impulse and ordered by tradition were creatively stimulating. It may even be that the recognition of his wit and conversational genius accorded by fashionable hostesses gave Gogarty some new assurance, yet it was Dublin, his friendships there, the hills beyond Dublin city, Renvyle House and Connemara, that provided the springs of Gogarty's song.

It was in these years that his friendship with Yeats really flowered, so that Yeats, sitting in Gogarty's office, could jot down some suggested revision of a line or two on the doctor's medical pad.[20] This was the apotheosis of the kind of poetic interchange on which Gogarty flourished. In a letter to G. K. A. Bell (January 8, 1905) Gogarty wryly observed, 'All those hours at the "Mermaid", the "Dog", the "Triple Tun", and other taverns are lost to us—years even. But they live in one or two songs of Fletcher's which he wrote in an hour but took a year to drink for.'[21] By the same token, the poems Gogarty published between 1923 and 1939 must be multiplied by the hours with Yeats, in English country houses, at London luncheons, in the Bailey tavern, at the salon of AE, on picnics, jaunts, and binges with Augustus John, in the Trinity chambers of Tyrrell or Macran while the wine flowed, on the parapet of the Martello Tower. The best poems of *An Offering of Swans* must be seen as a mature man's gleanings from all those hours and experiences.

Yeats was the master of a disarming prose style, and the apparently casual and characteristic manner of his 'Preface' to *An Offering of Swans* startles one by the sharpness of his insights. Just as one begins to assume that Yeats has become engrossed in a metaphor that he is pursuing, he rushes to the conclusion that poetry comes into being with 'the discovery of a region or a rhythm where a man may escape out of himself'.[22] And then he observes, 'Oliver Gogarty has discovered the rhythm of Herrick and of Fletcher, something different from himself and yet akin to himself.' Nothing could better illustrate the truth of Yeats's perception than the lyric 'Begone, sweet Ghost':

> Begone sweet ghost, O get you gone!
> Or haunt me with your body on;
> And in that lovely terror stay
> To haunt me happy night and day.
> For when you come I miss it most,
> Begone, sweet Ghost!

The economy of language, the grace of the rhythm, the wit of the oxymorons ("Sweet Ghost', 'Lovely terror', 'Haunt me happy') might, indeed suggest that the stanza was written by one of the 'sons of Ben'. On the other hand, the language of the stanza, with the exception of 'begone' and 'get you gone', which deliberately toy with the tradition that is being evoked, is essentially colloquial. The inversion with which the second and final stanza opens is more problematical, but the concluding three lines with their emphatic repetition of the lover's appeal, are completely successful, suggesting the mock extremity of his plight:

> O do but clothe you in that dress
> Whereby was young Actaeon killed;
> He died because of loveliness,
> And I will die from that withheld,
> Unless you take on flesh, unless
> In that you dress!

If Eliot's use of Renaissance lines, if Pound's characteristic use of archaisms, can be justified, then surely Gogarty's language can. For the tone of this poem is obviously one of banter, and those elements ('begone', 'get you gone', 'do but clothe . . . / Whereby was') that call attention to themselves as non-contemporary are an element in the playful irony of the poem. Gogarty can succeed in a poem like this, not because he is aping the manner of another day, but, as Yeats sensed, because he is entering a world of feeling by wearing the mask of a sensibility like his own yet different from it.

Not all of the lyrics of *An Offering of Swans* are as successful as 'Begone, Sweet Ghost'. Again, as Yeats observed, there were 'careless lines now and again, traces of the old confused exuberance',[23] and there is a group of sonnets ('Non Blandula Illa', 'Virgil', 'Liffey Bridge', 'Dunsany Castle'), a form to which Gogarty was always attracted but one that usually constricted his lyric talent, though the first two are perhaps his best in the form. Yeats admired, in particular, in addition to 'Begone, Sweet Ghost', 'Non Dolet' and 'Good Luck'. These he said he had been murmuring. The second of them has been compared unfavourably to Yeats's 'The New Faces' by T. R. Henn, who complained of 'outworn personifications' and confused syntax:[24]

> Our friends go with us as we go
>   Down the long path where Beauty wends,
> Where all we love forgathers, so
>   Why should we fear to join our friends?
>
> Who would survive them to outlast
>   His children; to outwear his fame—
> Left when the Triumph has gone past—
>   To win from Age, not Time, a name?
>
> Then do not shudder at the knife
>   That Death's indifferent hand drives home,
> But with the Strivers leave the Strife,
>   Nor, after Caesar, skulk in Rome.

It is regrettable that Gogarty chose to capitalise 'Beauty', 'Triumph', 'Age', 'Time', 'Death's', 'Strivers', and 'Strife'. He need not have done so, and the sophisticated reader probably dismisses the typography anyway. (There was always something nearly Germanic about the way Gogarty capitalised. One wishes

the publisher of *The Collected Poems* had corrected this tendency.)
The abstract personification has been treated with special scorn by
most of the critics who have shaped our tastes in poetry, despite
Yeats's willingness to use it when it occasionally suited his purpose
and Auden's frequent and brilliant use of it. Actually among the
capitalised words of 'Non Dolet', only 'Death' in 'Death's indifferent hand' is, in fact, employed as an abstract personification,
and the metaphor particularises the force with great intensity.
Yeats's judgment was right about the poem. The rhythm of the
whole, inextricable from the tone, is what makes it memorable.
Opening with a gentle reflectiveness, 'Non Dolet' turns wryly
ironic at the moment when we are pulled up short by the pronounced caesural pause combined with a run-on thought stress
that precedes and follows the last syllable of the third line. The
irony intensifies through the second stanza, and the syntax of the
poem mounts to a climax with the interrogative and periodic
structure (Who would survive. . . . To win . . . a name?). The
final quatrain then moves towards a resolution as it opens ('Then
do not shudder'), yet the poet has such control of his language
that his final metaphor and the verb 'skulk' that is central in it
drive home his ironic conclusion and the stoicism which is its
positive aspect.

Just as a poem like 'Non Dolet' derives its strength from the
poet's ability to confront the traditional subject by entering
imaginatively into a traditional stoic response—his, but not his—
so does 'Good Luck' depend upon a double sense of things. In the
case of this poem, the double sense of things is the very subject.
The opening stanza plays off its charming allusion to the race of
Melanion and Atalanta against a comic and mocking final line. It
is tempting to suggest that, given the terse impudence of the last
line, the poet is projecting against the classical allusion, an anti-
classical, a modern line and phrasing, as a way of seeing the
situation:

> Apples of gold the Hero dropt
>   As he was in the race outstript
> And Atalanta, running, stopt,
>
>   And all her lovely body dipt
> A moment; but she lost her stride—
> And had to go to bed a bride.

Indeed, the witty conclusion of the poem depends for its effect
(even more markedly than the first stanza) upon contrasting levels
of diction between the last lines and those which precede it:

> But where can I get Western gold,
>   Or posset of constraining fire?—
> I who am fated to behold
>   Beauty outdistancing desire?
> Aye, and to falter wonder-struck;
> There's no good love without good luck!

Some months after the publication of *An Offering of Swans*,
Gogarty wrote a column, 'Literature and Life. Style', for AE's
Irish Statesman in which he speaks of a recent portrait that does
not resemble him. (No doubt the first of two by Augustus John.)
'I was told,' Gogarty writes, 'that it was a very good so-and-so.'
He goes on to conclude, not as waggishly as it may seem, 'that,
perhaps, the secret of writing may also consist in putting something else in the place of the subject.' By way of illustration,
Gogarty cited 'The Bonny Earl of Murray', which he admired for
its 'selectiveness'. The subject of the ballad is the earl's death, but
'something has been put in its place. His death has not been
ignored, but it has not been mentioned except in the third line—
one out of 24—and there it is announced by the mouth of some
horrified choreagas.' Rejecting the notion that poetry is a 'criticism
of life' and convinced that it has the power 'to restore, to translate,
to transpose, and to transfigure life,' Gogarty, in characteristically
intuitive and light-hearted manner, approached a conception of
the whole poem if not as symbol at least as objective correlative.[25]
Well, one may ask, isn't this a bit pretentious: bringing Eliot—
actually Santayana by way of Eliot—to Dublin? Consider, though,
a poem like 'Golden Stockings'. Nothing could seem more transparent, less vexed by meanings than this simple lyric:

> Golden stockings you had on
> In the meadow where you ran;
> And your little knees together
> Bobbed like pippins in the weather,
> When the breezes rush and fight
> For those dimples of delight,
> And they dance from the pursuit,
> And the leaf looks like the fruit.

I have many a sight in mind
That would last if I were blind;
Many verses I could write
That would bring me many a sight.
Now I only see but one,
See you running in the sun
And the gold-dust coming up
From the trampled butter-cup.

Readers nurtured on the complexities, or at least duplicities, of much modernist verse may be inclined to ask for what 'something' these lines, almost childlike in quality, could possibly have been put in the place. Gogarty himself has given an answer, for in an essay published decades later, he commented—an exception to his practice—on the poem. In 'Poets and Little Children' he quoted his own poem, observing of it:

> Here is a piece which sets a little girl running in a meadow golden with buttercups. She is made into the spirit and personification of the golden things in Nature, the gold of the meadows the gold of the fruit, the gold of the leaf. And to give these things life she is made to run in the sunshine. And she is isolated by the simple device on the part of the poet of closing the eyes and seeing in the mind's eye only her. Thus is the stillness produced which the powder of the buttercups can dust with gold.[26]

A poem like 'Golden Stockings' is a hazardous operation. The least uncertainty or imprecision in its execution, any excess or crudity in its utterance, would be fatal. In less certain or less tender hands the matter of the poem could turn to sentimentality and banality of the worst kind. In the midst of a period during which Donne was probably the most admired of English poets, Oliver Gogarty chose to write like Herrick! (Incidentally, 'Poets and Little Children' opened with a tribute to the inspired tenderness of Herrick's 'A Baby's Grace.') Yet as Gogarty's own commentary reveals, the central image of the little girl, her dimpled knees and buttercup-stained stockings, expanding through association with the image of the bobbing yellow apples, should release a whole complex of feelings and associations, creating for the reader a moment of golden and pure joy.

Among the 'other' poems added to the 1924 *An Offering of Swans And Other Poems* is one, 'The Casting', which realises and expresses the effect Gogarty now sought in his poetry:

> I pour in the mould of rhyme
>> All that my heart would hold:
> The transient light on the tower,
>> The moat in its wintry gold,
> Sunlight, and a passing shower.
>> The gleam of your garments' fold
> That baffles the eye as you pass,
> Formless and lovely things
>> Look speech that breaks in a laugh;

The sensibility behind those lines—as remote from Buck Mulligan as anything could be—is one quickly and intensely responsive to the most delicate and evanescent of moments, sights, and sounds. Doubtless influenced by Yeats' metaphor and ideal in 'The Fisherman' ('I shall have written him one / Poem maybe as cold / And passionate as the dawn.') Gogarty celebrates the union of passion and discipline in art:

> I heat them with more than heat,
>> Because they must glow in the cold;
> I puddle the white-hot mass,
>> And praying with words retold,
> To temper beauty from Time,
>> I pour them into the mould.

Though not all of the poems added to *An Offering of Swans and Other Poems* are equally successful, in poem after poem one finds the balancing of delicacy of feeling by terseness of expression, of emotion by irony, of tender sentiment by the discipline of the form:

> I, as the Wise Ones held of old,
>> Hold there's an Underworld to this;
> . . . .
>
> The generations of all Time
>> And all the lovely Dead are there.
>>>> 'Sunt Apud Inferos Tot Milia Formosarum'

. . . In barbarian lands,
Roman where Rome no longer stands,
This altar to your hard won love:
Earth, and the Nymphs and Springs thereof.
                    'Nymphis et Fontibus'

Enough! Why should a man bemoan
A Fate that leads the natural way?
. . . .
But have not little maidens gone,
And Lesbia's sparrows—all alone?
                    'Per Iter Tenebricosum'

Memory, enfold her and cling!
    And I will go forth against odds.
But heart, forget her and sing!
    This is no place for the Gods.
                    'To Ethne'

There are too, among the 'other poems', a number of addresses,
very different from these Roman 'mask' poems; the addresses are
Gogartian versions of the Horatian epistle. One of these, 'To My
Friend the Rt Hon. Lorcan Galeran', actually appeared first as 'The
Feast' in *Hyperthuliana*; it demonstrates Gogarty's early command
of the relaxed form of the address and of the mock-heroic tone.
Subtitled 'A Great Householder', this exuberant work plays tribute
to a 'Meridian man, Enstomacher, / For whom the whole world's
fruits are fare.' In the 1924 volume, Gogarty rewrote a number
of lines, at Yeats's suggestion,[27] substituting more natural phrasing
for an inversion, rewriting another line to improve the cadence;
he also sacrificed one stanza, substituting two new ones for the
sake of continuity. Celebrating not only food and wine but
the food for thought of a talented company, this *jeu d'esprit*
shows us how this Dubliner could enter in imagination a
mythic classical world and yet play with its mythology and
conventions:

O Tableland! O plain of Troy,
Whereon we wage the wars of joy!
You, Agamemnon to our force,
Big-bellied as the Trojan horse!

At the climax of the poem, in a marvellous comic conceit, Lorcan Galeran is warned of a possible apotheosis:

> Once like your Body bulged the Earth,
> Pear-shaped, before the Moon had birth,
> O keep your tropic waistcoat tight,
> Your Belly may fly off to-night!
>
> And, mounted to that heavenly dome,
> Another Moon would light us home,
> Fair as the ocean-shell that rose,
> And harvest-full and grandiose!

Yeats's attitude towards these occasional poems was curious, for he did not include 'The Feast' in his selection for *An Offering of Swans*, though he contributed to its revision and, writing of Gogarty's poetry in his Preface to *Wild Apples* (1930) he indicated that he believed 'public events—some incursion of Augustus John, perhaps, benumb his poetry.'[28] Yet Yeats also contributed to the revision of 'To Augustus John', and Gogarty preserved the revision Yeats jotted down on his medical pad. In Yeats's hand we find the couplet 'What better than a far ideal / To help one with the near and real?' Also in Yeats's hand are another couplet, 'Or a Viking who has steered / All blue eye and yellow beard' and the lines 'Looking on a mountain fellow / Or the gifted Robin Hood / Driven from his sheltering wood.'[29] Slightly modified by Gogarty in each case, the revisions entered the finished poem. In *The Whole Mystery of Art* Georgio Melchiori has suggested that Gogarty's 'To the Liffey with the Swans' and his 'Tell me Now' were among the complex of forces, themes and associations working upon Yeats when he wrote his great sonnet 'Leda and the Swan'. He also argues that after Gogarty's *An Offering of Swans* operated as 'catalyst for the images that went into Yeats's "Leda and the Swan", the debt was amply repaid for the myth of Leda recurs with obsessive insistence in Gogarty's later poetry.'[30] Doubtless Melchiori is correct in arguing that Gogarty's allusions in the poems he cites were involved in Yeats's imaginative process. But he both overstates the place of the Leda myth in Gogarty's later poetry and understates the degree to which Gogarty contributed to 'Leda and the Swan'. The myth of Leda was well established in Gogarty's poetry earlier than Melchiori assumes. It appears not only in the very passage of 'To Augustus John' that Yeats revised but also in 'To a Cock', a poem that Gogarty dedicated to John in *Hyperthuliana*; and, as I suggested earlier, Yeats's 'burning roof and tower' is closely related to the imagery of 'To a Cock', which Yeats would have read as he went through the poems of *Hyperthuliana*. In effect, both the contribution he made to the final form of 'The Feast'—'To Lorcan Galeran'—and 'To Augustus John' and the images he absorbed from the latter and 'To a Cock' suggest that Yeats found something compelling in these works but that the Horatian address was not a kind of poem he was able to appreciate fully.

Both 'To Augustus John' and 'To My Portrait, By Augustus John' are among Gogarty's successes in the 'other poems'. The former of these recounts in burlesque trimeters a wild automobile ride and the picnic following it:

> When you kept the gears in mesh
> Driving on through Lettergesh,
> And I kept not very far
> Behind you in another car—
> Not that I would cast a slur,
> No; but accidents occur,
> And your driving not your drawing
> Was what there might be a flaw in.

The occasional form of the address permitted Gogarty the kind of spontaneous and exuberant effects—deliberately outrageous rhymes, for instance—he enjoyed and this poem is filled with them. In the following lines, for instance, there are comic references to the charms of an unnamed beauty likely to have been noted by the philandering John, and to the characteristic dissonantal rhyme Yeats introduced into modern poetry.

> Well! you need not rail at me,
> For you could not watch the sea,
> Nor the purple mountain drawn
> Like the neck of . . . ;
> Nor the Hawk of Achill strung
> Like a cross-bow as he hung
>
> Half invisible in blue;

> All these things were lost to you
> For your eyes were strictly glued
> On (a Yeatsian rhyme) the road.

Like 'To My Portrait', this address obliquely implies a more serious theme, the contrast between the romantically idealist sensibility (here, Gogarty) and the realist (John), 'Beauty's Bolshevik' who knows 'how to undress / And expose her loveliness.' But it is necessary to the tone of the whole that the resolution arise from a comic gesture. In this case, Gogarty releases John from 'profoundest gloom' brought on by the reality of a picnic he finds tedious:

> . . . There is no need to tell
> How I broke the gloomy spell,
> What I was inspired to give—
> By bread alone doth no man live,
> And water makes a man depressed.

More subtle in its effects are the lines addressed to his portrait, 'Image of me according to John / Back from the world behind his brow.' Here Gogarty manages to suggest both the special qualities of many of Augustus John's paintings and yet his own dismay at an image he does not recognise as his own:

> But on your face a pallor rests.
> The opals of Elysian skies
>   Such as he paints around his friends
> Are not reflected in those eyes,
>   In vain that coloured peace descends;
> And never in the meadows where
>   He sets his women great with child,
> And dew has calmed the atmosphere
>   And all the willowy light is mild—
> O never in his mind's Provence
> Did you come by that look of yours!

Yet the painting and the painter's subjective vision of another's vulnerability have to be accepted with assured wit and grace: 'No matter by what devious track / My image journeyed, there is fame / In that it surely has come back.'

The best of the occasional addresses added to the edition of

1924 was also the most recent: 'To the Poet W. B. Yeats, Winner
of the Nobel Prize, 1924'. The tone of this address, which urges
Yeats, as the subtitle suggests, to build a fountain to commemorate
his victory, is beautifully controlled. Neither mock-heroic nor
comic, the Roman triumph parallel on which the poem rests pays
a graceful tribute to Yeats. The three beat line, an interesting
contrast to the comic trimeter of 'To Augustus John', is light
enough to suggest gaiety yet measured enough for the occasion:

> What should you do with your wealth
>   But spill it in water and stone;
> With a Dolphin to scatter the spilth,
>   To be for a sign when you're gone
> That you in the town of your birth
>   Laboured and hewed at a cup
> To hold what the clear sky spills.

Evoking the gestures of 'Caesars and Cardinals', the address
encourages Yeats to provide 'For children to dabble and splash, /
And break the bead at the brim; / For sparrows to shudder and
swim.' The poem concludes, reminding Yeats of the symbolic and
mythological significance of the dolphin and paying high tribute
to the poet's lineage:

> For his back to a poet he gave,
> And he follows at Venus' heel;
>   He comes from the depths at a song;
> O set him on high in his place;
>   For he stands for what flows in the lovely and strong
> And a sign for the Julian race!

Yeats himself would remember those lines, years later, when, in
'Byzantium,' he wrote, 'Astraddle on the dolphin's mire and
blood, / Spirit after spirit!' In so doing, whatever might have been
his recorded attitude towards Gogarty's addresses, he was demonstrating that genius may pay its own tribute to a fancy that delights
and charms.

4

A Crop of Wild Apples

'IT IS not often', began AE in an introduction to the American
edition of *Wild Apples*, 'that a friend of many years enchants us
by the revelation of unexpected beauty.' AE went on to explain
that 'Oliver Gogarty had for two decades delighted his intimates
by a wit from which nothing was immune' and that, 'We were
hopeful that the art which bedazzled us would some time incarnate
in a form where we could share our laughter with the world.' But,
AE explains, though he had expected almost anything from
Gogarty in the comic novel or drama, 'I did not expect beautiful
poetry.' Perhaps, though, it is when AE describes the manner in
which Oliver Gogarty 'published' his poetry that he makes his
most interesting observation. Having accustomed his friends to
broadly comic verse, Gogarty 'began shyly to show us verses of a
different character, and one by one these lyrics entered into
memory and created in us a new imagination of our friend.'
Imposed upon too long by Buck Mulligan and by the legendary
Gogarty, we too require a new imagination of him. And that new
imagination must take into account that he entered the world of
letters not as an 'artist' but as an impatient doctor profoundly
drawn to poetry but uncertain of his reception as a professional
poet in the market place of literature. Only Dublin among modern
cities could have brought a Gogarty into being; only Ireland in the
age of Yeats could have nourished his talent. For, if Gogarty and
his friends were quite capable of saying *anything* about *anyone*,
they were also capable of great generosity. The responsiveness of
AE and Yeats to Gogarty's first proffered 'serious' lyrics gave him
the encouragement he needed in order to see himself as 'poet'.
Moreover, it was not merely that George Russell was telling him,
as early as *Blight* that 'you have a couple of masterpieces tucked
inside your skull somewhere,'[1] or that he opened the pages of

The Irish Statesman to his friend's poetry or that Yeats criticised Gogarty's lines and published him through the Cuala Press, but that they helped to create the ambience necessary to an art like his.

Wild Apples demonstrated that this ambience would continue to sustain the lyric talent manifested earlier in *An Offering of Swans*. The publication history of the volume is somewhat confusing, for the three separate editions bearing the title differ so markedly from one another that they must really be considered separate and distinct works. The Cuala *Wild Apples*, 1928, was a collection of twenty-seven new poems, only thirteen of which were to survive to the *Collected Poems*. The second Cuala edition was published in 1930 with a Preface by Yeats and was, in fact, a selection made by him. It contained thirty-three poems, thirteen of which had appeared earlier (in *The Ship* and *An Offering of Swans and Other Poems*) and the rest of which had appeared in *Wild Apples*, 1928, excepting for five new poems. To further complicate matters, the beautiful American edition of *Wild Apples* (1929) published by Jonathan Cape and Harrison Smith, with a Preface by AE, contained forty-seven poems. Nineteen of these were poems that were not included in either of the Cuala editions, and most of the nineteen were recent work. So, in speaking of *Wild Apples*, everything depends on which edition one means.

In a fine monograph, *Yeats as Editor*, Edward O'Shea has observed that if Yeats promoted minor poets in his Cuala Press editions he had very little time for 'mindless imitators'.[2] Nor did Gogarty respond to Yeats's interest with the flattery of imitation. Admiring Gogarty's 'Ringsend' as much as he did, Yeats must have seen how completely its matter and manner responded to and then opposed 'I will arise and go now, and go to Innisfree,' with 'I will live in Ringsend / With a red-headed whore.' Yeats was, moreover, very nearly ruthless in his editorial role, so much so that Gogarty could refer to certain of his poems as ones 'uncensored' by Yeats.[3]

The correspondence with Gogarty over what was eventually to be *Wild Apples*, 1930, incomplete because most of Gogarty's letters have disappeared, is full enough for us to see how Yeats managed to have his way, combining an engaging flattery of his own with an inflexible authority. A letter of 6 January 1928 apparently so provoked Gogarty that he answered Yeats back on the margin. 'Now about the poems,' Yeats writes, 'I shall be very glad to have a book from you for Cuala, but I cannot put it in until after my own book which is just finished . . . Lolly . . . might not be able to begin your book for three months, can you wait so long?' It was next to this suggestion of a delay that Gogarty wrote in the margin, 'I'm not going to.' And apparently sensing that Yeats might have a larger edition in mind than he himself had, Gogarty added, 'Besides an edition of 25 is enough for my public.' Yeats's letter continues, exuding charm but revealing a fixity of purpose:

> You are much too eminent a person for me to ask to see your manuscript as I do generally before accepting a book for Cuala. Whatever you write will be valuable to the Press, but I would like for my own pleasures' sake to see your book.[4]

In the complicated publication history of *Wild Apples*, Gogarty seemed to have gotten his way at first. Cuala first produced a private edition of fifty copies apparently 'uncensored' by Yeats. But Yeats persisted over a period of two years when he was at times in desperately poor health. By early May, 1929, it seemed that Gogarty actually had more than twenty-five or fifty readers in the United States. Jonathan Cape and Harrison Smith were producing their enlarged edition. At the same time, Yeats was at work on a preface for a Cuala volume. 'I doubt if my preface would be of any use to Cape,' he wrote, probably in response to a request from Gogarty, 'I shall write about a selection chosen by myself and no doubt give my reason for my preferences and Cape will publish your total work or at any rate "Wild Apples much enlarged".'[5] Late in 1929, Yeats was still making additions to his preface.[6] Apparently, though, Gogarty was now thinking in terms of another private edition of a small group of new poems that he had submitted to Yeats. He should not have been. On 20 February 1930, Yeats wrote from Rapallo, shifting his tone from one of authority to ribaldry, to criticism, to flattery, as he needed, to make his argument:

> I suggest that you allow me to select from the collection, and from the privately published Cuala book and from that part of Spottiswoode's book which my sisters [*sic*] edition of 'Swans' did not contain. This would make a fine book for Cuala and one helpful to your reputation. If you like I will take responsi-

bility for the selection and declare that your erotic verse is
chaste . . . or that it contains a criptogram [*sic*] declaring the
hiding place of the crown jewels. Anything you like. The
present little batch is too small . . . and only two or three times
do they come off. I have gone through it all and made suggestions on the margin. Of course you could publish it privately
with my sister . . . but much better let me select giving only
your best. Lennox Robinson tells me that you are getting a
reputation in America especially among people who collect
things hard to get at. Another little Cuala book—300 copies—
would be just the thing to keep their interest. Let me select you.
I want to praise you.[7]

Later in the year, the third version of *Wild Apples* appeared,
selected by Yeats, of course, and with his preface. 'Oliver Gogarty
is a careless writer,' Yeats wrote of the quantity of material from
which he had sifted his selection, 'often writing first drafts of
poems rather than poems but often with animation and beauty.'
Why did he praise Gogarty? For giving, as we have seen, a sense
'of hardship borne out of pride and joy.' This was the quality
he found in particular in Gogarty's 'description of his own
verses when he compares them to apples and calls them a "tart
crop".'[8]

Certainly the demands of craftsmanship and critical selectivity
that Yeats made on Gogarty were to the latter's advantage. According to Frank O'Connor, 'Gogarty once invited me to come to
Yeats's flat with him—"He's writing a few little lyrics for me,
and I'd like to see how he's getting on." '[9] Not so bent on tossing
off a witticism but just as wryly, Gogarty might, in his correspondence, refer to Yeats's 'censorship'; and he might, in mockery
of his situation, describe to one of his correspondents 'Yeats editing of my verses:—simplicity restored to my open text and
destroyed quite laureate efforts as I imagined.'[10] Yet it is clear
from his tone that he appreciates Yeats's attention. Nor is there
any mistaking his pride, when he writes in another letter, 'Yeats
is so bent on giving his country of his best in the Senate that he is
neglecting his writing. Here is a poem of mine which he passed
for metre, etc.'[11]

It is not the case that Gogarty accepted all of Yeats's suggestions
for revision nor that Yeats was invariably right in the selections

he made. Probably his suggestions for individual poems and his standards mattered most. His *Wild Apples* (1930) perhaps deliberately neglects nearly all of the very accomplished work that had appeared in the American edition a year earlier and passes by some of the very wittiest and most engaging poems in the volumes from which he drew much of his selection. The Gogarty Yeats emphasised in his selection was the pure singer, the poet closest to the Renaissance lyrics.

Wild Apples, 1928, and the 1929 American edition are thus the editions that shall concern us here, for they contain most of the new poems. Of the two editions, the first Cuala is the less substantial, since it contains a number of poems Gogarty eventually chose not to include in his canon, 'To George Redding', for instance, a number of love lyrics and descriptive poems. Two sonnets in praise of AE ('To a Friend' and 'To AE Going to America') and three heptameter quatrains 'To James Stephens' were carried over to the *Collected Poems*. Pleasant enough as occasional pieces to admired friends, these three seem a little bland. At this stage of his career, though, even the less inspired pieces may be lighted up by a particularly good line or passage, as, for instance, when the lines to James Stephens suddenly come alive with 'A mind that lit the Liffey could emblazon all the Thames.' Still, one regrets that while these three poems were preserved, Gogarty chose not to carry over two sharp-tongued epigrams, 'Upon Horan' and 'Upon Dawson', which are really more accomplished. Written with the left hand, as Robert Graves has described the Muse poet's satiric pieces, the first of these satires lauds the fertility of one whose 'bastards, through some failure in your force, / Were prematurely born or early buried.' The second mocks another Dubliner, somewhat—but not much—more gently, for his and his father's literary pretensions:

> No need to boast yourself well-read:
> The gift's hereditary rather;
> 'I read, before I go to bed,
> CHAPTERS of Sappho' : Thus your father!

Gogarty was like Robert Graves's Muse poet also in that he produced a great deal of impromptu verse with an unfinished quality and even published many good but uneven poems. Certain of the first poems in *Wild Apples*, 1928, illustrate his propensity to experiment with Greek measures in English. 'With A Coin from Syracuse' begins beautifully:

> Where is the hand to trace
> The contour of her face:
> The nose so straight and fine
> Down from the forehead's line . . . .

The second stanza begins on the same level, flags in the second and third line, where the language is uninspired, but picks up with the fourth—a line as assured as it sounds:

> The curved and curtal lip
> Full in companionship
> With that lip's overplus,
> Proud and most sumptuous. . . .

But in the third stanza, Gogarty permits himself the kind of word division and rhyme that, among English poets, Hopkins characteristically employed, though Gogarty's precedent was Sappho.

> Which draws its curve within,
> Swelling the faultless chin?
> What artist knows the tech-
> nique of the Doric neck. . . .

'Admonished' by Edward Marsh for splitting a word in this manner, he defended himself by citing three precedents in Sappho 'from whom I cribbed the trick, or the tech.'[12] The real problem with the passage, however, is that the rhyme in English has a strained and comic effect that is not appropriate to Gogarty's subject; the poem flounders and does not really recover until the concluding stanzas.

The poem following this one in the volume, 'Portrait with Background,' which develops a parallel between 'Dervorgilla's supremely lovely daughter' and a modern beauty, is written in Sapphic stanzas and is technically interesting. Yet, despite some fine efforts its two subjects jostle one another: the tribute to 'long limbs . . . and golden hair' and the attack on the Irish political situation, on 'the men of a few acres / Ruling a country'. The political element in the poem, first evidence of a pressure that would grow in intensity, might easily be confused, as Yeats's idiosyncratic political position so often (and sometimes deliberately) is, with Fascism. There is shrillness in the language of the poem to be sure; and 'I would have . . . drilled the Too-many and broken their effrontery' sounds authoritarian. It is, of course, but it does not evoke, as Fascism does, the mystic communion of mob and leader. The political attitude behind 'Portrait With Background' was reactionary in the sense that the poem was a reaction to the apparent attempt on Gogarty's life, to the burning of Renvyle House, and to assassinations, civil disorder, burning and pillaging that had taken place—actions one can not regard as those of humanitarian liberals. The political element *within* 'Portrait With Background' is part of a hyperbolic and conditional tribute to a beautiful woman that is highlighted and developed to such an extent that it takes over the poem. One has also to consider the aesthetic connotations of 'Gogarty's' wish to build 'once again the limestone lordly houses'. Gogarty, like Yeats and like another middle-class writer with whom one would not expect to compare him, Evelyn Waugh, was wont to employ the great house as a symbol of nobility, order, and grace; and these are the aristocratic values Gogarty poses against the anarchy or the mob, the petty ambitions, narrowness, and greed that he saw disguising themselves as patriotism. Nevertheless the artistic problem one senses in 'Portrait with Background' is that Gogarty actually wanted to write a poem about the contemporary shabbiness of motive and demagoguery he regarded as a betrayal of Ireland; and, in this case, the lissome blonde was not the right object to put in the place of the real one!

Closely following 'With a Coin from Syracuse' and 'Portrait with Background' in the collection, however, is another 'Portrait' subtitled 'Diana Clothed'. And in this poem Gogarty's touch is perfectly controlled. Though he was to banter with Yeats, when the latter was producing the *Oxford Book of Modern Verse*, pleading that he not immediately precede Hopkins, and was later to insist that Hopkins had introduced the hiccough into English poetry, this 'Diana' poem demonstrates that he could successfully assimilate some of Hopkins's techniques.[13] Hopkins's characteristic compound modifiers, his syntactical counterpointing of thought stress with line structure, his 'springing' of a conventional metrical beat are so thoroughly adapted to Gogarty's own voice and form that few readers can have sensed the technical closeness of this poem to the work of the Victorian Jesuit. The image of the woman in the portrait is superbly captured, as is the emotion of the *persona* while he discovers the meaning of the image. The lyric opens with a breathless rush of words describing the stunning costume of 'Diana' and suggesting the moment of discovery:

> Who would have thought
> That your mottled and your speckled,
> Wavering and dappled,
> Leaf-brown costume in the light,
> Held at the shoulder
> By an orchid's freckled anther,
> Covering a bosom of an interrupted white,
> Was but the pelt
> That the Maiden, the Resistless,
> Light of Heel, the Huntress,
> Yes; . . .

That 'Yes' of certainty and the pronounced caesura brilliantly render the halt of recognition. The pace resumes, qualified, first, by the pause and, then, by the lengthening of the lines:

> Yes; the tall Toxophilite,
> Skinned in the brakes
> By her fatal arrow's flight?—
> Nothing to do with a merciful mild amice;—
> Too well I know, and it needs no second sight!

The witty punning on 'second sight', the vividness of the mythological reference to that huntress chaste and cruel, the deliberate harshness of the 'k' sounds that precede the final admission of mingled terror and delight, the ambivalence of emotion in the conclusion, all of these attest to the imaginative intensity of the poem:

> Ah now I know;
> I should long ago have guessed it
> From your way who wear it,
> It is nothing more than this:
> Cruelty clings to it—
> It is nothing but the chlamys
> Covering and showing up
> The breast of Artemis!

Among the other most successful poems of the collection, there is further evidence of Gogarty's stylistic range. For instance, 'Marcus Curtius' pays tribute to a Roman who 'In response to an oracle which declared that a gulf recently opened in the Forum could only be closed by casting into it that which Rome held most dear . . . mounted his war-horse and plunged into it.' His conviction that Rome 'held dearest . . . her chivalry' and his gesture serve far better to express the poet's admiration for heroic action and Stoic endurance than the lady's beauty in 'Portrait with Background'. Here the restraint of the quatrain and the epigrammatic terseness embody the theme of an inner discipline on which such action depends:

> From softness only softness comes;
> Urged by a bitterer shout within,
> Men of the trumpets and the drums
> Seek with appropriate discipline,
>
> That Glory past the pit or wall
> Which contradicts and stops the breath,
> And with immortalising gall
> Builds the most stubborn things on death.

Resting on a paradox comparable to this association of sacrifice and nobility, 'The Crab Tree' does not evoke a classical mode or myth. As disciplined, however, as 'Marcus Curtius', within its freer stanza, it is a joyous introduction to the entire group of poems:

> Here is the crab tree,
> Firm and erect,
> In spite of the thin soil,
> In spite of neglect.
> The twisted root grapples
> For sap with the rock,
> And draws the hard juice
> To the succulent top:
> Here are wild apples,
> Here's a tart crop!

A song with a cunning irregularity in its rhythm that appropriately expresses its theme—the beat on which that rhythm moves being a curious amphibracic dimeter—'The Crab Tree' celebrates nature and solitude, past and present, passion and order. More epigrammatic than imagist as it develops, the language of 'The Crab Tree' remains firm and vital. Gogarty's 'great tree of Erin' :

> . . . takes from the West Wind
> The thrust of the main;
> It makes from the tension
> Of sky and of plain,
> Of what clay enacted,
> Of living alarm,
> A vitalised symbol
> Of earth and of storm,
> Of chaos contracted
> To intricate form.

David Clark has written a nice analysis of the intricate rhyme effects of the poem but argues that in parts of the poem, content is at war with metre. Clark's notion is that, as he describes the tree, Gogarty needs a 'wider' line. Yeats's 'O chestnut tree, great rooted bloomer' seems better to him. Even something like 'Under the spreading chestnut tree the village smithy stands' would be better, he states—even though Longfellow wrote instead 'Under the spreading chestnut tree / The village smithy stands.' Clark's analysis seems to me to rest upon what has been too pompously called the fallacy of imitative form.[14] It is an approach that, once taken, could lead one to reject any fixed stanza or beat, or even to argue that many lines of Yeats's 'A Prayer for My Daughter' are insufficiently turbulent and windy for the storm depicted in them. In considering the form of 'The Crab Tree' on Clark's assumptions, I would want to attend to what Gogarty actually does to his dimeter lines when he moves from ones like 'Here is the crab tree / Firm and erect' to ones like 'A forest tree spreading / When forests are gone'. To my ear, given the metrical and quantitative norm, the lines do, in fact, expand. Moreover, I would want to attend to the relation of the form to the *persona*'s emotional response to every aspect of the tree, since that response is the real subject of the poem. Considering that response, the *persona*'s sense of firmness, bleakness, sharpness, hardness, tartness, thrust, contraction, acerbity, grimness, and even sweetness seems appropriately realised in line and beat. In essence, the crab tree is an image of Gogarty's own art throughout the collection, of the qualities Yeats discerned when he spoke of 'a hardship borne and chosen out of pride and joy'. The concise interrogative of the final stanza is answered by the poem itself and the best of those that follow: 'What sapling or herb / Has core of such sweetness / And fruit so acerb?'

The mingling of acerbity and sweetness was an essential aspect of Oliver Gogarty's poetry. 'Aphorism', which became 'Ringsend', demonstrates again the intensity of utterance and effect the mingling of these apparently antinomial qualities can achieve. Gogarty never wrote a finer poem. Yeats said of it, he 'would be certain of its immortality had it a more learned rhythm' and he added, 'as it is, I have not been able to forget these two years, that Ringsend whore's drunken complaint, that little red lamp before some holy picture, that music at the end.'[15] A metrical tour de force in which a light anapestic beat does things it is never supposed to do and ironically subtitled 'After reading Tolstoi', 'Ringsend' takes us into the milieu of Realism. It evokes by its naming of one of Dublin's dingiest neighbourhoods and by its succinct and assured 'imaging' of the (inevitably) broken panes over the door and of the red light Yeats noted, a whole atmosphere of squalor and poverty. The lyric opens with a declaration of commitment to this 'reality', its excited anapestic movement restrained in the first four lines by a number of subtly stressed syllables in compounds ('Ringsend', 'fan-light', 'hall-door'):

> I will live in Ringsend
> With a red-headed whore,
> And the fan-light gone in
> Where it lights the hall-door;
> And listen each night
> For her querulous shout,
> As at last she streels in
> And the pubs empty out.

The lyric movement is slower in the next lines—due to an iambic foot and the hovering of accent following it—but it quickens in the adjectival passage, then slows for the superb conclusion as accent and sound quality complement the image:

To soothe that wild breast
With my old-fangled songs,
Till she feels it redressed
From inordinate wrongs,
Imagined, outrageous,
Preposterous wrongs,
Till peace at last comes,
Shall be all I will do,
Where the little lamp blooms
Like a rose in the stew;
And up the back-garden
The sound comes to me
Of the lapsing, unsoilable,
Whispering sea.

Brief as it is, 'Ringsend' is an immensely accomplished poem. Sensitive as always to the quality of Gogarty's work, Yeats argued that inasmuch as it is both 'clear and inexplicable' it would be misjudged.[16] Like his own frequently misjudged early poem 'The Lake Isle of Innisfree', to which its opening alludes by way of contrast and with which it shares the archetypal image of water as purifying release, 'Ringsend' reaches below the level of consciousness. What could be simpler than it—or more profound? One can sense the rightness of Gogarty's simile of the lamp blooming 'like a rose in the stew'; because even granting the ambiguity of the simile, we recognise the aptness of the figure to the particular tawdriness it adumbrates, just touched by a kind of vulgar 'prettiness'. One can tell, too, just how that series of sibilants works in the final image of the sea, its sounds echoing what the language portrays. But can one with any exactness articulate everything connoted by the whispering of the unsoilable sea as its sound comes up through the garden? The power of Gogarty's conclusion is that it evokes with extraordinary delicacy everything we have ever known or sensed about the racial memory, the amniotic fluid of the womb, the origin of life in the sea, the pre-existence of the soul, and, even, the state of innocence. 'Ringsend' is not *symboliste* but it is symbolic; it affects no learned rhythm, but its rhythm is that of experience and wisdom. At its deepest level and in the economy of its length and style, it reflects Gogarty's metaphysical vision of the condition of the soul in the world of Becoming; that soul, as he sees it, may transform even the boozy stew of our existence through the power of art—'old-fangled songs'—yet it is haunted by a sense of pure and unsullied Being.

But, if symbolic, 'Ringsend', it must be added, is not allegorical. What it connotes or suggests, it expresses *in* its unique cadences and images. Among the poems of *Wild Apples*, 1929, is 'This Kip', a sonnet—one of his best—that Gogarty regrettably chose not to include in *The Collected Poems*. Bearing an epitaph from Villon's 'Ballade de la Grosse Margot', 'Ce bourdel ou tenons notre estat', and suggesting, through its situation, slightly archaic diction, and harshness of imagery, the tone of Villon, this poem *is* close to being allegorical. It is also very closely linked to 'Ringsend' and yet a very different poem. 'This Kip'—the title being Dublinese for brothel—opens with a bold declaration of the conceit on which the poem is based: 'Whore-Master of the Body, O my Soul'. With a bitterness comparable to that of Villon, when, in a number of passages of the *Grand Testament*, he speaks of his affairs with prostitutes, this sonnet elaborates the conceit, describing the soul 'in loathsome ways constrained to move'. A man who did not disdain or despise life, Gogarty was able to accept existence, even on its basest level, as a manifestation of the divine. His own zest for experience, from his earliest days as a medical student, had given him a sympathetic knowledge of social and human realities; and yet there was in him, too, a powerful and idealist yearning for the transcendent. As early as 1905, he wrote in a 'Gospel' he sent to a friend, 'one becomes many, God becomes man, Being becomes appearance, the Root puts into leaf.' At the same time, he was also prepared to assert that, 'In the imagination all things are one. The imagination is the bridge between subject and simile; it is that which makes symbols possible and just; it is the One which remains; the sun.'[17] 'This Kip' is not the poem of a dualist who loathes the physical, but it is the poem of one who recognises a tension between the divergent poles of being. This whoring soul possesses the harlot Body and doles out coins, scowling contemptuously while, paradoxically, 'adding up the toll / Of sumptuous hours' and

Remembering that, capricious from her role
Of revel in the raucous, flaring kip,
She'll turn to you for solace from its rows;

For reminiscent sweet companionship,
To reach again to days, ere all was changed,
When there were fields to walk in unestranged,
And morning sun, and quiet in the house.

As in 'Ringsend', at the conclusion of the poem, all passion is spent; release and quiet are the solace the soul can bring to the harlot, life. More explicit and more limited than 'Ringsend', the sonnet is nevertheless imaginatively bold; the poems considered together indicate not only Gogarty's persistent themes but also the variety of poetic means at his command.

The Jonathan Cape *Wild Apples* is, in fact, a hoard of Gogarty's best. In addition to 'This Kip', there is another poem that should have been carried over to the *Collected Poems*: 'The Weathercock', a bantering love poem. Its tone is one of easy and engaging wit, yet this poem also explores a consciousness of opposite poles of being:

For I would, in those fields of air
Love you as in these fields of grass
And meet your moods and seem to veer,
Swinging around to let you pass . . .

Even the roistering and apparently ribald 'O Boys, O Boys!' plays off two realms of being, the mundane and the exotic, against one another: 'O Boys, the times I've seen! / The things I've done and known!' In this poem, the comic ironist who is the speaker may mock our workaday reality with hints of the adventures he has had: 'If you knew where I have been / . . . You never would leave me alone; / But pester me to tell, / Swearing to keep it dark, / What . . . but I know quite well: / Every solicitor's clerk / Would break out and go mad.' Still, while he insists we must reconcile ourselves to our routine, it is his final exclamation that entices us: 'So better go on with your work: / But Boys! O Boys! O Boys!'

Yeats has been described by Georgio Melchiori in *The Whole Mystery of Art* as a 'visual' and 'visionary' artist.[18] The terms could be applied to Gogarty as well, though the latter in a more qualified sense than Melchiori applies it to Yeats. No painter of the tulip's streaks but more responsive to scenes in nature and less abstracting and diagrammatic than Yeats, Gogarty had a delicate sense of the appearance of things, of nuances of colour, form, and motion. His poetry is filled with the imagery of sight. Though he seems never to have responded to Yeats's persistent interest in esoteric systems and, certainly, never to have experienced anything like the arcane vision of his friend, his poems suggest that he was a 'visualiser' in another and different sense—that his imagination was intense enough to summon up 'visions' of the real. There is, for instance, a minor poem ('Portrait'), an image of a child at play of which we learn, 'Sleep brought it back again / In its old sweetness.' And in 'The Plum Tree by the House' he appeals, having seen 'the clay break into bloom, / The black boughs all in white,' for the opportunity to entertain what his eyes have seen, on another level of vision:

> Then leave me while I have the light
> To fill my mind with growths of white,
> Think of them longer than
> Their budding hour, their springing day,
> Until my mind is more than May.

Again, in 'The Waveless Bay (Kiltymon)' a vision is consciously summoned: 'I close my eyes to hold a better sight, / And all my mind is opened on a scene / Of oaks with leaves of amber in the green.' All the sensuous details of the scene are evoked—mist of blue, calm azure bay, warm fields, stiff yellow gorse—as the vision detaches the *persona* from what surrounds him and lends to a moment of transcendence:

> It matters little what distraction drives
> Clouds through my mind and breaks the outer day.
> For all I know that distant water strives
> Against the land. I have it all my way:
> Through budding oaks a steadfast sun survives:
> Peace on the fading cape, the waveless bay.

One poem, 'The Phoenix', unsuccessful as a whole since the form and the image do not seem to be under control, quite specifically probes the visionary experience in its most appealing lines:

> But would there be the seeking for,
>   This wistful straining after things:
> Islands surmised from lines of shore,
>   Unless within me there were wings,

Wings that can fly in, and belong
  Only to realms revealed by song,
That bring those realms about their nest,
Merging the Seeker and Quest?

More interesting is 'The Emperor's Dream', a poem that shares
key details—the Emperor, the marvellous bird—with Yeats's
'Sailing to Byzantium' and 'Byzantium'. Probably it is no accident
that a later Yeats poem, 'Lapis Lazuli', which also concerns the
survival of works of art, came to include details, a Chinese carving,
an imagined scene, and the significant word 'gay', that Yeats
associated with Gogarty. Gogarty wrote:

When the internal dream gives out
I let my eyes wander about
Amongst the gay and the grotesque
Ornaments upon my desk . . .

Once glimpsed, the Chinese crystal bird stimulates 'internal dream'
again:

I sent my thoughts across the skies
Of regions where the Phoenix flies,
Where Past and Present are as one,
To bow before the Emperor's throne.

From this point on, 'The Emperor's Dream' develops the fable of
craftsman-artist and Emperor-God. The Emperor having commanded proof of the artist's genius—

. . . paused and solemnly averred:
The crystal wings without a flaw
Were those that in a dream he saw.

The artist's subtle flattery returns us to Gogarty's 'Gospel' of 1905,
according to which the imagination bridges the gap between the
one and the many, for the Chinese craftsman replies:

. . . in the Emperor's mind were held
Art's emblems; and, if one excelled,
Of those who mould, or carve, or limn,
His genius was due to him.
. . . at this the Emperor laughed,
Praising the master of a craft
Which had so worthily enshrined
Things hidden in an Emperor's mind.

Naïvely fabulous though this narrative may be, it is a metaphysical account of the nature and source of a visionary art.

The eight lines of 'Fresh Fields', however, are Gogarty's most perfect rendering of the visionary capacity through the faculty of sight. Here absolute simplicity of diction and economy of detail convey an experience that transcends reason:

> I gaze and gaze when I behold
> The meadows springing green and gold.
> I gaze until my mind is naught
> But wonderful and wordless thought!
> Till, suddenly, surpassing wit,
> Spontaneous meadows spring in it;
> And I am but a glass between
> Un-walked in meadows, gold and green.

One has to turn back to the seventeenth century to discover in English poetry the capacity to render an ecstasy such as this with such simplicity, grace, ease, and gaiety. While 'Fresh Fields' manifests none of the complexity of a poem like Marvell's 'The Garden', it depicts a comparable experience—as a Cavalier poet might have known it. In Gogarty there was just such a mingling of spirituality and sensuousness as there was in Andrew Marvell, and a comparable capacity to render details, emotions, and experiences of exquisite fragility. He differs from the metaphysical poet tremendously, of course. The directness and swiftness of 'Fresh Fields' are nothing like the intricacy of thought and feeling in Marvell's poem. Nevertheless, the image of a transparent mind that Gogarty summoned up in these four couplets is as close as any poet of our century has come to the annihilation of 'all that's made / To a green thought in a green shade.'

Among the new poems of *Wild Apples*, 1929, were a number devoted not to the heavenly Aphrodite but to her earthly manifestation. 'The Nettle', comic and erotic in a way that an imagination coming to maturity among the Edwardians could be, recounts how 'my Love was stung, / My girl-Adonis on the thigh by nettles.' The conversation of the lovers is appropriately risqué and elliptical:

> O what a bore! I must sit down, said she;
> I cannot walk! . . . O darling, what's the matter?
> A nettle stung me where you must not see,

Just where my stocking ends and thigh grows fatter.
But I will shut my eyes before it gets . . .
And you shall guide me so I shall not miss it—
Before the poison in your system sets
I'll press my lips and very gently kiss it.

The passage that follows is innocently depraved, perversely
delicate, for the lover proceeds 'Before the poison in your system
sets' to 'press my lips and very gently kiss it':

The little blister white upon white
Of sudden snow where violets were peeping,
Was reddened by the cure which set it right.

The final lines of this excellent piece manage to parody Donne
and travesty the classical convention of metamorphosis:

Now if, years hence, you find they are not keeping
My grave with all the reverence that is due
To one whom Beauty's smile in Life elated,
O, Busybody, trouble not! Can you
Be sure the nettle waves to desecrate it?

At least at present it seems unlikely that ever again will a poet be
able to tap such sexual attitudes as Gogarty does here. This poem,
in which matter is negligible, frivolity of manner everything, is a
triumph of archness, a demonstration of the sheer delightfulness
of tone Gogarty could achieve.

Equally successful in its command of tone is 'A Pithy Prayer
Against Love'. Although Yeats offered Gogarty a ten-line revision
of six lines of this poem, introducing a garden motif, Gogarty
exercised his independence—rightly I believe—by rejecting nine
of Yeats's lines and then proceeded to exercise his judgment—
again rightly—by adopting one of them ('Give her a clout of it').[19]
In this priapic prayer, Gogarty's classical learning rests lightly
upon him, and dactyls and trochees dance a randy exorcism:

Gods, get me out of it!
Spirits of laughter
Come to my aid now
And exorcise it!

> O you, Priapus,
> Stand till you're skyward,
> Stand till you're all staff
> And cannot rise it!

Following this paradox, surely one to be fully appreciated only by the phallic divinity himself, such unromantic erotics as 'Blowing Jack Falstaff' and young Hippocleides are summoned to aid the reluctant lover. It is that 'Chiel' Hippocleides, though, whose obscene dances and cry of 'I don't care,' released him, according to Herodotus, from a marriage contract, who best illustrates the successful exorcism of the tormenting passion. In a beat that mimics both the incantation of prayer and the growing wildness of the cordax, Gogarty imagines how Hippocleides,

> Dancing incessantly,
> Dancing indecently,
> Danced, till he danced off
> A cure for all heart-aches
> (Dancing the cordax!)
> . . . .
> He danced off his marriage;
> Danced to surmount his
> Fate with: οὐ φροντίς [ou phrontis]!
> Teach me his courage.

AE once wrote that he doubted if 'Oliver was in love with any of the women he praises' and he insisted that 'he sees the lovely girl, but he suggests, however remotely, the psyche within the flesh.'[20] It is true that most of Gogarty's beautiful women are ideal images that have been put in the place of something else. Still, these last two poems are indicative of other attitudes towards woman and love. The 'little blister white upon white', however delicate, was upon substantial flesh; and the priapic laughter of 'A Pithy Prayer Against Love' mocks romantic idealism. 'Let your preposterous / Pole fall upon her : / That for her honour!' It is the sexual dance itself that provides a release from 'Love'. Indeed, the epigram 'On Troy', which also appeared in the 1929 collection, indicates an even more disenchanted realism : 'I give more praise to Troy's redoubt / For Love kept in than War kept out.' Another epigram, far more deadly, 'To "Aphrodite" ' did not appear until 1933, but is surely related to 'On Troy'. Here, even the title is cruel, the quotation marks themselves conveying scorn. And the epigram itself does not disappoint expectations created by the title: 'Venus I called you when your love began; / And I was right; and you Pandemian.' Precisely because this poet's imagination could move so freely between the Heavenly Aphrodite and the Common, such a range of tones and attitudes as we have seen was accessible to him and enlivened the three different *Wild Apples*.

D

Ireland and Troy

IN 1933 Macmillan published Gogarty's *Selected Poems* in New York, with forewords by AE and the American critic Horace Reynolds; this publication was an indication not only of the doctor's productiveness during the twenties and the first years of the thirties but also of a growing public for his poetry. Of the approximately one hundred poems selected for the edition, twenty-four were new; the rest had been gleaned from earlier volumes, including those privately printed. *Others to Adorn* which was published in England in 1938, very nearly corresponds to the *Selected Poems*, with minor changes and some additions. In substance, it is the English edition of the *Selected Poems*, graced with an appealing title from Spenser. Reading either edition now, one understands how Gogarty's fellow poet James Stephens could write to him just a few years later, 'in the English-speaking mode, you are the sole example of the classical poet writing anywhere today.'[1] In making that observation, doubtless Stephens had in mind both that Gogarty had found his models in Greek and Roman poetry and in English Renaissance poetry under the same influences and also that Gogarty found his subjects and themes where poets in the classical tradition have always found them. The beauty of woman, the delights of the natural landscape, the aptness of mythology, the power of time and death and change, the celebration of friends and occasions, the permanence of art: in these he found timeless themes just as he found in such forms as the epigram, the song, the polished quatrain, the freer Horatian epistle, the elegy, the mock-heroic narrative, the means to embody them. The playfulness of his imagination, even when most robust and bawdy—indeed, the tough realism he often manifests, far from being inimical to his classicism are an aspect of it. As he himself queried at the very outset of his poetic career, 'was there ever a classic composed in the modern sense, i.e. austere, colour-less, unromantic[?]. . . . This modern admiration for the cold and classic only exists because it is modern and the classics are old. Landor is "Greek" and "classic" but is more "classic" than Aeschylus or Euripides . . . we call the white marble classic. It was coloured once.'[2]

Among the new poems included in the *Selected Poems* of 1933 are a number that might have appeared in earlier Gogarty collec-tions and that demonstrate a balance of traditionalism and in-dividualism. Thus the sestet 'Death may be very gentle', in theme at least, would fit the *Greek Anthology*. It closes, however, with a carefully restrained paradox which is Gogarty's own and with a kind of sudden tenderness of which he was master: 'And he has with him those whose ways were mild / And beautiful; and many a little child.' Another poem, the brief 'Back From the Country', has the lyric simplicity and nearly child-like quality Gogarty found in certain of Herrick's poems; its good humour and its homely imagery, though, are entirely of its present moment and place:

Back from the country
Ruddy as an apple,
Looking ripe and rural
As the maid a farmer seeks;
Fresh as an apple
Shining in the pantry,
Back you came to Dublin
Whom I had not seen for weeks:
How I hid my laughter
Fearing to offend you,
Back from the country
With your apple cheeks!

Even a far different poem, the facetious 'Choric Song of the Ladies of Lemnos', takes as its subject an episode in the life of Hercules and renders the episode in a strophic structure that merges with the traditional ballad quatrain. Reminiscent of the playfulness of *Hyperthuliana*, the 'Choric Song' praises the virility of the hero in a language appropriate to Irish street song:

> Often strong and silent men,
>   With sorra much to say,
> Are with young and old women
>   Winsome in their way.
>
> Tis the great Tirynthian groom,
>   A boyo hard to parry!
> Rather ask the question whom
>   Hercules will marry.

On the other hand, in a mordant adaption from the Persian, 'To Shadu 'l-Mulk', the timeless and the contemporary are indistinguishable as a mistress who has taken a second lover is dealt with appropriately and the lover's vanity appeased, by a metaphor from barnyard or stable:

> Thus for the dam's rebellion,
> The ostlers often try her
> With a jackass, till the stallion
> Strikes the cobbles into fire.

More easily seen, to be sure, is the element of individuality involved in the startling modification of a traditional form. 'New Forms', for instance, which opens—'I gathered marble Venus in my arms'—in Gogarty's most classical and timeless manner, turns into a piece of satiric raillery, mocking a favourite contemporary target: rationalism as the enemy of imagination. The wrenching of accent (and less certainly of syntax) in the conclusion is justified by the irony: 'Alas, she fell and broke to many pieces: / Discovered later by a Professor, / He cried, "New Forms, new forms!" And wrote a thesis.'

In the face of these lines, it may be impertinent to suggest that while such poems as we have just examined remind us that Gogarty already had made a variety of poetic manners his own, other poems in the Macmillan volume show that he was moving out in new directions. Always responsive to the beauties of place in Ireland and to the heroic element in Irish history, particularly to the Norman past, he had a man of taste's disdain for the vulgarised forms of national symbolism. Steeped in the classicism of his masters at Trinity, he was, at the turn of the century and for some time thereafter, critical even of the enlightened nationalism and folk interests of Yeats and Synge. So it is intriguing to find him now trying his hand at a version of 'The Old Woman of Beare', the anonymous tenth-century Gaelic classic. In theme and tone, this lament of an aged woman which is also a randy celebration of life and sexuality, was well-suited to his earthy and ironic side. A free adaptation, nineteen quatrains as opposed to the thirty of Frank O'Connor's translation, and yet true to the essential metaphors, tone, and form, Gogarty's version opens with a paragraph stanza reminding us that the spirit of the old woman lived in Dublin's kips earlier in the century: 'This today had been Fresh Nellie, / For she had as wild a belly; / Or a kind of Mrs Mack, / For she had a bonnie back.' The first quatrain of the adaptation establishes a tone of regret qualified by earthy vitality:

> Now my ebb of youth is gone
> And my ebb of age comes on;
> Though the sonsie may be happy,
> I'm no longer soft and sappy.

Frank O'Connor's translation is both faithful to the original and accomplished as a poem in its own right. Yet there are stanzas where the Gogarty version is more alive. For instance, O'Connor has this:

> Though today they ask so fine
> Small the good they get of it;
> They are worn-out in their prime
> By the little that they get.[3]

Gogarty's stanza is more grotesque and more vivid:

> Now each bargain-driving clown
> Wants two ups for each go down;
> God, if I reciprocated,
> They would think themselves castrated!

O'Connor's conclusion, which is prolonged over five quatrains, is a sober and moving one. Here Gogarty firmly compressed, wishing apparently to insist upon the presence in the original both of a stoic acceptance of the inevitable and of a protest against asceticism:

> Every foot that moves must stop;
> Every acorn has to drop;
> For the blazing festive sconce
> Darkness now, and prayer's response.

Cups of whey at night and morn
For the crescent drinking horn;
But the nuns and all their whey
Have not washed my rage away!

Interesting less for what it does than for what it indicates is a
far slighter poem, 'Connemara', in the same popular stanza though
untouched by the irony that gives a bite to the old woman's complaint:

West of the Shannon may be said
Whatever comes into your head;
But you can do, and chance your luck,
Whatever you like West of the Suck.

What is interesting about the fifteen quatrains of 'Connemara' is
the fact that Gogarty is now associating the spirit of a particular
place with Irish legendary material and with a cherished theme,
the theme implicit in *Blight* and in the 'visionary' poems: his
longing, as in 'The Plum Tree by the House', for 'The Perfect,
the Forbidden City, / That's built—ah, God knows where!' This
particular nexus of themes—'You must not ask what kind of
light / Was in the valleys half the night,' and '. . . never ask the
right or wrongs / When mountains shake with battle-songs'—
suggests that Gogarty was reaching out towards a more intricate
development of subject in a longer poem. 'New Bridge' and
'Limestone and Water' support this view of a new development
in the poetry, for both of these, longer and more intricate than
most of his earlier 'serious' poems, express theme through the
exploration of a scene. In each of these, the thought emerges
gradually as he explores a particular place or landscape, the details
of which imply meanings beyond themselves. 'New Bridge' is a
meditation on the transitional, on the attraction and fearfulness of
the archetypal 'crossing'. It is at its best when most oblique: 'The
black bright water over there / Is flaked beside the brink. . . .
And underneath an arch I see / A long grey gleaming reach.'
'Limestone and Water', the most accomplished of these three, is
also the freshest and most original in image and diction. In the
opening stanza, the stone itself, man (by synecdoche), and the
buildings of man are brought into relation:

This is the rock whose colours range
   From bright to dark when wet with rain,
Clear as an eye whose colours change
   From smoke-grey blue to dark again:
This is the limestone base of earth
From which the best things come to birth.

Through the development of these particulars, the speaker, whose eye explores the landscape and its significance, comes to recognise not only the vital identity of all things but the generosity of time and the power of art:

The castle by the shallow ford:
   In ruin, but the upright line
Above the tangle keeps its word:
   In death the unbroken discipline!

If 'Connemara!' and 'New Bridge' may be taken as an effort to write a kind of poem new to him, 'Limestone and Water' has to be seen as an indication of Gogarty's success.

Among another group of the new poems, there is further evidence of a reaching out to what had not been done before, and even some evidence of strain. 'To Ninde' of all the poems in this group is most like earlier tributes to women's beauty, and all its terms of comparison evoking the charm of maidenhood are taken from the classical world. Yet a second motif ruffles the calm surface of this apostrophe: 'O young and lovely! Now I'm left / With old ideals gone; / Bereft of power to praise, bereft / Of high comparison.' Another poem, 'I Wonder' develops a related theme—man's love of woman and the discrepancy between past and present. The heptameter and octameter lines of this poem seem forced; and, despite its classical allusions, the poem is essentially discursive thought. In 'Faithful even unto Freud', however, Gogarty regains his wit. Like 'To Ninde' and 'I Wonder', this poem deals with a love into which an element of conflict has entered, a conflict far more mundane than any that has hitherto touched the love poetry. (The bitter epigram 'To "Aphrodite" ', mentioned earlier, with its contrast between love imagined and its reality, typifies the fundamental difference between these and the earlier poems addressed to women.) In 'Faithful even unto Freud', an ironic argument that fantastically elaborates the details of dream imagery is the means by which the subject is controlled:

> . . . If you came in
> To the Liberties of Sleep
> Where as proud as Saladin
> A preposterous state I keep;
> Would you ever guess each bride
> Was your own self multiplied?

Despite its psychological persuasiveness and wit, this poem ends ruefully, 'But nothing cures / Love the loved one still abjures.' 'Applied Poetry' is also developed through clever argumentation; and, as in 'Faithful even unto Freud', tone and manner are the necessary means by which Gogarty achieves distance from his subject. The quatrains of trimeter and dimeter lines and the light banter of the dramatic monologue may seem sheer play:

> So let us find a bank . . .
>   What's this? You won't?
> You think I mean to rank—
>   Indeed I don't—
> Doll Tearsheet with yourself,
>   My dear, you're dull!
> How could a lanky elf
>   Suggest a trull?

But the lightness of the tone masks a serious concern, explained by one of the quatrains: 'The only way to capture / What may not be expressed / Is turn it into rapture / Or turn it into jest.'

Of this group of poems of troubled love, 'Sub Ilice', which handles its subject most obliquely, is the most successful. The long line that did not quite come off in 'I Wonder' here seems perfectly adapted to the dramatic monologue form and to the meandering thought pattern of one on an imaginary stroll in Italy. Gogarty's literary allusiveness, casually exhibited as it mingles with the distracted thoughts of a 'tourist' responding to the sensuous appeals of the Southern landscape, was never better or more comically used:

> Is that Alba Longa? Yes; and there's Soracte.
> Soracte? Yes; in Horace: don't you 'vides ut', you fool?
> No! She's not a model . . . you will have her husband on us! . . .
> Though her buttocks are far better than the Seven Hills of
>   Rome!

A fantasy of a romantic encounter with 'a tall fair student girl from Dresden / Whiter than a cream cheese, credulous, and O / Earnest, and so grateful for the things that I might teach her,' leads to a guided tour. This ramble permits Gogarty to indulge his love of Virgil ('Rhythm's mountain ranges rose to sunshine from his page') and his erotic fantasy even more fully. The *persona* alludes to Eclogues Nine and Three:

'Virgil was Menalcas: let me call you Phyllis.
Now look up the Idyll where they tried what each could do;
There! "Vis ergo inter nos", and "turn about's" "Vicissim";
My pipe though not wax-jointed can play a tune or two.'

At this point, there is an abrupt break in the poem, as the speaker, addressing his friends explains that an ilex, a 'togaed exile' in Dublin, has precipitated the engaging yet erotic fantasising. The concluding lines of the poem, however, suggest the intensity of emotion that the fantasy—erotic and literary—has displaced: 'I turn to human grandeur's most exalted voice for reasons, / And not the least, that Virgil led a soul estranged from Hell.' The revelation of the final line comes with a shock; yet, having read it, we sense the troubled necessity that has impelled the estranged *persona* to such apparently spontaneous mental play.

'Europa and the Bull' and 'Leda and the Swan' appear untouched by the emotional pressure implicit in these poems. Nevertheless, they concern themselves with passions, divine and earthly. Both are accomplished examples of light versification and a distinct development of the talent Gogarty had earlier shown in the more broadly comic 'To a Cock'. In both, Gogarty has an assured control of tone and pace. Both are delicately and unobtrusively mock-heroic, or perhaps one should say mock-mythic.

'Europa and the Bull' is the longer of the two and the more overt in its implication. Gogarty's comic ploy was to treat the myth without limiting reference to a particular historical time but in terms of certain of the conventions of a modern provincial society. The dactylic measure, varied by the substitution of an iambic line that opens with an anapest, is the perfect vehicle for the exuberant narrative as for the passages of dialogue. At the poem's beginning, the king expresses his concern that 'Little Wide Eyes' has been allowed by her nannie to visit the farmyard, not because he fears the animals, but because,

Girls of county families,
Of men in my position,
With grooms are so familiar
It's as bad as man and wife!

And then there is this Never-to-be-
Too-much-deprecated
Tendency towards bringing
Only daughters up as boys; . . .

Convinced that he must spare Wide Eyes the fate of Connie Chatterley and protect her from the gross realities of the farm, the king sends her off to the shore. The mode of the poem is free enough to permit this delicate rendering of the scene:

Do you see that wave there,
Where the crescent curves lift,
Transilluminating
For a second into green
Miles of crystal daylight,
Then, the hissing snowdrift:
Light so water-tangled
That its sightless self is seen—?

Just as delicate is the way Gogarty balances the world of myth and the mundane reality. Europa, both 'the Archer Goddess' and a 'tomboy / With the scratches on her shins,' is filled with wonder to see 'A Bull, where nothing ever / Drew a furrow but a sail!' His touch is also certain with the minimal but telling erotic detail: For instance, 'Silky-soft' the bull's hide tickled, 'When she held the strong beast / Tight with either thigh' and 'Bulls are ill-directed / When you take them by the horn.'

In another kind of poem the didactic passage that follows the ravishment of Europa would not do, but here the license of a comic 'application' is permitted the narrator, who yet insists that 'the tales that suit me best / Are tales without a moral.' Still, he finds it possible to read the myth as a mockery of 'men who separate Mankind / From Universal Nature— / For what eloping god to-day / Would turn into a Ford?' If our age has a faith, jibes the narrator, it is in the abstract mathematics of the Einsteinian universe. In the myth of Europa, as retold here, sexuality, miracle, nature, and man are seen as inseparable. Farmstead and god may be poles of existence, but, as the king learns, existence is one.

Even more tactful and poised is Gogarty's comic touch in 'Leda and the Swan', where the stanza and the beat of 'Europa'—the latter that of the nursery rhyme 'Goosey Goosey Gander'—are quite different, lighter yet and more glancing in quality, and the mock-mythic is even more understated. Many would feel that it was an act of *hubris*, after the publication of Yeats's 'Leda', for Gogarty to have published his poem. But Gogarty stated that he wrote his 'Leda' first, and the poem does not challenge comparison with Yeats's.[4] Indeed, the two poems are so completely different in matter and manner that evaluative comparisons would be fatuous. Yeats's stunning sonnet depicts the very rape, dramatises the moment at which the supernatural enters the natural world; it is historical, metaphysical, cosmic in implication. Gogarty's poem depicts the human but extraordinary beauty of the maiden and the approach of the swan; it avoids the actual rape. It reverses, in short, the emphasis of Yeats, contented to explore the ordinary, very human, but lovely world in which the miraculous event innocently transpires—despite its fateful consequences. His Leda is a naïve girl, sporting in an Irish stream. She is both an impulsive and a sensuous maiden and the very essence of fragility and evanescence:

> In without a stitch on,
>   Peaty water yielded,
> Till her head was lifted
>   With its rope of hair;
> It was more surprising
>   Than a lily gilded,
> Just to see how golden
>   Was her body there:
>
> Lolling in the water,
>   Lazily uplifting
> Limbs that on the surface
>   Whitened into snow;
> Leaning on the water,
>   Indolently drifting,
> Hardly any faster
>   Than the foamy bubbles go.

Only a perfect control of tone and attitude could carry off a poem like this, ranging as it does from the banality of Leda's addressing the swan in nursery language as 'Goosey-goosey gander' to its delicate evasiveness in handling the consummation:

> Apple blossoms under
>   Hills of Lacedaemon,
> With the snow beyond them
>   In the still blue air,
> To the swan who hid them
>   With his wings asunder,
> Than the breasts of Leda
>   Were not lovelier!

Above all, though, Gogarty succeeds with his 'Leda' because in his comic imagination the commonplace and the miraculous, Ireland and Troy, could be one. Perhaps the exclamation of Leda's mother—uttered, one wonders, how often each day in Dublin or Connemara, less ambiguously, but never more appropriately than in this telling of the myth—best illustrates the consummate wit of the poem: 'What was there to say but: / Glory be to God?'

6

The End of an Age

WHEN Gogarty prepared the English edition of the *Selected Poems, Others to Adorn* (1938), he added very few new works; but, with the exception of 'Reflection', which was not carried over to his *Collected Poems*, they were substantial poems. Indeed, 'High Tide at Malahide' and 'The Mill at Naul' were the culmination of the longer 'visionary' landscape poem essayed earlier in 'New Bridge' and 'Limestone and Water'. The first of these is a poem of effulgent light captured near sunset; the second is a poem of night and dream. In both, a subtle form gradually adumbrates metaphysical nuances that cannot be reduced to statement.

In 'High Tide at Malahide' Gogarty has adopted a measure that is conventional but very free inasmuch as the iambic trimeter of the opening expands to an apparently much longer line of anapestic trimeter. The poem starts with an evocation of a moment between sunset and moonrise and captures the combination of dazzling light and mist so characteristic of Ireland. 'The luminous air is wet / As if the moon came through.' The *persona* of the poem, standing 'beside the tidal river' and responding to the 'ebb and flow' of the air, is responsive to another tide: 'And every axon of my brain / And neuron takes the tide again.' Such correspondences between the ebb and flow of ocean, air, and brain cells should prepare us for the vision that follows—a miracle rather than a calculation. It is a vision of the Irish past, of conquering warriors, Norman or Norse, returning to Malahide:

They are Norse! For the bugles are wild in the woods,
Alarms to the farms to look after their goods:
To bury their cauldrons and hide all their herds.
They are Norse! I can tell by the length of their swords—

Oh, no; by their spears and the shape of their shields
They are Normans: the men who stand stiff in the fields
In hedges of battle that no man may turn;
The men who build castles that no one may burn.

Like almost every other significant Irish writer of his time,
Oliver Gogarty was excited by the heroic possibilities of man and
by the heroic dimensions of his nation's history. 'We Irish,' wrote
Yeats, 'born into that ancient sect / But thrown upon this filthy
modern tide / . . . Climb to our proper dark, that we may trace /
The lineaments of a plummet-measured face.'[1] Too ebullient to be
tormented as was his erstwhile friend Joyce by the nightmare of
history and too volatile to desire, as did Yeats, a cosmology,
Gogarty was yet just as conscious as they of the unheroic quality
of modern society and just as compelled by the theme of rebirth.
In his own way in this poem, he climbs above the modern tide to
measure the dimensions of the heroic:

The founders of cities,
The takers of fields,
The heroes too proud to wear armour or shields,
Their blood is in you,
As it cannot but be,
O Townsmen of towns on an estuary!

Apostrophising the Swords River that has given him one of the
images of his vision, Gogarty finds in river and sea, in weed and
water, in ether and sound, in science and myth, assurance that the
greatness of the past survives, that all process is One, and that
implicit in flux are preservation, transformation, and eternal
return:

For sight and sound like a bubble tost
On the high tide no more than on ether is lost:
No sight or odour or country sound
Lately reflected or long ago drowned,
But rises again, and as beautiful
As the golden weed when the tide is full.
. . . .
For all that you brought from the fields of home,

Is saved, not lost, in the fields of foam,
And rises again, for it was not dead
Here where meadows and waters wed.

'The Mill at Naul' ends in no such certainty, but in tantalising
questions about the nature of reality. Once again, as in 'High Tide
at Malahide', the protagonist moves through the stages of his
vision as he speaks. To evoke sleep, he calls to mind the ruins and
river at Naul, these suggesting to him not time the destroyer but
time the preserver:

For keep above and mill below
There is no further way to go;
They have already gone so far
With Time, that as the hill they are,
Or as the mill-pond by the mill,
Which, though it flows, is standing still.

At this moment of stasis and motion, the speaker realises that he
is prepared to relinquish ego: 'And I can leave my pride which
raged / Too long here, in the keep besieged; / And let my love
descend to spread / Through lowly roofs the gift of bread.'
Neither fixed as allegory nor developed so fully as symbols, the
poem's images imply meanings beyond their own particularity.
(The poem is like Robert Frost's 'After Apple Picking' in this
respect.) Sleep, of course, is by natural association analogous to
death; semi-consciousness, by the poem's suggestion, to supra-
rational vision. And the mill, in the course of the reverie, becomes
a paradigm of the universe and of the creative mind:

I see the way, now half awake,
The protons and electrons take
To spin the world, and bring the grist
To wild dreams of the scientist,
Who knows, for all he hopes to know,
That round a myriad mill-wheels go
From some far pond, unplumbed and still,
Which breaks to power and moves the mill.

At the climax of the poem, dream becomes reality; the mill

trembles into power, and provokes not only a question that would
have delighted Bishop Berkeley but, beyond it, questions about the
soul, immortality, and the foundation of Being:

> I wonder now will this go on
> When light, when light is quite withdrawn;
> And if, when sleep is deeper still
> The Mill without the Miller will?

On the threshold of sleep and in the context of the vision-reverie,
these rhetorical questions—neither 'philosophy' nor systematic
thought but intuitions and hints—have a naturalness and inevitability about them as does the fact that the poem should end
without an answer. Indeed, commenting on the poem to an
American friend, Gogarty noted that he had 'tried to be light and,
at the same time to involve questions which no one can answer'.
But he stressed that the poem 'is and after all should be, a light
entertainment of dream and scene'.[2]

One other poem added to *Others to Adorn* was 'Aeterne Lucis
Redditor', formal in stanza, essentially 'classical' in metaphor and
allusion. Did Oliver Gogarty realise when he wrote it that he was
not only memorialising his beloved Trinity Master, Robert
Yelverton Tyrrell, but his own youth, Dublin's greatest age, a
world now irrevocably gone? 'Aeterne Lucis Redditor' is, indeed,
the epitaph to such an age, to such a humane and lively ethos,
that, however attractive we may find it, we are unlikely to know
soon again. Like all good elegies, this one is less concerned with
its particular subject than with those generous humanist values
associated with him and still important to those who have survived. Not that Tyrrell, wit, beloved friend, restorer of 'light by
which blind Homer saw', who had brought the glories of the
ancient world and its art alive for Gogarty and others, is not amply
complimented. Essentially, though, it is the image of a more serene
and spacious turn-of-the-century world and the classical tradition
in letters that are both mourned and celebrated here:

> You shared with us the mood serene
> That ruled the universal scene
> When Peace was guardian of the poor
> And only rusty was the door
> Of Janus, and the pillared shade

Revealed the studious colonnade :
The toga with the purple hem,
The temple that with quiet flame
Acclaimed the distant Emperor,
Aeterne Lucis Redditor.

Conscious of the cataclysm of violence then about to befall Europe,
and already experienced in Ireland during the 'Troubles', Gogarty
must have known just what he elegised when he concluded :

And not again in this our time
Shall sound magnanimous the rhyme;
The wolves have torn our pleasant folds,
And the Great Wall no longer holds,
But Love can bridge the Stygian shore.
Aeterne Lucis Redditor.

The great wall of civilisation was indeed falling, when Gogarty
composed his elegy. In addition, the Dublin world he had known
and loved was fast disappearing. In 1932, de Valera had at last
come to power in Ireland; in 1936, with Gogarty protesting until
the last minute, he abolished the Senate—and the notion that such
men as Yeats and Gogarty might have a place in the councils of
the nation. In 1933 AE left Ireland, ill and disdainful of the
repressiveness of the new regime; in 1935, Gogarty at his bedside,
AE died.[3] In the same year Gogarty published *As I Was Going
Down Sackville Street*, in effect, a memoir of the Revival. A
literary success, the book was in another sense a disaster, for it
provoked a libel trial and a financial judgment against Gogarty at
a moment of financial crisis. In 1939, Yeats died while Gogarty
was on a lecture tour in America. Gogarty's Ely Place residence was
sold the same year also, an indication that Gogarty already con-
templated exile. It was in 1939 too that *Elbow Room*, the last of
Gogarty's Cuala Press volumes, was finished.

Given Gogarty's productiveness throughout the thirties and
given, in particular, the strength of such poems as 'High Tide at
Malahide' and 'The Mill at Naul', *Elbow Room* is a considerable
disappointment. But as the thirties came to a bitter close, Gogarty's
creative energies were being devoted to prose works, to *Sackville
Street* and the two volumes that quickly succeeded it, *I Follow St
Patrick* (1938) and *Tumbling in the Hay* (1939). *Elbow Room*

contained an even dozen poems: and only a few of these are comparable to Gogarty's best.

According to Ulick O'Connor, the poem 'All the Pictures', one of the weaker poems in the group, was written in London, immediately upon the doctor's leaving surgery.[4] The poem is based on the stoic response of one of his patients on being told he did not have long to live, and it bears the traces of hasty composition. Yet the weakest line in the poem is an added one that violates the couplet pattern and employs an archaic word for a strained rhyme effect ('And woman's love not any mo'). This line does not appear in a manuscript version that has survived; and so the weaknesses one observes in certain of these poems may not entirely be the effect of hasty composition. Even the title poem of the group, an engaging declaration of faith by an incorrigible optimist, that reads like a reply to Frost's 'Desert Places', seems to me to be flawed by a bit of flippancy in the diction: 'Abhorrent and inhuman this / Chineses call, "The Great Abyss".'

Among the best poems of the collection are the relatively brief lyrics, 'The Blackbird in Town', 'Anachronism', and 'Thinking Long'. In these we find elements of extreme emotional pressure well-contained by the form. Yet there is unmistakable evidence of intense conflict. In 'The Blackbird in Town', for instance, the bird, 'Golden bill. . . . / With his gurgling beak,' which has legendary associations with valour in Ireland, is heard 'Here behind the huddled houses / Which the squalid gardens break'. In this sordid atmosphere, the bird defines poetry, 'Careless, sweet, and independent / Of all circumstance of Time' and defines an attitude for the speaker, 'Loudly whistling my defiance / In the slums of circumstance'. 'Anachronism' is more oblique in developing its theme of frustration. Here the early morning is shattered by the roaring of a mad beggar; as a response to this mad roar, an ironic vision of Homer reciting to an audience rises in the imagination of the speaker. 'And then, indignant, down the lane / The great dark beggar roared again.' His roar, in effect, expresses the frustration of the *persona* and of all modern men who find themselves in the 'slums of circumstance'.

Equally ironic is 'Thinking long', a poem that completes the group of troubled love poems we have seen in *Selected Poems*. Though it owes something of its opening and tone to Yeats's 'When You are Old', it is not at all closely imitative and it seems perhaps the most personal of all Gogarty's love poems. It opens gently enough, 'When children call you Grandmamma', and proceeds to recreate the image of the beloved's hair in youth—'glorious smouldering bands of sullen gold'. But the image is evoked only to reveal

> . . . this message from the Past :
> "Tis love that counteracts decay
> And lights and makes all Beauty last.'

The thought in these lines would be little more than a truism were it not for the painful twist of the conclusion. The beloved is made to

> . . . wonder if the love you spared
> To starve the light-heart man of rhyme
> Has left him low and you grey-haired,
> Though you are old, before your time.

Understatement—'love . . . spared / To starve'—could not be more bitter. At one and the same time the beloved is praised for what little she has given and terribly reminded of the consequence of her coldness. As a result, the commonplace truism one might otherwise regard as too explicit is revealed in all its inadequacy to the actual situation.

Elbow Room also included two poems more broadly comic in tone than witty that point towards the light verse of Gogarty's American years; and these are, in their own way, quite successful. 'Time, Gentlemen, Time' is filled with the roistering spirit of a good Dublin pub and protests against the rule of mechanical clock time :

> It makes me wonder whether
> In this grim pantomime
> Did fiend or man first blether :
> 'Time, Gentlemen, Time!'

'Sung in Spring' has a comparable quality of exuberant good nature in its allegory of our planet as a ship in space :

> No question can prevail on
> The Master of the Ship;
> He won't say why we sail on
> This never-ending trip :

> Though young and old and ailing
>> Hold contradictory views
> I think that simply sailing
>> Is the meaning of the cruise.

It is the comic tone of the poem and the frankly allegorical mode that permit Gogarty so explicit a conclusion, his statement of continuing regard for the Heraclitan notion of flux.

Yet in several of the poems of *Elbow Room* one discovers that the impulse to surrender to discursive thought is now strong in Gogarty. In 'The Forge', which is the strongest poem in the collection, this impulse is itself the subject of the poem; and, again, it is the comic tone that licenses the element of statement in the poem. Still, 'The Forge' is not comic in its opening, which rings with the beat of the hammer on the anvil and glows with the image of the blacksmith's fire: 'The bellows blows on the dampened slack, / The coal now glows in the heart of the black.' It is as if 'The Forge' began as a poem in the manner of 'High Tide at Malahide' and 'The Mill at Naul' and, failing to achieve the poise of these, turned into a wry examination of the difficulty of fusing feeling and thought. With gusto, the speaker, who has taken the hammer in hand, puts Bishop Berkeley to the test:

> I swing it up in my bulging fists
> To prove that the outside world exists;
> That the world exists and is more than naught—
> As the pale folks hold—but a form of thought.
> You think me mad, But it does me good,
> A blow is the measure of hardihood.
> I lift the sledge and I strike again
> Bang! for the world inside the brain; . . .

The landscape-vision poems had been able to embody their metaphysics in image and detail; but in 'The Forge' metaphysic vexes, and one thought leads to another, specifically to the difference between man and his maker—'Man may fashion but he cannot create.' Self-mockery provides a release from 'philosophy'; and an image from the beginning of the poem, the molten shoe, the witty 'turn' of thought:

> No wonder Pegasus cast a shoe
> When I succumbed to the English curse

Of mixing philosophy up with verse.
I can imagine a poet teaching;
But who can imagine a poet preaching?

Gogarty thus is able to bring 'The Forge' to a successful and paradoxical close in which he preaches the cause of non-didactic poetry, of 'song that is lovely . . . light and aloof, / As the sparks that fly up from the well shod hoof.' But the very means by which 'The Forge' succeeds, by becoming a poem about Gogarty's own poetic crisis, were means that *could* succeed only once! One other alternative, we have seen, was the light versification of 'Time, Gentlemen, Time!' or 'Sung in Spring'. Yet another was the badly flawed and 'serious' 'Fog Horns', which ends, after landscape and vision, in a few lines of overt preaching. Curiously enough, however, 'Angels' which seems an unabashedly impassioned sermon is a powerful poem, one almost on the level of 'The Forge'. Its opening is understated:

In an old court-yard,
Seen from a lane-way,
Down by the Liffey,
Somewhere in Dublin,
Whitened with stone-dust
Dwells an Italian;
And he makes angels.

The poem starts to pick up emotional force, though, as Gogarty remembers the 'Winged amorini, / Angels of Venus,' he has seen in Pompeii and then thinks of 'Hermes the Angel, / After his flight from / Crystal Olympus.' By association, his imagination then evokes Dante 'drawing an angel' and then the 'Grim civilisers'—'Dreamers of angels'—of the Italian Renaissance. At this point, Oliver Gogarty, singer of pure song, departs, and Oliver Gogarty, social reformer and author of *Blight*, returns. The latter exclaims:

O for ten thousand
Gifted Italians
Dwelling amongst us
Just to put angels
On the black fresco

Of this most dismal
Reasty and sunless
Town. . . .

. . . .

God send an angel!
Not a mere figment
From childhood remembered,
God, but a far-flashing
Terrible creature,
An awful tomb-shattering
Burning Idea
Of Beauty and Splendour,
A Winged Resurrector. . . .

Indeed, the author of *A Serious Thing* reappears in those lines, as once again an Irish writer cries out for national transformation, for the Redeemer to emerge from his tomb. Given the date of the poem, its celebration of things Italianate, and its appeal to God to 'Raise up a man' even 'if he must shout from / The mountebank platform / To gain him a hearing,' it is surprising that the poem has not been cited as evidence of the 'fascism' of Gogarty and his friend Yeats. However tempting it may be for the simplistic ideologue to see the poem in that light, I think it should be noted that the former Senator was alluding (albeit disdainfully in the case of the first) to Irish elections and Georgian architecture and not to the corporate state; he was protesting against an illiberal regime's failure to respond to social need or aesthetic possibilities. In fact, as the poem reaches the climax, it is more akin to the innocent bourgeois fantasies of Leopold Bloom ('Build up with gladness / The house individual / Set in its garden / Detached and uncrowded') than it is to those of General O'Duffy and his Blueshirts. The poem's ideal is the City of God on earth, with no churchy undertones but with strong Graeco-Roman overtones, which always appealed to Gogarty's sense of grandeur. Its aim is social justice; its enemy, totalitarianism, 'The living damnation, / Which comes from the crowding / That leads to the Commune.' Above all, its impetus is a heroic vision of man and his proper setting that an Ireland now being exploited by land and housing developers and a Dublin now being destroyed by port-developers and office-blockers would do well to ponder:

Why should the sons
Of the Gael and the Norman
Be huddled and cramped
With broad acres about them
And lightning-foot cars
At their beck to transport them,

Which overcome space
Like the sandals of Hermes?

Nations are judged
By their capital cities;
And we by the way
That we fashion an angel.

Seldom has the slum seemed nastier: the suburb more grand. But 'Angels' gives us the poet preaching, not the poet singing experience. It is, in Yeats's sense, 'rhetoric' rather than poetry, a quarrel with others rather than with the self.

Sackville Street and the Search for a Hero

ONE of the scenes in *As I Was Going Down Sackville Street*
(1937) depicts Gogarty as he is urged by an American publicity
man to prepare his memoirs. *Sackville Street* does seem to have
been undertaken in response to such prompting. When Gogarty
submitted some portions of the manuscript to the publicist's firm,
the editorial staff apparently had some difficulty finding any
'necessary counterpoint' in the material; moreover, the editors had
even more trouble locating the names they had expected Gogarty
to drop for them. 'It is evident', Dale Warren wrote from
Houghton Mifflin in June 1935, 'that the book will have legs of
its own, and not be hung upon a string of big names. Yet I think
that all the chief contemporary Irish figures and personalities
should be introduced, both as a matter of record, and because your
readers will expect you to give them the low-down.'[1] Later in the
year, Warren even provided a list of topics his firm's literary
advisers 'would want to find as well as expect to find' in the
volume of reminiscences.[2] Gogarty's own marks on the list suggest
that he made some use of it in writing *Sackville Street*, but the
completed book was nevertheless one that stood on its own legs,
its complex structure depending not in the least upon a string of
names or the real 'low-down'. Furthermore, as Gogarty worked on
the book, rich and varied as it became in the range of its characters,
scenes, and subjects, it assumed a distinctly political character,
condemning the disastrous consequences of 'politics' in modern
Irish life but demonstrating the importance of the individual to
the *polis*.

Widely anticipated before its appearance, *Sackville Street*
created a sensation in Dublin. In May 1937, Yeats wrote Dorothy
Wellesley:

Have you read Gogarty's book? Here everybody is reading it. A publican down the quays told a customer, 'You can open it anywhere, like the *Imitation of Christ*'. It is not all wit, one can say of much of it, as somebody said I think of Raleigh, it is 'high, insolent and passionate'. None of its attacks on things I approve vex me and that is because they are passionate. His only attacks are on modern Ireland. He is passionate not self complacent so we forgive him.[3]

Passionate those attacks on modern Ireland are, and the book's political perspective is so insistent that it must be considered first. *Sackville Street* is, in a special sense, a 'reactionary' work. Yet as a recent Irish historian has argued and demonstrated, 'Irish politics were extremely complicated during the "thirties".'[4] It would be altogether easy on the basis of individual elements within Gogarty's attack to oversimplify his position and to misapprehend it. After all, early on in the book, the Gogarty *persona* encounters General O'Duffy, who had led his Irish Brigade off to fight for Franco by the time *Sackville Street* was published; and, in the course of the ensuing dialogue, the *persona* agrees with almost everything the General has to say about the political situation. The General, who complains of de Valera's government, 'We have Moscow's anti-God and anti-mother love and anti-family,' also denounces the 'little commissars', the 'firbolgs' and the 'Plain Men' who are its administrators, in a rhetoric that is unmistakably of the extreme right. Throughout the book, Gogarty himself manifests contempt for 'bagmen' and 'bogmen'—that is, for de Valera's followers and the IRA. Perhaps the nicest thing he has to say about Eamon de Valera is to be found in an ironic passage defending the Long Fellow's Irishness: 'He is perhaps more Irish than any of us seeing that he looks like something uncoiled from the *Book of Kells*.' Add to all this Gogarty's celebration of the aristocrat, even of English aristocrats, his praise of Yeats, who wrote—we all know by now—three marching songs for O'Duffy's Blueshirts. Add to these pieces of evidence, such scenes as the one in which Gogarty encourages Yeats to join him in wearing a silk hat at the first official function of the Free State. All the proof is there, if one is seeking it, to raise the kind of cry that occasionally has been raised against Yeats: Snob, Middle-Class Climber, Fascist.

The difficulty with such an interpretation is that it fails either to account for the complexity of the book or of Irish politics. Ireland in the thirties refuses to fit the convenient Right-Left dichotomy. For instance, O'Duffy was, following the defeat of Cosgrave's party by de Valera's Fianna Fail, briefly leader of the emerging and centrist Fine Gael party; and his short-lived Blue-shirt organisation originated, at least in part, to protect freedom of speech and assembly, both threatened by extremists of the IRA. De Valera, himself known as 'the Chief', never adopted the pose of the Common Man, even if his colleagues did. Indeed, he appeared at public meetings astride a white horse and wearing a black cape; he was widely regarded by his opponents as an incipient dictator. Scarcely a liberal reformer during the thirties, he adopted policies that were theocratic, isolationist, protectionist, and conservative. Not for decades did his party, Fianna Fail, espouse substantial reformist measures.[5]

Gogarty's own political attitudes, as they emerged during the twenties and the thirties, do not seem to lend themselves to simplistic categorisation. Could one expect so paradoxical a sensibility to be other than politically idiosyncratic? Bent, however, upon a rather superficial political classification and unable to distinguish the impulses of a moment from an intellectual commitment, one could demonstrate a drift to the extreme right by a man formerly of reformist tendencies. As early as 1923 and as late as 1935, Gogarty was able, in the Senate, to imply that he approved of Mussolini. Indeed, in 1932, he went so far as to write an American friend that 'what we want is a fellow like Mussolini'. But in the same letter surveying the Irish situation, he also concluded that 'three commissioners could run the country';[6] and when he spoke, in 1935, on the Italian invasion of Ethiopia, he did so to ridicule the inconsistency of de Valera, now, he mocked, merely the gullible instrument of English foreign policy. Describing de Valera in 1933 as 'this Mussolini of Miseries', he certainly intended no compliment either to the Italian dictator or to de Valera.[7]

In the perspective of time, it is certainly difficult to consider the positions taken by Gogarty over his years in the Senate as representing an extremist ideological commitment. During the Civil War, he supported the Public Safety Bill, the harsh measures of which were designed to halt Ireland's drift into anarchic violence. In 1932 he argued that Ireland should remain in the British Commonwealth and 'keep with the nations who understand that the first principle of freedom is a freedom that does not permit interference with the personal liberties of the citizen'.[8] He was consistently hostile to government efforts to encourage the revival of Gaelic. He indicated his belief that Irish industries should be protected against international trusts. Conceivably, some or all of these stands might be regarded as reactionary or conservative—depending, of course, upon how one might define a liberal stand in the context. Gogarty supported the Shannon Scheme for the development of electricity, emphasising in his speech its importance not in industrial development but in providing the public with the light needed for education. He defended the proposed Electricity Supply Board against the charge that it was socialistic. He urged national upkeep of roads, pointing out that, in time, road travel would replace the railway; and he urged a national policy of reforestation. He also supported Land Banks for farmers. Conceivably some or all of these positions might be regarded as sane, moderate, even progressive. Gogarty advocated measures to protect farm animals against cruelty, to extend public health to the schools, to improve school buildings and the educational system. He also supported measures to eliminate slums and to protect female workers from exploitation. Conceivably, some or all of these stands might be regarded as sensible, progressive, perhaps even liberal. In 1929, Gogarty emerged as the Senate's most devastating critic of the successful effort to impose censorship of publications—'the most monstrous proposal that has been made in this country,' he called it.[9] And in 1934, he stood alone to suggest that there might be some medical and prophylactic justification of contraception. 'The alternative', he said 'is in disease, in child outrage and in the fate of any illegitimate child.' And he asked, 'Is prevention not better than murder?'[10] Whatever label one might want to attach to these various specific stands, I think it would have to be said of the man who, in that time and that place, rose to his feet to declare himself on the subject of censorship and contraception that he had an inspiring courage and that he gave the Irish Senate at least two moments of human greatness.

One of Gogarty's early notes to James Joyce was addressed to the latter as 'Scorner of Mediocrity and Scourge of the Rabblement';[11] in that greeting to Joyce, he caught the mood of an artist who was about to exile himself from his family, his nation, and his religion and who defiantly recognised the necessary isolation of the artist. Gogarty, himself, though he bowed to convention in the career he chose, recognised an inevitable solitude and apartness in the creative individual. 'What a pity', he wrote more than a decade after his mock apostrophe to Joyce, 'this Socialist pose is among the writers who wish to be and are popular—Shaw, Wells, Anatole France, Chesterton. Cannot somebody be a great writer and not mind popularity? Yeats is honester than these. It is so easy to fool all the people, if they have been to the Board Schools. The "Daily Mail" gives them their daily bread. This accounts for their inanition. It's ignoble of G.B.S. I told him so. Why impress the proletariat? It is bad enough for Statesmen to be reduced to it, but for *serious* people!'[12] Gogarty's own Senate career demonstrates how ill-equipped he was to make an appeal to the masses, or even completely to identify with a single party. Though he acted at times as spokesman for Cosgrave's Party—on the Public Safety Bill, for instance—his record in the Senate was essentially that of an individualist, not of a party ideologue. Like Yeats's, Gogarty's was essentially a party of one. He seemed to recognise this uniqueness as his radical commitment, when, thanking Yeats in 1929, for the Preface to *Wild Apples*, he wrote, 'Prophetically as usual you herald a movement which is coming against the drilling, the marshalling, the robotising of mankind, and point out that the lonely were the creators.'[13]

If the political rhetoric of *As I Was Going Down Sackville Street* sometimes seems in excess of the political facts of the time, inasmuch as a de Valera and his Party scarcely approached Socialism let alone Communism, we still need to inquire into just what it was that provoked Gogarty to passionate, political utterance in his book. Even today, Ireland has not escaped from the terrible heritage of the Civil War that racked the island following the Treaty with England; and it is in the events of that period that Gogarty's animus had its origin. Though one may have to conclude that the economic and foreign policies of de Valera in the thirties and forties eventually worked to Ireland's advantage, it is difficult to dismiss Gogarty's reading of the role the former played in the Treaty negotiations and the Civil War, even if what happened was more by accident than by design. As that role is depicted in *Sackville Street*, de Valera with Machiavellian astuteness allowed Griffith and others to negotiate with the English, and then, independence gained, provoked a Civil War over the Oath of Allegiance, an oath easily enough repudiated when Ireland might choose but providing de Valera with the issue that was to bring him to power. For Gogarty, as the *Sackville Street* scenes involving Arthur Griffith and Michael Collins reveal, it was these men who had led Ireland to independence, the latter through his brilliant military strategy against the Black and Tans, the former through his efforts as editor of *Sinn Fein* and then as a negotiator. Griffith, taciturn, deliberate, almost the opposite of the volatile Gogarty was, as I have indicated earlier, a man the latter worshipped. And for Gogarty, Griffith's untimely death was caused by the mental anguish of civil strife deliberately provoked by de Valera; Collins's death, by an IRA assassin's bullet.

Other details in *Sackville Street* suggest further reasons for Gogarty's detestation of de Valera and the Republicans. When Gogarty reports the burning of Sir Horace Plunkett's house, Kilteragh, by the IRA, he dwells on the loss of the philanthropist's collection of books and paintings and goes on to blame this loss on 'resentment':

> This resentment is not necessarily political at all, but is born of the under-dog's envy of the man who can build his kennel. Dull resentment against the cultivated and apparently ideal and leisured figure is an attitude of mind not at all confined to Ireland, but found in almost every country where there is civilisation, for civilisation is the enemy of the under-dog. And its disappearance will not help him. Civilisation is a veneer on the unremitting forces that seek to drag down all that is elevated.

Certainly one can point to personal reasons for the Senator's hostility to the IRA and to the course of Irish politics in the twenties and thirties. Had Griffith lived, Gogarty felt he might have filled the ceremonial office of Governor General, a post that would have permitted him to encourage cultural links between England and Ireland, as he did at the time of the Tailltean Games.[14] As we have seen, because he was a prominent supporter of the Free State government, Gogarty's life was threatened and his own Western house, Renvyle, was burned. In *Sackville Street*, he has far less to say about his famous escape from IRA 'corner boys' than about the destruction of Renvyle:

> Memories, nothing but memories. In that house was lost my mother's self-portrait, painted when she was a girl of sixteen. Her first attempt in oils. And her sampler of the big parrot, made with a thousand of beads, outcome of patience and peaceful days half a hundred years ago, under the tuition of the nuns of Taylor's Hill. . . . Books, pictures, all consumed: for what? Nothing left but a charred oak beam quenched in the well beneath the house. And ten tall square towers, chimneys, stand bare on Europe's extreme edge.

It is not the destruction of property as such, distressing as that must have been, but the injury done to the values and emotions it embodied that Gogarty protests. His *Sackville Street* reaction against 'modern Ireland', whatever the terms in which it was couched, was an attack on climbing, trimming, and vote-buying in public office; on drabness and mediocrity as national values; on a rigid and joyless and enforced Puritanism; on national indifference to culture, except at the level of cottage skills; on isolation from the civilisation of England and Europe. When he and Yeats donned morning coats and silk hats, they were making a deliberate symbolic gesture (too easily misunderstood as social affectation and pretension) in favour of a code of behaviour, of forms that would invest public life with distinction, in favour, if you will, of custom and ceremony and certainly of the exceptional.

In Chapter ten of *Sackville Street*, Gogarty depicts one of his 'at homes' which takes place in the midst of 'the Troubles'. Among the guests are Michael Collins and AE; around Ely Place are posted seven guards who, as Gogarty quips, 'draw the Republicans' fire and the Free State Government's pay'. A machine gun periodically sweeps the street. At one moment, a 'piece of moulding became detached and fluttered to the carpet'; the guests pretend to ignore it. In this context, at once violent, commonplace, and bizarre, the gentle visionary George Russell speaks to the political issue that is a central concern of the book. Yeats not being present, AE has ample opportunity to speak:

> 'The English mistrust genius in high places,' AE announced. 'They choose forceful average men as leaders. Intensely in-

dividual themselves, they fear the aristocratic character in politics.'

Having established his credentials by this criticism of the English, AE proceeds to argue that 'They have gradually infected us with something of their ways, and, as they were not truly our ways, we have never made a success of them.' The way is now clear for AE to advance his positive programme:

> 'We must fall back on what is natural with us, on what is innate in character, what was visible amongst us in the earliest times, and what, I still believe, persists amongst us—a respect for the aristocratic intellect, for freedom of thought, ideals, poetry and imagination as the qualities to be looked for in leaders; a bias for democracy in our economic life. . . .'

And, he continues, his language sharpening, as he contrasts the ideal with the reality: 'We were more truly Irish in the Heroic Ages. We would not then have taken, as we do today, the huckster and the publican and made them our representative men.' As AE's monologue is developed from this point, the element of fantasy gradually displaces fact, and there is a comic clash between Collins and the mystic. Thus AE's words about the Irish political scene and the qualities he regards as most 'Irish' must be taken as an element within the total context of the book and AE cannot be regarded simply as a spokesman for Gogarty.

Conversation, as handled in this work, is never static; like reality, as apprehended by *Sackville Street*'s dominating *persona*, it waxes and wanes. The Gogarty *persona* explains to the dazzled girls from Bryn Mawr who also had been at his 'salon' that, 'It has been said of AE that he is one of those rare spirits who brings to us a realisation of our own divinity and intensify it. He enlarges the Joy that is hidden in the heroic heart. He is a magnifier of the moods of the soul. . . . He is an artist. He teaches nothing. He communicates himself.' But in the entire context of the work, the words of AE have a moral substantiality about them that cannot be ignored. They both communicate the qualities of George Russell's moral being that should have entered Irish public life and they support the developing political thesis of the book: that de Valera's Ireland—indeed, modern urban society—seems incapable of respecting the free and imaginative mind.

When Gogarty addresses himself to the subject of aristocracy, he is disarmingly and comically frank. He admits to the worst of charges that can be pressed against him:

> There must be something if not of the courtier, then at least of the flunkey, in my composition. I like to have people better than myself about me. They radiate on me a security similar to that Julius must have felt when he had men about him of his own liking. Every Irishman loves an aristocrat. In all the sagas of Erin there is not the name of a commoner mentioned. Even the charioteers were noblemen. Let my critics digest that. Anyway, I dearly love a Lord, and I think I can analyse the reason: he stands for an established order of things, for an household of continuance with the obligations its traditions confer.

There is a boldness in the self-mockery of the passage that is so persuasive one is forced to abandon an initial judgment of snobbery and recognise the positive values Gogarty commends. (As he offers praise to a 'household of continuance', he reveals a kinship of sensibility, earlier remarked, not only to Yeats but to Evelyn Waugh.) Going one step further in his self-defence, Gogarty pleads directly with the reader: 'Blame me not at all or as much as you like when I honestly betray what may not be called a weakness in me, but a yearning towards the better than myself, to the "Beyond Man".' The comic strategy that he has employed here scores its point, I believe, and necessitates that we see him not as a conservative upholder of the *status quo* nor as a totalitarian but as an admirer on one level of aristocratic *panache*, and on another and more important one, of an ideal beyond the self. Mercurial as Joyce imagined him to be, Gogarty does not hesitate to make a *volte-face*. Having won us to his side by a comic frankness, he just as frankly reverses himself: 'But too much hero-worship is bad for the worshipper. It makes him lean his weight upon the hero at the cost of his own responsibility and power of initiative. Wait a minute, I assured myself, and I shall recover and contradict myself.'

Nevertheless, like so many other works produced by Irish writers in the early part of this century, *Sackville Street* is fundamentally concerned with the hero. Haunted by memories of the tragic defeat of Parnell, a martyrdom frequently associated with Christ's, the Irish imagination produced an extraordinary number of powerful works that probe the nature of the heroic and, indeed, the very question of its possibility in the modern world. The subject deserves a book in itself, one ranging from Wilde to Beckett, but one need only mention Synge's *Playboy of the Western World*, Yeats's Cuchulain dramas and later poetry, Joyce's *Ulysses*, Shaw's *Man and Superman*, O'Casey's *Red Roses for Me* and his autobiography to suggest how pervasive the theme is. Even the cheerful and unreverential Gogarty, when he alludes to the Bailey Tavern, where Arthur Griffith had once met his friends, writes, 'Griffith was dead and we, his disciples, meet but rarely in the upper chamber.' And elsewhere in a context where he applies the mocking epithet 'heroic' to himself, he alludes to Griffith—a nice bit of Biblical typology—as one who 'fell among thieves.' Clearly the admiration expressed in *As I Was Going Down Sackville Street*, for certain aristocrats—Talbot Clifton, hunter, man of action; Lord Dunsany, 'leader of men', poet; Lord Birkenhead, athlete, rake—impinges on a heroic ideal of Being as active rather than passive. Even Sir Horace Plunkett, who is always faintly comic and more than faintly dull as Gogarty depicts him, takes on a heroic stature, as he braves the Black and Tans in an automobile: 'As the small, fearless figure sat beside me, I remembered the suit of armour in Dunsany Castle where Sir Horace was born. I thought that it was only a figure such as his that would fit into it. Back into the Past I rejected him—the beginnings of his family tree, a Norman knight repelling a raid.'

Archetypes of the quest are pervasive in Gogarty's mature works. There is even a curious unfinished draft of a poem called 'The Quest' in which Gogarty apparently tried—and failed—to fuse Christian elements ('Sir Christ', 'Lady Mary's Sleeve') with the pagan ('The Queen of Beauty'). Style, subject and handwriting all suggested that the poem was a very early effort[15] and that the archetypal search was long gestating in his imagination.

Sackville Street itself is a quest for heroic value, for an active identity that will lift its questing *persona* above the 'pigmies' of de Valera's Dublin. Towards the close of the book, Gogarty describes his return to Dublin from London where he has been hob-nobbing with aristocrats. (The time is probably 1924.) Dublin is the loved town 'where every man is a potential idler, poet or friend'. Still, he has to ask himself, 'Where are its aristocrats?' He is led on by this question to the realisation that the Irish never

E

identify property with aristocracy; 'yet they have their chieftains, their aristocrats'. Long descent is simply taken for granted by the Irishman, and does not confer distinction in itself. It must be then in certain personal qualities that the 'hero' is to be defined. (One scarcely notices that 'aristocrat' has given way to 'hero' in Gogarty's analysis.) The heroic qualities, as they are listed, are not at all startling:

> First of all he must be physically great, big-bodied, burly, the full of a door. His personal courage must be outstanding and unquestionable, he must be rosy, generous, and chivalrous. He must have some noble, endearing fault which is easily forgiven, extravagance for choice. But outside battle, he must be gentle and courteous and capable of comradery.

Those traits, the traits of Goll and Finn and Conn, even of less burly Cuchulain, he is prepared to find in certain of the figures of the resistance to the Black and Tans—Sean McKeon, Dan Breen, Charlie Dalton. A rather deflating conclusion one must feel, however one might admire the bravery of such fighters, for, after all, not even to the book's *persona*—doctor, Senator, poet—is a military role accessible. Surely the warrior is not the only answer to the pigmies?

We have already seen one figure in *Sackville Street*, not a man of action like Griffith, or Collins, or any of the aristocrats, capable of evoking a sense of the heroic: AE 'who enlarges the Joy that is hidden in the heroic heart'. There is another, as well. It is he, Gogarty writes, whose 'mind provides me with a realm of beauty beyond the beauty of Woman'. He is 'the greatest poet of this and of most of the last generation'. It is with him Gogarty would stand 'and resist the lapse from grandeur with dignity'. On the street, a chance allusion by a friend to a poetic image reminds Gogarty of 'the mind of the man I loved. A mind full of imagination, with all the charm of all the muses at its call . . . a mind to which myth and metamorphosis were as present as if he were a denizen of a translunary world.' It is, of course, Yeats of whom these words were written.

There is, in fact, a constant impulse in *Sackville Street*'s author himself to achieve imaginative release from the terrestrial. 'Contact. That is the thing I wish to be rid of—contact with earth, for a while,' he muses as he sets off in his plane for a flight that is of the imagination as well. Again, when he departs in his car for a visit to Yeats, he praises 'Speed for speed's sake. Soon our minds will realise the electric nature of our being and deliberately direct our bodies' movements towards the All-Mover, the Primum Mobile whose glory thrills and penetrates the universe.' One of the funniest sections of the book recounts Gogarty's discomfiture when he is forced by Talbot Clifton to stalk deer, prostrate in a puddle, while wearing a new and elegant hunting suit, when he would clearly much rather be in the library or lecturing Clifton's son on Virgil and Pindar. Gogarty asks, 'Is there no middle way between Helicon and the heather?' And he answers, 'Men like Lord Dunsany prove that there is.' Still, if Dunsany could bridge the gap between Sean McKeon and William Butler Yeats; and even if Oliver St John Gogarty himself aspired to fuse the heroism of action and the heroism of imagination, the very structure of *Sackville Street* would suggest that the second is the more accessible and necessary alternative. In the passage following immediately upon his analysis of the Irish concept of the aristocrat and his definition of the hero, he asserts of Goll, Finn, Conn, and Cuchulain, 'Deep in the heart of the Gael these heroes are enthroned.' Then, just as he reflects that the Irish have not raised monuments to conquerors and soldiers, his thought is interrupted:

'Excuse me, Senator,' a sailor said, as he wound a cable round a mushroom-like protuberance on the quay 'there's a few stanzas in my pocket that I would like you to look over if you have time.'

The purport of this climactic passage is inescapable. The loquacious author of *Sackville Street* has left behind him the aristocracy of extroversion. 'What is wrong here,' he had thought in London, 'is the absence of the metaphysical man.' He has returned to Dublin, where even an ordinary seaman may be touched by the heroism of the imagination, that inspiration of AE and Yeats.

When Joyce attached the soubriquet 'Buck' to Malachi Mulligan in *Ulysses*, he was suggesting that Oliver Gogarty resembled eighteenth-century Dublin's swaggering men-about-town, the 'bucks' of the Hell-Fire Club. Yet—whatever may have been his social presence as a young man—Gogarty's poetry suggests that he might have been at home in the earlier seventeenth century. When

one seeks for some precedent or parallel for *As I Was Going
Down Sackville Street*, curiously enough one even thinks of such
seventeenth-century works as Robert Burton's *Anatomy of Melancholy* and Sir Isaac Walton's *The Complete Angler*. Of course,
George Moore's *Hail and Farewell* provided an immediate
stimulus to Gogarty's imagination and choice of subject, and it
strongly influenced the way he handled dialogue. *Hail and Farewell* itself, however, has to be seen as a fascinating and successful
blend of novel, autobiography (or confession), and anatomy (or
Menippean Satire) in which the novelistic elements are strong.
(The terminology I use will be recognised as that of Northrop
Frye.) Gogarty's *Sackville Street* blends the same fictive modes
lacing them with romance, but, in it, anatomy—episodic, satiric,
and impure enough to include passages of poetry—and confession
are the dominant elements; and romance is far stronger than novel.
If one turns to this account of life in Dublin from 1915 to 1935
anticipating the narrative sweep and novelistic form of George
Moore's masterpiece, one can only be horribly disappointed; and
Sackville Street will seem the most chaotic, digressive, and formless of works. Seen properly—and in the literary tradition to which
it adheres—*Sackville Street* is much more than a useful source
book for the cultural historian; it is an impressive and highly
individual work within its tradition, a tradition that embraces
writers in English as diverse as Samuel Butler, Thomas Love
Peacock, Jonathan Swift, Lawrence Sterne, Robert Burton, and
Isaac Walton, and that extends back in time to Petronius Arbiter
(one of Gogarty's enthusiasms), Apuleius, and their predecessors.
Gogarty himself described his book as 'something new in form:
neither "memoir" nor a novel'.[16] Unique *Sackville Street* certainly
is and unusual among modern works, but, in another sense, it belongs to narrative modes far older than the novel.

The American and English editions of *As I Was Going Down
Sackville Street* are strikingly different; and it is the English
edition that best represents Gogarty's original design. Although
the firm that first proposed to Gogarty that he write the book did
not finally handle it, the editors of the American firm that did
made some faulty decisions, reducing the number of chapters from
twenty-five to twenty-three, making two extensive cuts and a
number of minor ones, and telescoping certain chapters. In the
process of telescoping and cutting the fourth and fifth chapters of

the English edition, the editors managed to obscure a fundamental structural division and a substratum of implication. As Gogarty wrote to Horace Reynolds, the structure of *Sackville Street* 'is a paradigm backwards of the Divinia Commedia'. Thus the three parts of the *Commedia—Inferno, Purgatorio,* and *Paradiso,*—are implied in Gogarty's work in reverse order, each 'representing', as Gogarty put it, 'a decade of my decensus down Sackville Street, that is from the Anglo-Irish civilisation to the Gaelic going native in a town which no Gael ever built'.[17] In the English edition, the first part concludes, as it properly should, with an ironic echo of Dante's star reference at the close of the *Inferno.* As the *persona* of *Sackville Street* turns into Stephen's Green, he leaves behind Grafton Street 'with its temple of Fortune and its cinema crowds seeking solace in their shadowy stars' and we leave behind the hell of Dublin in the thirties, to pass into the purgatory of the twenties. Perhaps by accident, the oblique allusion (at the end of the eighteenth chapter in the English edition, of the sixteenth in the American) to the release from Purgatory survived the attention of the American editors: 'You know that Ireland is a place or state of repose where souls suffer from the hope that the time will come when they may go abroad.' Responding to the buried clue, we should realise that in the last chapters of the book we will enter Paradise—the world Gogarty knew before the twenties.

Other allusions in *Sackville Street* enrich its ironies. One epigraph to the work is the exclamation of Odysseus on his return to Ithaca, as Gogarty irreverently and colloquially adapted it for a friend, 'Oh, where the hell am I now?'[18] The exclamation is echoed later in the purgatorial section. When Shamus deBurgoe bursts out in the Bailey Tavern, 'Jayshus! What kind of kip have I come into at all?' the *persona* reflects, 'The very question Odysseus asked of his home.' Playing on a metaphor that he always found compelling (in 'This Kip', and 'Ringsend' for instance), Gogarty suggests that Dublin is a fallen state into which the soul has descended and that the Odyssean *persona* of *Sackville Street* now can scarcely recognise his native land. (As we shall see, this metaphor will return again to complete the thematic development of the book.)

Gogarty gives additional clues to the structure of *Sackville Street* in epigraph and text. 'We Irishmen', Bishop Berkeley is quoted as saying in a second epigraph, 'are apt to think something and nothing are near neighbours.' This citation of Berkeley and the narrative point of view of the book are designed to draw our attention to the fact that, as Gogarty told Horace Reynolds in explanation of the form and tenses of the book, 'The only world that exists is my own consciousness: and the dead are in that, as much alive as the living; more so when they are remembered more vividly. Hence thirty years of life all contemporaneous.'[19] It is more than likely, too, that in his effort to render a 'continuum of consciousness' in space and time, Gogarty was drawing upon J. W. Dunne's philosophical-mathematical treatise *An Experiment With Time*—not for argument or analysis but for insight.[20] In the Shelbourne luncheon scene with the American publicist, Gogarty promises that he will produce a book with no perspective; he will 'treat this town . . . in the way the Chinese treat their pictures.' *Sackville Street* will unroll backward in time, 'like a Chinese masterpiece where everything has the same value in space', giving 'past and present the same value in time'.[21]

As *I Was Going Down Sackville Street* has probably most often been read as a garrulous and gossipy kaleidoscope of social and intellectual life in Dublin. On one level it is just that, and ought to have an appeal to anyone who enjoys good Irish gab or a nice bit of gossip. The first four chapters, for instance, constitute an initial rhythmic unit in the whole; and these, as I have indicated, depict how the author lived in the mid-thirties in Dublin. Opening with a description of Endymion, a notable Dublin eccentric, *Sackville Street* moves on to recount Gogarty's visit to the National Library where the Librarian's anecdote about a priest and the tantalising lingerie of a neighbouring rector's wife leads to a discussion of, among other subjects, the Docetic heresiarchs; Gogarty then strolls on and encounters a series of lively talkers, including the bombastic General O'Duffy. The chapter ends with a visit to Fanning's pub, behind Trinity; as politically enraged as O'Duffy, Fanning nevertheless invites the doctor to 'Gyroscope yourself down into a region of calm' and wins us by his 'Abso-bloody-lutely!' The second chapter continues the saunter and introduces a collector of graffiti, a lunatic promoter of kaolin deposits, and a grotesque street rally of Republican stalwarts. Following this rowdy gathering, Gogarty fortunately conducts us in the next chapter to Merrion Strand for 'an hour's canter' and a reflection on the charms of the landscape; thence we follow him on his hospital rounds which provoke a Rabelaisian essay about hospital administration, the educational well-being of invalids, and the social function of humanitarianism in England and Ireland. In chapter four, a flight of fancy and an aeroplane flight precede a luncheon at the Shelbourne Hotel, where the American encourages Gogarty to write his memoirs and is regaled by anecdotes treating of such diverse matters as Lowell of Harvard, temple prostitutes, and Irish politics, as well as by certain satiric verses (which in combination with one passage of prose and some additional lines of poetry provoked a libel suit against Gogarty). We are then conducted to a cocktail party where the Embassy crowd mingles with the intelligentsia as a Grand Duke dances a bear dance, but Gogarty fails to convince his hostess that George Redding, his friend, is fact rather than fiction. A stop at the Bailey introduces another set of friends, a contest over the poetry of Seumas O'Sullivan and James Stephens and an encomium of alcohol and good company. The next chapter opens with a remembered visit to Tim Healy, first Governor General of the Irish Free State, at the Viceregal Lodge; it is followed by another view of Endymion, paying tribute to time as he salutes the Ballast Office clock. In the past now, though in the present tense, Gogarty devotes a chapter to Sir Horace Plunkett, absurd and brave; and, in the chapter that follows, he is prompted by an invitation extended by Tim Healy to motor to Rathfarnham, where he chats with Yeats about George Moore and persuades Yeats (by comic psychological devices) to attend the Free State function to which Healy has invited him. The chapter concludes with a full-scale account of an earlier dinner at the Viceregal Lodge.

Interesting in itself, this apparently diverse material is given formal significance by metaphor and structure. Endymion, as Sighle Kennedy has suggested in her study of Samuel Beckett, doubtless had some shaping influence on the kind of character Beckett was to exploit in his mature fiction. Beckett knew *Sackville Street* well enough to give testimony against Gogarty in the libel trial over the book, yet he not only found Endymion useful but went on in his first novel *Murphy* (1939) to develop a theme based upon the mechanical nature of time and upon the concepts of 'nothing' and 'naught', a rather bleak reflection on Gogarty's notion of 'nothing' and 'something'. Here is Gogarty's Endymion:

He wore a tail-coat over white cricket trousers which were caught in at the ankles by a pair of cuffs. A cuff-like collar sloped upwards to keep erect a little sandy head, crowned by a black bowler some sizes too small. . . . Under his arm he carried two sabres in shining scabards of patent leather.

This description of Endymion opens the book, and Endymion is one of the guests at the picnic that closes it; he is seen or mentioned at intervals throughout. He is, in fact, a simulacrum of Doctor-Senator Gogarty who had, as most Dubliners and most readers of *Ulysses* would know, 'saved men from drowning'. Endymion's lunacy is the consequence of an act of gallantry: He plunged into a vat at Guinness's brewery when a companion fell in. The vat, alas, proved to contain only carbon dioxide gas. Endymion was 'touched' but only slightly; he has chosen by garb, gesture, demeanour and word to indicate that not he but the world is mad. The cuffs on his ankles manifest that he is standing on his head and walking on his hands; greeting a sentry before the Senate, he shouts, 'Noom to me, and moon to you.' In short, he is going 'backwards in time' and 'reversing in space'. The only sane man in an insane world, he has, like the author of *Sackville Street*, through fantasy, commanded fact. He has adjusted 'Reason to the phantasmagoria of Life'. 'After all,' Gogarty muses, remembering the fissure at Delphi, 'if the wisest nation of the world once set its course by the noxious fumes, why not Endymion?' And why should not Gogarty set his course in *Sackville Street*, well, not by noxious fumes, but by the 'Atlantic vapours' that turn Irishmen who 'live in this vast vat of fumes from the lost Atlantic' into 'mystics, poets, politicians and unemployables'. Why should not Gogarty, for whom 'Past grew as considerable as Present' when he and his comrades at the Bailey strove 'to keep the intellect afloat', inspired by imagination, move backward in time and space? Never a man to ignore the earthier possibilities of a metaphor, the Senator describes with gusto the responses of the Dublin crowd at a Republican rally. As the Man of the People rises to a pitch of enthusiasm for a United Front and appeals to his audiences to 'Rally round the flag', an urchin emerges from under a wagon. She carries

a rusty tin of Jacob's biscuit suspended from her neck. One side bore the faded legend, digestive. On the top of it, she beat a

brisk tattoo breaking the silence, singing in a childish treble:
Rally, men, rally,
Irishmen rally!
Rattle a fart in a band-box!

Other vapours, other fumes, excite the imagination of *Sackville Street's* narrator, and away from this political rumble in the bowels of contemporary Ireland he leads us paradoxically to 'journey ever onward to the Golden Age'. So, moving backwards and forwards at the same time, we move with Gogarty to the time of the Troubles, to the West of Ireland and to threats on his neighbour Talbot Clifton's life, to the warning he himself received that he had been 'marked' by the IRA, to a salon at his Ely Place house, attended by Michael Collins and AE. Never moving quite in a linear fashion but in loops of time, though almost always in the present tense, we learn of Collins' death, of Gogarty's attendance on Arthur Griffith in the hours before and after his death, of the burning of Gogarty's house, Renvyle; and then we move back to a yet earlier time, to a seance and a ghostly appearance at Renvyle, during a visit by Yeats and his wife. Again, we backtrack: in four chapters Gogarty recounts his stay with Clifton, the season in London during which he kept a second office in order to avoid the violence at home; we read of visits to Augustus John and George Moore and of his return to Dublin. In the third part of the book now, we move back to the days of the Treaty negotiations, to the occupation of Ireland by the Black and Tans, to the arrest of Lord Dunsany, to the performance of Gogarty's anti-imperialist Abbey play, *A Serious Thing*, to Dr Tyrrell, to Griffith in his prime, to AE in the theatre, to James Joyce and the turn of the century. Another loop moves us forward slightly to an uproarious dinner with Gogarty's Ely Place neighbours, George Moore and Sir Thornley Stoker, and to a near adventure with Horace Plunkett. The book concludes with a picnic in the Wicklow mountains, involving a large number of colourful friends, Gogarty's wife, and her sister. Pastoral and idyllic, this gathering is the 'golden age' to which we have been led. One of the final details in Gogarty's description of the picnic concerns his Trinity mentor, R. Y. Tyrrell. The worthy and now wobbly classicist has to remove 'a fruit salad that threatened to slide down and enfillet with crescents of orange and green, the dear old doctor's supernal brow'. The detail is

comic but its implications are also Dionysian and joyous; and it is
designed too as an ironic contrast to the flag of green-white-and-
orange that Endymion carries in the opening lines of the book—
a symbol of the strident politics of the day. We realise that our
quest has been to rediscover this Graeco-Roman version of Eden
before the fall. It is a pagan and spontaneous world, the polar
opposite of the rigid, doctrinaire, and puritanic society of the
Ireland depicted at the start of the book.

My concern in these pages is with *Sackville Street* as a literary
work. *As* a literary work, Gogarty's book does not even demand
of us that we accept its judgments, only that we be willing to
accept the validity of the *persona*'s response to things *as* a possible
human response. Yet *Sackville Street* does raise certain vexing
issues, ones related to the critical hostility from which Gogarty's
reputation still suffers; and into these issues it is necessary to probe.
Into the whole complicated history of the libel suit over *Sackville
Street*, an appalling morass, I do not intend to enter. Yet the suit
was based upon details in the book and to that extent must concern
us. Briefly stated, the suit was brought by Henry Sinclair, who
claimed that he had been libelled by two passages of poetry quoted
by Gogarty and by one passage of satiric prose describing the
usurious grandfather of the twin brothers satirised in the lines of
poetry.[22] The vices ascribed to the figures satirised in these brief
passages seem fair enough game for satire: cupidity and child
molestation. Furthermore, the lines of poetry quoted in the book
were written by George Redding, had circulated to the extent that
they were widely known in the Dublin literary world, and were
even, on reliable testimony, recited by Gogarty in the presence of
Henry Sinclair, without protest from him.[23] Their appearance in
Sackville Street was thus no distortion of Dublin experience.
Furthermore, the passages are related to dominant motifs in the
book and can be justified as thematic development. When, for
instance, Gogarty quotes the second of the two poems by 'George',
he goes on to analyse the rhetorical aspect of the poem and to
dwell upon the way in which imagination enlarges events, impart-
ing significance to them: 'And the organ-note in that "Twin
grandchildren" which endows their infamy with grandeur until it
almost equals the fame of the Great Twin Brethren, Castor and
beneficent Pollux. "Verse calls them forth" from vulgar obloquy.'
When his hostess inquires 'Who are the Great Twin Brethren?'

Gogarty replies 'Consummations of the poet's dream. Shadows invoked by sound. Men that do not exist.' In the context of his observations, the quoted poems and the satiric description in prose can be seen not only as another manifestation of the element of social satire in the book but of its central thematic contrast between fact and fantasy.

Still, the passages on which the suit was based could be identified with three rather unsavoury Dubliners, one of whom was still living at the time the book was published. (That the plaintiff acknowledged his grandfather as one who 'interfered' with adolescent girls is surely revealing!)[24] There is reason to conclude that the judgment went against Gogarty not because of the isolated passages but because of the expressive freedom of a book published at a time when the impulse to censorship was rampant in Ireland, and because of Gogarty's Senate attacks on de Valera. Nevertheless, Gogarty's use of the material raises the same difficult questions raised by Moore's *Hail and Farewell* and Joyce's *Ulysses*. What are the emotional, psychological, and moral consequences of fictive detail that may be associated with living persons?

One consequence of the lawsuit to Gogarty—aside from the financial strain—was that attention was drawn to an element of anti-Semitism in the Redding poems ('Two Jews grew in Sackville Street', 'grandchildren of the ancient Chicken Butcher'). Readers of Joyce's *Ulysses* have not failed to notice that some of Buck Mulligan's language ('Jewman', 'sheeny') and his response to Leopold Bloom seem overtly anti-Semitic. (It has, however, usually escaped notice that Joyce did not hesitate to use the term 'Jewman' in correspondence;[25] more surprisingly, it is seldom remarked that the Leopold Bloom who describes Reuben J. Dodd as 'a dirty Jew' is himself anti-Semitic.)[26] Both in public and in private, Gogarty did, throughout his career, make anti-Semitic remarks. To some extent these were a reflection of commonplace stereotyped notions rather widespread among writers of his period. One need not cite the lunatic extreme of Ezra Pound: the attitudes of figures like Hemingway or E. E. Cummings or Evelyn Waugh were far more typical. Because it is perhaps too easy today and too smugly self-congratulatory to condemn anti-Semitism for those who have been able to survey its consequences under totalitarian regimes in Germany and Russia, it is worth attending to the more specific reasons for Gogarty's attitudes. One source of his anti-Semitism was certainly the Sinn Fein movement with which he was associated at the opening of the century and which identified Jewish banking interests with English imperialism.[27] On another level altogether, but at approximately the same moment in his intellectual development, Gogarty made a sharp distinction between the Hellenic and the Hebraic, between the Graeco-Roman and the Judaeo-Christian. With the latter of these he associated Puritanic moralism, anti-physical dualism and asceticism, intellectual dogmatism and authoritarianism, rationalism, mental abstractionism and schematicism, and ideological fixity: in other words, all those qualities and characteristics he disliked. These feelings were further reinforced by his acceptance of the distinction Yeats made between the Western and the Eastern, between that which is conducive to the development of individual being as opposed to that which loses the individual in the mass. Perhaps the writer Gogarty most closely resembles in these attitudes and his way of expressing them would be Aldous Huxley in whom Philip Thody has remarked 'a recurrent anti-semitism which shows itself not only in incidental remarks in books and letters but also in his approach to a number of religious, philosophical, and historical questions' and who constantly opposed Greek civilisation to the Hebraic. One might conclude of Gogarty's anti-Semitism what Thody concludes of Huxley's: 'The most that can be said in defence of . . . [his] more extreme remarks is that they are directed less against the Jews . . . than against a set of mental and spiritual attitudes which he would have found equally objectionable in any group of people.'[28] In the particular case of *Sackville Street*, one can only regret that the trace of stereotyped prejudice in the provocative passages should have detracted from the book's essential qualities.

Like so many of Gogarty's early poems, *As I Was Going Down Sackville Street* is a true *jeu d'esprit*—mental and verbal play at its freest. A prefatory note to the book informs us that 'The names in this book are real, the characters fictitious.' In fact, not even all the names are real, for Gogarty has modified some of the original names. (His university tutor Macran becomes McGurk, for one instance.) This vagary should draw attention to the subtitle of the work 'A Phantasy in Fact' and to the complex and ironic and often whimsical playing upon the contrast between appearance and reality throughout the work. The publican Yeats mentioned to Lady Dorothy Wellesley who felt that it was possible to open

Sackville Street almost anywhere was not far wrong; it is also possible to open it almost anywhere and to locate an incident, anecdote, or allusion that expresses this contrast between appearances and reality. When Gogarty hears from the librarian Lyster of how Father McQuisten, tormented by the undergarments of the rector's wife, "loaded his twelve bore . . . and let fly, not at the para-virginal cami-knickers, but at four of the Vicar's shirts (hanging upside down) which in the interval good taste and modesty perhaps had interposed for his lady's lingerie,' he exclaims, 'Appearances were against him.' Appearances are definitely against George Moore late in the novel, when the doctor plays an elaborate joke on his petulant friend, persuading him, to Moore's obvious delight, that an attack of weeping eczema may be a memoir of his dead youth and that he must be confined for a week if he is to recover. Then Gogarty arranges for Moore to receive a series of coveted dinner invitations during the course of the week. Earlier in the book, Gogarty's hostess at a Dublin party insists upon believing that the 'George' Gogarty so often quotes is an invention, even when Gogarty leaves and brings him back to the party. But not all the contrasts of the book are amusing. For instance, when Gogarty arrives at a nursing home where the beloved Griffith lies ill, he climbs the stairs to find 'President Griffith, the man who believed in the Irish people . . . on his back'. It is not the real man but a semblance. In perhaps the bitterest words of the book, the doctor exclaims, 'Take up that corpse at once.'

These are but a few illustrations of how the implications of the epigraph from Bishop Berkeley pervade *As I Was Going Down Sackville Street*. It is Gogarty's underlying irony in the work that 'something'—for instance, the expedient Irish politics of the thirties, a rumble in the bowels—is often 'nothing'; and that 'nothing'—for instance the ghost of Athelstan Blake who appears to Mrs Yeats at Renvyle—is often 'something'. Renvyle House itself is 'nothing' after the IRA has finished with it, and yet Gogarty's memories of it, like all the memories of the book, are 'something'. *Sackville Street* does not evade reality or fact, though it does imply that often what is thought most real is insubstantial. In one episode, Sir Horace Plunkett tries to persuade an American of the importance of his newspaper, given the threatening political situation. The following passage then appears:

A bomb fell at the other side of St Stephen's Green or just behind Ely House. 'Echoes,' I murmured. It might have been a cork popping for all the deflection it caused in Sir Horace's flow of speech.

By contrast to this vacuousness, in which neither the violence nor the words can mean anything, consider an episode in which imagination works first upon 'nothing' and then upon 'something'. When Gogarty arrives at Yeats's house in Rathfarnham, far from being in a state of waking dream, Yeats is apparently in the mood for gossip. He has been reading Moore's *Memoirs of My Dead Life*; and he has a question: 'Do you think Moore was impotent?' As the discussion between the two develops, with all the interest of literary gossip, it becomes clear that Yeats is concerned with the relation between Moore's experience and his art. 'Moore never tells what the woman did. Why?—pointing and shaking his finger at me—Because she was not there!' After the discussion on Moore has run its way, Gogarty gets to the matter at hand, his effort to persuade Yeats to accept Tim Healy's invitation. His first ploy, as we have seen, is to excite Yeats with the symbolic significance of the silk hat. Yet he knows that more is needed to compel this imagination, and so he limns the 'clean and wholesome' butter-girls who will be present. And he proceeds to describe one of these at the churn:

> She had buttocks like a pair of beautiful melons. Her sleeves were rolled up. She had churned from early morning. Her neck was pink with exercise. Her bosom laboured, but she could not desist, for the milk was at the turn. Up and down, desperately she drove the long handle: up and down, up and down and up and up for a greater drive. The resistance grew against the plunger. Her hips and bosom seemed to increase in size while her waist grew thin. In front of her ears the sweat broke into drops of dew. She prayed in the crisis to old forgotten gods of the homestead! Twenty strokes for ten! Gasping she sang:

> Come, butter!
> Come, butter!
> Come, butter,
> Come!

> Every lump
> As big as
> My bum!'

Beating time to the chant, Yeats agrees to go; and, as Gogarty departs, the master is murmuring 'Come, butter, come, butter.' The meaning of all this could be made (probably fatally) explicit, but it is not necessary for Gogarty to explain what he has rendered implicitly. His visit to Yeats, amusing just as a look at the man behind the masks, explores the relation of art and reality. Moore, the artist who fantasised his own psychic inadequacy into works of art, is examined by one who exercises his imagination upon the relation of 'nothing' to 'something', and then proceeds, fascinated by Gogarty's account of that very substantial buttermaid, to transform 'something' into a rhythmic imagining.

As I Was Going Down Sackville Street in its entirety is a paradoxical exercise of the imagination upon 'nothing' and 'something'. It satirises the present, and offers us, in its concluding chapter, a joyous moment in the past, a moment of freedom and spontaneity, untouched by conflict: a redemption of time. The Puritan sensibility would probably protest against that conclusion that it is an evasion of reality. But *Sackville Street* is for all its satiric jibes neither a rejection nor an evasion but rather a joyous celebration of life, as recreated by imagination; and the picnic on Mount Kippure, a Platonic banquet, has much of the charm and all of the symbolic import of pastoral idyll. Surely the writer who had 'Shamus' Burke introduce the word 'kip' into the book as an ironic metaphor for life in society and who prefaces the picnic on the mountain by a discussion of banks and kips wanted us to be aware of a pun in the name of the Wicklow hill where this varied company refreshes itself. That company—the grotesque Endymion; the bibulous Trinity classicist, W. Y. Tyrrell; Professor McGurk, Gogarty's devoted Trinity tutor; the Hegelian H. S. Macran; the painter Sir William Orpen (who called the sketch he did of Tyrrell at this gathering 'Pic-Nic on Parnassus'); a number of others esteemed by Gogarty as companions or eccentrics; the ladies, even including one appropriately named Sylvia—revels in good food, beverages sacred to Bacchus, conversation, and landscape. Gazing out, in his imagination, over the hills of Wicklow, the bay of Dublin, the city itself, Gogarty exclaims: 'The dear

and fog-crowned Athens of my youth!' Gossip and anecdote, witty
exchange and quotation enliven the scene. The music of Homer
and Milton, of Endymion's fiddle, and Dublin street song mingles
with the trees.

The title chosen for this anatomy of a time and a place blends
an allusion to Horace strolling on the Via Sacra with the title of a
notorious song, a satiric ballad well known on the pavements of
Dublin. Gogarty's version of 'Sackville Street' opens:

As I was walking down Sackville Street,
    Hey, Ho! me Randy O,
Three bloody fine whores did I chance to meet,
    With me gallopin' rearin' Randy O.

Alas, the singer of 'Sackville Street' pays dearly for his pleasures,
enduring a hot poultice for his pox. Yet his spirit is not extinguished:

'Oh Nurse, Oh Nurse! It is too hot!'
    Hey, Ho! me Randy O.
'Ye didn't say that when gettin' the pox
    In yer gallopin', rearin' Randy O.'

But now that I'm well, I feel quite game,
    Hey, Ho! me Randy O.
If I meet wid me whore I'll have her again
    Wid me gallopin', rearin' Randy O.[29]

In a cryptic passage lamenting the fate of Arthur Griffith, Gogarty
adds this comment: 'Ireland has three characters, like the three
ladies whom the hero of the old Dublin ballad "As I Was Going
Down Sackville Street" informs us that he "chanced to meet".'
For the sake of the living and the dead it may be tactful not to
explain that political comment in particular and in detail. Suffice
it to say that the ballad with its randy theme of rejuvenation is
relevant to the concluding lines of the book and to the state of the
nation as well. Like Joyce's Shawn the Post, who floats down the
River Liffey which Senator Gogarty once swam, the *persona* of
Sackville Street has moved backward in time. But like Joyce's
Shawn and his Anna Liffey and like the River Liffey in Gogarty's
last chapter, the *persona* of the book is recreated at the end of his
journey. Relaxing in the sunlight, after the pleasures of the picnic,
this extraordinary talker nods by a warm rock,

Until there came to me the image of a little child with velvet suit and lace collar in a public house tempted by a coachman and wondering at the drink proffered to him in secrecy, sweet and bitter, sanguine as Life.

'Would you care for another raspberry cordial, Master Oliver?'

'By 'Gis and by St Charity if it leads to a great calm like this with friends like these above the world in spite of the danger of its becoming a habit, I would say "The Same Again!" and chance again my lucky stars.'

Pantagruelian and optimist that he was, Oliver Gogarty in one of the great books of the Irish Renaissance, led his readers backwards in time, through appearances and realities, in quest of an imagined moment of calm, so free, so spontaneous, and so real, that it persuades the railing narrator of the book to quaff again the sweet and bitter liquor of life.

8

A Saint for the Nation, Patrick, the Roman Gentleman

WHEN *I Follow St Patrick* (1938) was reviewed in the excellent *Dublin Magazine* (edited by Gogarty's friend Seumas O'Sullivan) by 'A.K.,' who was clearly all at sea. Taking issue on a number of minute archaeological points and protesting at the disturbing digressiveness of the work, 'A. K.' nevertheless had to admit that 'it is a most enjoyable book to read'.[1] Years later, writing his sympathetic account of Gogarty's career, Ulick O'Connor described the book as 'a study of St Patrick' and as 'a blend of light scholarship and Gogartian discursiveness'.[2] One can imagine the quandaries of librarians when the book arrived for classification. Hagiography? Travel? History? Autobiography? Digressive only to the extent it ought to be and, according to Gogarty, 'by no means a "Life",' *I Follow St Patrick* is as enjoyable a book of its kind as one could imagine. Its scholarship, lightly worn, is all charm; indeed, it makes no pretence to scholarship at all. In effect, Gogarty has asked: 'What can a man of imagination and sensibility with a memory for classical literature, a considerable but non-professional reading on the subject at hand, a unique vision of national greatness, and a vast delight in his island's beauties, learn about Saint Patrick's significance from following his footsteps to whatever extent he may discern them?' The answer he gives us in this fiction, to the title of which we must attend. With only the slightest trace of either novel or romance, *I Follow St Patrick* is confession and anatomy. Indeed, taken together, the three books Gogarty composed at the close of the thirties illustrate beautifully not only Northrop Frye's four forms of prose fiction but his observation that 'The forms of prose fiction are mixed, like racial strains in human beings.' Judged as archaeological treatise, saint's life, or history, *I Follow St Patrick* is an appalling botch. Seen as what it actually is, an account of Oliver St John Gogarty's highly personal quest and conclusions, it is a discovered delight. And once one has seen that it is no saint's life, one can see that, like the books which preceded and followed it, this one is 'political', cultural, and metaphysical in its concerns. Gogarty could not possibly be clearer on the nature of his book than he is in the opening passage. There he states that: 'his aim is, by describing the places which the saint visited and sanctified in our island, to draw from these, as from well-springs, inspiration which shall be truly traditional, pure, and undiluted by modern distractions and fatuous ideas of patriotism'.

It was never Gogarty's intention to trace all of Patrick's 'journeys through the length and breadth of the land'. Instead, he follows him, after an initial account of his capture as a youth, his captivity, and his escape, 'from his incoming to Tara and . . . across the country to the lands "beyond which there is no man", to Croagh Patrick and Murrick in Mayo, and furthest west out to Cahir Island'. In short, he follows the saint on the principal stages of his journey and episcopacy, giving appropriate attention to those places uniquely linked to him by biography and legend.

But it *was* Gogarty's aim, exercising his imagination and sense of probability upon the available evidence, to achieve some sense of the culture to which Patrick carried the new faith, some sense of the culture he imported, and of the elements in the indigenous culture most responsive to it. When, for instance, Gogarty wants a mental picture of the raiders who carried Patrick into slavery, he seeks to determine whether they carried bronze or steel swords. Artifacts and carvings in the National Museum, his own knowledge of Roman antiquities, the judgment of the Director of the National Museum, the experience of a Dublin metallurgist with bronze and steel weapons, all these are weighed before he decides that the raiders carried weapons of steel. On the other hand, when he considers the legendary magical combat of Patrick and the Druids at Tara, neither the total silence of Patrick on the subject of 'miracles' nor his own sense of natural probability permits Gogarty to dismiss the legends. Not to be accepted literally, the legends imply both 'antecedent customs' and extraordinary powers on the part of the Druids and Patrick. Drawing upon J. B. Bury's classic *Life* of the saint, on more recent authorities who are generously quoted, and on his own speculations, Gogarty's book makes no show of authority, except in its argument that 'When scholars

are divided, contradictory, and uncertain, the only appeal that remains is to what is not yet fully appreciated, and that is the veracity
of legend and local traditions.' In effect, not claiming accuracy,
I Follow St Patrick depends only upon the veracity of the *persona*'s
response to things.

Those who have confused Buck Mulligan or the Dublin myth
of the outrageous Doctor with the far more interesting Gogarty
have probably been puzzled by this book. To the pious and
doctrinaire it must have seemed a kind of blasphemy that he
should even write about St Patrick. And to admirers of Gogartian
irreverence, it must have seemed another kind of blasphemy, a
betrayal of his scepticism. Yet the attitude of the Gogarty *persona*
is entirely consistent with attitudes expressed in other prose works
and in the poetry. *I Follow St Patrick* is no surrender to institutional pieties, church fetishes, or naïve nationalist symbols.
Indeed, it is an answer to these.

Although Gogarty was a medical practitioner, he was never a
scientific materialist. Nor, on the basis of *I Follow St Patrick* or
anything else he wrote, was he an orthodox Roman Catholic or
Christian. 'Being or God', he wrote in 1905, 'has human attributes
because it is felt by men. Many names has this being been called
by, owing to its visitation and the results. It is nameless for a name
is a symbol and no symbol alone can symbolise that of which all
things are symbols.'[3] Still a supernatural naturalist or naturalistic
supernaturalist and no system maker, he asserts more than thirty
years later, 'I believe in miracles from a scientific or a rational
standpoint too—that is, from a consideration of our godlike
Reason and immortal mind; and because, in spite of science, I have
retained my imagination . . . I believe in miracles because I am a
miracle.'

This fundamental belief in the unity of all existence does not
lead Gogarty to sobriety in *I Follow St Patrick*, but rather to comic
variations—to those digressions which are really the most important part of the book, though they proved so confusing to
'A. K.'—on the theme of matter and spirit. One of these concerns
Hadrian 'that Emperor who, in spite of his Roman gravitas, could
be gentle and gay and turn a lyric (Herrick-like) with the best'.
One senses that Gogarty is much closer to Hadrian than to Patrick,
as he praises the Emperor's breadth of spirit, his openness, his
acceptance of death. Above all, he is delighted that Hadrian's

famous lyric, 'Animula, blanduala, vagula,' tender and terse in its address to the soul 'may for all I know be touched with a little cynicism and a little irony at the expense of the soul'.

More than a little irony at the expense of the flesh is expressed by the author himself. For instance, inspecting the site where Patrick is said to have jumped from Skerry to Slemish, Gogarty leaps and twists his ankle. Later, crossing Lough Corrib to the grave of Patrick's nephew, he takes an oar:

> I was beginning to . . . shed 'drops of onset'—as the politest of poets puts it—from my brow.
>   'Am I coming back too far?'
>   'No, everything is all right.'
> Is it? Well, every stroke is shifting her six feet, anyway. And two yards into five miles is . . . Well that has finished my left hand. I had too tender a palm. . . . 'Palmam qui meruit ferat.' It seems that I am beginning to rave, to become somewhat delirious. I must take a pull at myself. But myself was taking too many pulls—that was the trouble . . . hic labor! After all I am doing this for St Patrick.

Punning in two languages at once, Gogarty mocks the frailty of the flesh and unabashedly admits his brazen response to the boatman's compliment: 'Nothing, nothing at all, my man. In fact I would row you back but for a slight blister.' The chapter immediately following this one recounts Gogarty's ascent of Croagh Patrick, with other pilgrims; here, once again, he makes broad comedy out of the physical difficulties of the climb. Neither poetry nor Latin succour him this time though, for when, 'badly winded', he encounters Father Paddy (Monsignor Browne) and exclaims 'Excelsior', the latter points out that 'there's no such word in Latin. . . . It may have been "altius" Longfellow was trying to say.' As much a punster as the author, Father Paddy invites Gogarty to partake of spirits as they finish their ascent, and adds to the irony by a paradox, when he observes, 'And when your spirit is refreshed, it will be time enough to think of your body.'

On one level these digressions that mock the frailty of the flesh are comic strategies to remind us there is 'only one saint at a time in this book and he is not the author!'—in short, that we are getting *a* truth not *the* truth. On yet another level, they are related to an extensive ironic metaphor of 'wind' first developed when, in an early chapter, Gogarty meets Father Paddy on July the 'twalth', the Orange holiday, on the train from Portadown. Elaborating a whole series of *double entendres* on air or vapour that start in ridicule of the Orangeman's drums—empty inarticulate air—Gogarty prepares us for the later encounter with Father Paddy. What is foolishly thought by man, the substantiality of his individual physical world, to be most real is dependent on Hadrian's pathetic 'sprite' and is often little more than empty air; what is deemed least substantial is of more substance: the dreams of Southern Ireland as opposed to the drums of Belfast, for instance. Gogarty stands at sunset on the Hill of Slane, where Patrick challenged the primacy of the Druids on Tara: 'A strange sense, from days long before St Patrick, of memories pressing on the mind, messages ancestral, not to be comprehended by modern man, invaded my spirit, and I felt the weight of immemorial dreams.' The relation of that paradox to *Sackville Street*'s governing metaphor of 'something' and 'nothing' should be apparent.

When Joyce depicted Gogarty in the opening chapter of *Ulysses* by means of a rhetoric of volatility that suggests constant change and when, in addition, he associated him with the ocean, that element of phenomenal flux so loathed by Stephen Dedalus, he had a sharp insight into Gogarty's psyche, even though he chose to ignore the connection between Buck Mulligan's 'materialism' and the Platonic transcendentalism he posited for him elsewhere in the novel. Water—the streams Patrick must have forded, wells associated with him, pools, lakes—is everywhere in *I Follow St Patrick*. Gogarty himself jokes that he 'would seem pathological to Professor Freud, so fond am I of wells and waters in general'. More spiritual than sexual, however, Gogarty's water imagery from his opening allusion to 'well-springs' of inspiration to his observation that 'Like dew on the fields of Erin, the name of St Patrick has saturated the very land,' is entirely traditional in its association of the element with life-giving energies. And at its most intense and moving level, the comic conflict between the flesh, or matter, and the spirit is expressed through water imagery. Though intuiting the oneness of all being, the talker of this book also assumes different modes of being. Gazing into 'one of the loveliest rivers in Ireland, the Blackwater, bright and dark with its mild, deep stream', he longs 'to get rid of my body that is . . . at the mercy of external conditions, and turn myself, a mind only, into a river to flow forever, slowly and silently, luxuriating through the rich land'. Always willing in this book to digress on some beautiful natural detail, Gogarty imagines, in a periodic sentence that flows like the river itself, 'lush grasses', 'wavering reeds', the 'grey-green budding trees'; he imagines himself rising 'with the sap of the lilies that flower on the dark untroubled pools' and dropping 'from the bent alembic of the willows in daedal and beneficent dew'; above all, he imagines holding 'within me all that passed with the seasons of unending years! If I could be only a mind and flow forever like a river that is perennially replenished by the same substance and conscious only of change without it, itself forever fresh, exempt from age, identified and made one with the Perpetual Flux!' The experience rendered here is closely akin to the ecstatic visionary moments of poems like 'Fresh Fields' and 'High Tide at Malahide'; and whether one takes it as wish-fulfilment fantasy or, as I am inclined to do, as a metaphor for numinous perception, its function in the book is to suggest the *persona*'s desire to be free of what Gogarty's Hegelian Master, Macran, described as 'contingent and nugatory idiosyncracies'. As metaphor, it embodies both Gogarty's sense of the unity of being and the Heraclitean doctrine of flux. 'So I who am touched by Eternity, a minion of That Which is Ageless, mused, and with the waters I murmured παντα ρει .'

Perhaps these apparent digressions, so characteristic of the anatomy, are more closely related to the quest for Patrick than they might seem to be. Of course, it is such digressions that reveal the nature of the quester to us and the values that are his. And these we need to know. But, in addition, essence and contingency are being distinguished from one another. Through the flux of time and the shifting shapes of legend, Gogarty seeks the essential Patrick; through the multifarious ways in which Patrick has pervaded a culture and a people and the innumerable ways in which he has been 'used' historically, Gogarty seeks what is uniquely Patrician, 'pure and undiluted by modern distraction'.

When, for instance, Gogarty turns to the subject of St Patrick's Purgatory, he dwells very little on its fearsome aspects and very much on its archetypal significance: 'For like to the way Odysseus went and Aeneas after him, it gave entry to the underworld.' Indifferent to its special Christian associations with sin and purgation, he views Patrick's Purgatory as a 'response to the urge of curiosity which has beset mankind since the world began,' and, as if to emphasise the continuity of experience and the universal archetype adds, 'From immemorial times down to the days of Homer, Virgil, and Gregory the Great man has sought to penetrate behind the Veil and to still the obstinate questioning of Fate.' Indeed, the devout might feel that Gogarty's Patrick has far more in common with Odysseus and Aeneas than with Hell's Harrower, that he is presented as a link between the civilisation of Greece and Rome and the modern world rather than as the bringer of the mysteries of the Trinity, Incarnation, and Resurrection.

When Gogarty wishes to gain some sense of the primitive world into which Patrick introduced notions of charity and law, he— reasonably enough—visits Belfast for the Orangeman's 12th July parade! Even were one to question the anthropological significance of his evidence, could one possibly question the validity of his Southern Irish irony? This superb passage, expressive of the drummer's fierce passions (and deriving one or two hints from Vachel Lindsay's poem) should have a symbolic force, except for the humourless:

They held sway over the circular dun of their drums, and they beat the imprisoned wind until it roared and retched in thunder and bellowed back in rage like Typhon under Aetna, or as if the old demons of the land had been caught up, impounded, and battered in the great circular cell. Whack! The Flagellants scourged the drums and they punished themselves in their frenzy. Blood flowed and splashed from bleeding wrists and stained a hand's breadth of the drum where the tendons of the adept came in contact with the rim. Boom! And the jailed giants roared and erupted sound like a volcano. Outside, the careless notes of the fifes and flutes led on. But the Typhonic thunder of the drums drowned all. The fifes wailed like panic-stricken furies from all this Congo of the drums. Boom! Boom! Blood. Boom! The crowd cheers. The wagonettes respond with druidical dignity.

. . . .

I am in luck; I can see the faces of the drummers at close range. With heads thrown back and eyes closed they wait, tranced in silence, for the signal to begin. Slowly the great sound is re-awakened. 'Wul! Wul!' Drumtaps no more. But the lambegs are muttering, 'Wul! Wul! Wul! Wul!' Then, when the self mesmerism has worked, challenging, triumphant, bang go the drums!

WULLUM PRINCE OF ORANGE! It is all so very marvellous. They are exalting William and the Battle of the Boyne. Aye, but the sounds of battles long ago are here roaring in the wind, magically caught up, treated by the Water of Life, *usquebaugh*, and by the incantation and pious memories of the immemorial past, when the Picts fell on Roman Britain and extinguished the *Lux Aeterna* and broke her world-wide Peace. The battle-noises of all time are here: the groans of the dying and the screams of the flying hags that scour the dark, the Choosers of the Slain. Wul! Blood! Boom!

In this appalling ritual of wind, Gogarty hears the echo of the ancient violence, demonic, bestial, of the chaos into which Rome (and he does not mean the Papal See) brought order. 'To a savage culture', he writes, when he sums up the accomplishments of Patrick, 'he introduced civilisation.'

For him, in short, Patrick is not really missionary and defender of the faith but a Promethean bringer of light. He came to the poor, 'houseless, unsanitary, . . . unsegregated from maniacs and leprosy and lupus, half-naked, untreated for even the simplest maladies, subject to the terrors of witchcraft . . . devoid of hope . . . chattels to be bartered . . .' not simply to console with a message of eternal life. Gogarty the social reformer and man of medicine speaks here, as he asserts: 'To these slaves he brought a soul, and to their kings he gave a conscience.' Moreover, as Gogarty views the saint's accomplishments, Patrick was a bringer of new ideas, which were to free the island from its tribal limitations and 'parochial outlook and unite it to the civilisation of Europe'. The political nature of the book is manifest here; for, insisting upon the Roman, European, and broadly cultural significance of Patrick, Gogarty is rejecting, once again, the narrow kind of nationalism he always disdained. He cannot, for instance, prevent an indignant outburst that modern Ireland spends 'millions on Woolworth Irish—call that language Gaelic if you will' but is indifferent to its real past and fails to transmit it through education. And useful though he finds local legends in attempting to trace Patrick's steps, he cannot resist protesting that 'We have the most credible and accountable past in the heroic period of any nation's glory. What have we done with it? We have left it to legend.' To the historicity of Ireland's heroic period, he returns again and again; and the book itself serves as both a demonstration of the means by which reason and imagination may be brought to bear upon the flux of time and the vapours of obscurantism and also as a plea for the apprehension of what is essentially and uniquely 'Irish' and human.

It might be said, of course, that Gogarty set out in quest of St Patrick and found himself. Certainly his saint is very much a man after his own heart, a Roman aristocrat, a vessel of culture rather than a divine agent. He is everything that is generous, humane, noble, and enduring, a counter to Woolworth culture and Woolworth nationalism. Furthermore, he is used by Gogarty to mock the levelling tendencies of the times, in a line that surely scores a point: 'Bear with me if I maintain that "one man is not as good as another," our Pelagians' way of saying that our worst is equal to our best.' On the other hand, in the concluding pages of the book Gogarty suggests that Patrick is every Irishman's familiar and that 'Every person in our island shares something of the personality of that steadfast and enduring man who is spoken of more frequently with affection than with awe.' In short, St Patrick's aristocratic equalities of mind and spirit have pervaded the common life of the people. An endorsement not of the common man but of the patrician in every Paddy, Gogarty's conclusion indicates that, despite political reverses, the Senator was more fully identified with the national spirit than he knew.

9

Merging the Seeker and the Quest

AN author's note to *Tumbling in the Hay* (1939), reminiscent of that which prefaced *Sackville Street*, informs us that 'The time of this book is approximately the beginning of the present century and all the characters are fictitious.' A 'fiction' *Tumbling in the Hay* certainly is, and nearly in the same way as *Sackville Street*. In this recounting of his days first as a B.A. candidate at Trinity College and then as a medical student—the years between 1898 and 1906—Gogarty may seem to have fictionalised more completely than in *Sackville Street*. The narrator of this book is, after all, Gideon Ouseley—even if most of the other characters in the book are identifiably 'real' people and even if Gideon Ouseley was the pseudonym Gogarty adopted for his two Abbey plays. But if Gogarty's point is to be granted him—as it must be—it should be granted for the right reason. Neither more nor less fictive than *Sackville Street*, *Tumbling in the Hay* is another work of the imagination, a selection from 'reality', a transformation rather than a transcript. A blend of confession, anatomy, and romance rather than novel—though with much more of the novel's interest in manners than its two predecessors—it deserves, like *I Follow Saint Patrick*, to be rescued from the undeserved limbo of neglect into which Gogarty's best prose works, other than *Sackville Street*, have passed.

Almost untouched by the political bitterness and raillery of *Sackville Street*, except when Gogarty's account of Arthur Griffith and the early days of *Sinn Fein* move him to assert that, 'Human sacrifice has never quite died out in Ireland,' *Tumbling in the Hay* is also less concerned with the imagination than with the things the imagination can realise, less concerned with 'nothing' than with 'something', less concerned with ideas than with persons, places, and things. It is not that Gogarty is any less responsive to the discrepancies between reality and illusion or any less dedicated to the creative imagination than in the earlier work but that the mood of the work is expansive and comic and that it revels in the way things were. A portrait of the artist as medical student, *Tumbling in the Hay* is also a picture of a world—turn-of-the-century Dublin—its author relished, even when it piqued his sense of irony.

According to the publisher's blurb on the dust jacket of *Tumbling in the Hay*, 'Gogarty—and for a second time—has dared to write as he has always talked. And for the second time he has triumphed.' Certainly the Gogarty voice is as unmistakably present as in *Sackville Street* despite the assumed mask of Gideon Ouseley. The conversational quality of the prose, or of the *persona*'s narrative voice is no mere matter of raciness, or of informality, or of colloquial idiom, or of terseness. Rather it results from a complex of elements. Gogarty's 'talk' has little of the elegance or artifice of that earlier Trinity wit, Oscar Wilde, but its spoken quality is not easy 'naturalness' any more than it is the consequence of carelessness. It is formed to achieve its effects. Consider the following passage, for instance:

> 'I don't know what things is coming to at all,' said Mrs Mack. 'Lookit that now.' I followed the direction of the bedizened arm, which pointed, as it seemed, to the centre of a bare floor covered with oilcloth which had been newly waxed. The room was empty save for two forms of benches on either side, and a pianist who sat with his face turned to the wall in front of a cottage piano on which stood a half-empty pint measure of stout. He sat on a revolving stool with his toes turned like the toes of an organist; and, judging from his inept legs and in-turned toes, he was an advanced case of locomotor ataxia. But the poor are kind to one another; so are the whores. Doubtless in his day he had gone 'into the breach bravely with his pike bent bravely', and had come 'halting off'. But he had got a job as pianist at Mrs Mack's. Over the mantelpiece two gas jets lowered economically illuminated an oleograph of Dante meeting Beatrice by the bridge of the Arno and gripping his left infra-costal space.

Developing, just after the Dublin Cockney dialogue of Mrs Mack, two loose sentence structures that present the details of the charmless, cheerless decor *en masse*, the passage leads us up to the telling detail of the half-empty pint. A complex-compound structure then follows, depending for its effect on a retarding of the parallel elements in the second clause and on a sudden shift in the level of diction, with the introduction of a medical term, though a relatively common one. The next sentence, epigrammatic and brief in expression is very casually 'balanced'. Then an allusion to Shakespeare, itself mock-heroic and ribald in the context, is introduced by a mockingly formal and alliterative, 'Doubtless in his day'. The suddenness and colloquialness of 'But he got a job as pianist at Mrs Mack's' is even more deflating, prefaced and followed as it is by the literary references. And the final line of the passage in which detail is massed once again in a loose structure that has almost the effect of a periodic one, mounts to a comic crescendo, as the gesture of Dante (particularly ridiculous in the context of the brothel) is described with the inappropriate anatomical exactness of a medical text.

These effects are scarcely random ones; and they are not effects even a literate contemporary audience would associate with conversation. Yet by all accounts these effects were characteristic of a man who may have been the last of the great *diseurs*. Ben Lucien Burman, one of his American friends, has described how, late in his life, Gogarty's gaiety could charm the customers in a New York tavern, 'even though his somewhat formal manner and speech were so alien to their experience.'[1]

Actually, the Ouseley-Gogarty voice is only one of the voices in a book that is particularly rich in voices, from nearly every level of Dublin society. In effect, all the characters of *Tumbling in the Hay* contribute to a feast that is of language, accent, and idiom, as well as of conversation. The supremely learned and affected John Pentland Mahaffy defines the nature of the conversational feast and demonstrates one kind of conversational style:

'Weally, gentlemen . . . you are hardly fair to me, nor indeed to yourselves. Our good friend here might imagine I was the tywant of Antioch. . . . You remember, of course, how Antiochus Epiphanes would come and sit and drink and joke with his subjects as if to share their amusements. Let me tell you that he was disappointed, and they were far from being amused by his vagaries. His subjects mistrusted his familiarity. That conduct is wather out of date: none of us is subject to another, so let us keep the λεγόμενον ἐς μέσον , as the Greeks say. Pull your chairs closer to the fire. After all, we must remember that conversation means a feast to which all must contribute, an *eranos*, a contributory feast.'

By contrast to this formality, there is the playful fractured Latin of another classicist, the benignly cynical W. Y. Tyrrell:

'Pereunt horae et notantur: The whores passed by and are spotted,' he murmured audibly, much amused.

'It's a good rendering if not exactly a translation, for it conveys the warning. There would be no meaning in telling us that our hours were numbered if we spent them well. And whoever wrote that knew there were certain things that led to hours misspent. The very place for the motto is an oyster bar.'

At another level of society and rhetoric, where language becomes bombast, there is the plea of the Counsellor Bumleigh. Bumleigh first defends the City Coroner Friery ('one of the most respected and beloved citizens who ever held public office in any country. A friend of the poor, a general comforter of the distressed.') against the suit of Aggie Durkin ('a woman associated with those race-going gangs that infest the racecourses of England, and are about to begin their nefarious operations in our hitherto crimeless country.') Next Bumleigh pleads the case of the accuser:

'A woman thrice bereaved. . . . She entrusts her little legacy to the City Coroner, who, taking advantage of his high office and the confidence implied by it, squanders on the fortuitous field of Baldoyle the hard-earned money of this widow and thrice-bereaved worker. I do not know, nay I would not care to know that infamy could go deeper. I would not care to know,' he repeated, wagging his head, 'lest my faith in the truth and goodness of human nature be destroyed.'

Mr Golly, the estimable publican whose premises stand behind the Medical School, is also afflicted with gas. He suffers 'something shocking from flatulence,' but his language is not inflated; indeed, it is very close to the pavements of Dublin:

'The wife, a merry woman in her day, often called out, "Another balloon gone, Gus!" as if I was one of them ould

cods swapping balloons for rags and bones with the chisellers,
"Another balloon gone, Gus!" I used to be getting to be a trial
to her.'

Even closer to those streets is the language of that great bawd,
Mrs Mack, whose house is one of the liveliest in the Kips, Dublin's
Nighttown. Not that Mrs Mack is not refined! 'I declare to
Jayshus, the language of some of them doxies would make me
want to puke.' Given her sense of decorum, Mrs Mack is properly
distressed when one of her girls insists upon declaiming Adriana's
'lust' speech from *The Comedy of Errors*:

'How often have I told you to stop that yodelling! Ye'd
think ye was one of them gladiators gliding down an Alp. Isn't
it enough for ye that I was fined last week for a misdemeanour?
How the hell can I run a decent house with all this bloody Art
about the place? Ye'd think this was one of them disorderly
shanties up the street.'

In short, *Tumbling in the Hay* is a feast of language and of
voices. The witty discourse of a Trinity salon; the pedantries of
the lecture hall; the mordant sarcasms of the hospital; the *bêtises*,
the slanging and punning of the medicals; the garrulity of the pub,
the cockneyisms of the racetrack; the alien accent of the North;
the jargon of the lawcourts; the Paracelsan quotations of 'Kinch'—
James Joyce; the blather of the brothel; the polyphonic chatter of
the Hay Hotel in the early hours of the morning: all these Gogarty
mimics with an exuberance that pervades the book.

Verbal play of almost every kind abounds. Silly Barney and
Weary Willy (two of the 'medicals') diagnose Golly's complaint,
anticipating, or giving hints to, Samuel Beckett and learnedly
invoking the names of such famous men of science as Kundt and
Foucault with all too acute an awareness of the associative significances of their authorities' names; later they manage to insert in
the *Irish Times* an account of Golly's second marriage that contains an obscene Latin 'typo'—*in secundas nuces* (for favourable
nuts). Golly himself, despite the innocence with which he responds
to foreign words and phrases, is not without linguistic resources.
His 'Irish bull' in this discussion of an astronomy examination
taps metaphysical and cosmic depths:

'They might ask you "What's Space?"' '
'Easy enough. Couldn't you tell them it was Nothing?'

'But then they would ask you what was Nothing.'

'Easy enough.' said Mr Golly. 'You could tell them that it was a bung-hole without a barrel.'

Randy mnemonics, ribald limericks (fragmentary and complete), and scatalogical verses, which serve the medicals a practical purpose since they incorporate information, also contribute to this verbal play, both instructive and entertaining. Ouseley's 'grind' Parker, his 'crammer' for Anatomy, suffers more than one limerick but most amusingly in this:

> There once was a solar eclipse
> Which could only be seen from the Kips,
> As the daylight grew darker
> I thought I saw Parker
> Astride on a . . .

If 'prostitute's hips' do not complete the original limerick, they surely are in keeping with its spirit. The magnum opus of Gogarty's Trinity days, a parody of Coleridge and a catalogue of physical and chemical causes and effects that narrates the Odyssey of a syphilitic sailor in comically forced rhymes, appears in some regrettably few fragments. 'Sinbad' is eventually swallowed by a whale, the mercury in his system contributing something to the ecology of the earth:

> Where that cetacean defecated
> A continent was concentrated
> From all the food evacuated,
> Which was no mean land;
> And from its colour, when located,
> They called it Greenland.

Rich in conversation, accent, and verbal play, *Tumbling in the Hay* is also intensely visual and substantially detailed. Like other works in the tradition of Menippus and Petronius, its approach to its personages is largely external and ironic. It gives us types rather than three-dimensional portraits. Here, for example, is Gogarty's description of Hosanna Bumleigh, the barrister:

> He was a tall, thin, low-shouldered man with a sudden stomach like the protuberance of a sea-horse, and a mangy moustache and eyebrows, which he used for concentration or brow-beating, and full florid lips, purple and exuberant, suggesting a Moor

or a pair of earthworms on their honeymoon. An unblinking glass gave his countenance a fixed regard which suggested un-wavering loyalty and steadfastness. He was a ready barrister, with a voice which could rant like a street preacher or whisper as insinuatingly as a charwoman ordering a glass of plain.

The approach is that of caricature, but the selective strokes are such as to bring the character alive in the imagination as a physical presence, at the same time that his moral significance is being expressed through the irony.

Tumbling in the Hay is dedicated to the painter Augustus John, 'To you, Augustus, with your "Don't be afraid of life!" ' Both the painter and his imperative can appropriately preside over the book. Mrs Mack, the brothel-keeper is, for instance, both a voice and a presence; and as she is seen and heard, she is judged and understood :

> Her face was brick-red. Seen sideways, her straight forehead and nose were outraged by the line of her chin, which was undershot and outthrust, with an extra projection on it like the under-jaw of an old pike. There is a lot of rot talked about the effect of vice on the countenance. It gives some faces, if any-thing, a liberal look, but it largely depends on the kind of vice. Avarice was written by Nature's hieroglyphic on the face of Mrs Mack. I thought of the grasping ways of her and her like, which led to the establishing of the 'Whore's Bank' [a match seller on the Dublin streets] that the little starveling street-walkers might preserve a few shillings from the inquisition and the search to which they would be subjected on their return to the Kips.
>
> 'Ye can't dance be yerself. And there's nothing doing till wan of them hussies is disengaged.'

Yet the response to moral understanding is neither revulsion nor fear. It is not that Ouseley is either too detached to feel or too sanguine to apprehend. Developing his picture of the noted kip, for instance, he amasses enough solid detail to make it possible to reconstruct the 'office' he is invited to enter, as he awaits his friends :

> The room I entered had, opposite to the door, a large wash-stand containing two jugs in bright-yellow basins. The basins

F

were of the same pattern, the jugs were different, one of them being made of enamelled tin. A large bed hammocked with age occupied the space behind the door. Open trunks lay on the floor beside a mirror. A sewing machine, spools of silk, slippers, cigarettes, empty cigarette tins, greasy curl papers, a broken alarm clock and one that was busy ticking, together with half-a-hundred odds and ends of gauzy female gear lay in old chocolate boxes or on the table in littered heaps. On the mantle-shelf, mottled by the marks made through the years by numerous cigarettes, were several rancid tumblers and a photograph of a smart trap full of girls and another of Kit Malcomson's coach. A candle was stuck in the neck of an empty Guinness bottle to give light. A fly-blown mirror still held the decorations of a vanished Christmas—pink tissue paper and a card stating that Christmas comes but once a year. An empty matchbox lay in two halves in the empty grate. But magnificent on the dirty coverlet lay the satin nightdress case of Mrs Mack.

The picture we get here is as much of Mrs Mack herself as of the room and, by extension, of the establishment. And there is no doubt at all, that what is suggested is a profound disorder—not merely of taste but of the very existence of this being and the very being of this existence. The ironic juxtaposition of the intensely realised details implies the assessment Gogarty is making.

It is instructive, I think, to compare the conclusion of *Tumbling in the Hay*—the visit to Mrs Mack's, its aftermath at the Hay Hotel, the celebration shortly thereafter at the lying-in hospital of the recently qualified medicals—with the climactic Nighttown episode in Joyce's *Ulysses*. Doubtless Gogarty was motivated by a desire to set down his version of the way things were in Night-town; and, of course, there are innumerable connections between this book and Joyce's works. 'The Citizen', John Elwood, and Vincent (Cosgrave), two medicals who are close companions of Ouseley, are the Temple and Lynch of Joyce's *Portrait*; the latter, who also appears in *Ulysses*, there betrays Stephen Dedalus by deserting him in Nighttown. An early scene at the Holles Street Hospital, where there is some boozy and callous discussion of childbirth; the episode at Mrs Mack's; the fight in the street (during which Tiger Roche is knocked out by a Lancer); the drinking scene at Golly's, after which Kinch is abandoned, through his own indifference; the visit to the Coombe Hospital, where there is further roistering: all of these correspond to episodes in *Ulysses*. There they are treated in a different sequence and with far different emphasis and significance. While Gogarty manifests no particular enthusiasm for Kinch in this book, he is not markedly hostile to him; certainly there is not in this portrait of Joyce any of the deliberate cruelty of certain of the jibes in *Ulysses*. Yet Ouseley-Gogarty does insist that Kinch was rude, had 'poor manners', was contemptuous of others and, above all, entirely peripheral to the set of medical students. Subordinate details in the Gogarty work—his own poem 'Sinbad the Sailor', his character Mother Maher, Kinch's exclamation 'Rocks', these last two undoubtedly being accurate memories on Gogarty's part, particularly inasmuch as they followed by more than a decade the publication of *Ulysses*—were in Joyce's work elaborated into a texture of symbolic motifs central to the theme of the novel. At the climax of *Tumbling in the Hay*, one of the ladies who has been tumbling (quite literally), responds to the cook Maria's boast that all of her nick-nacks 'stand for something or other' : 'Here everything stands for something else!' Mrs Adrian's exclamation may be taken as an irreverent comment by Gogarty on the symbolic motifs of *Ulysses*. It is also a comic reminder that in *Tumbling in the Hay* everything actually is *what* it is, that persons, places, and things have a substantial reality. Because this is so for him, although Gogarty comprehends Mrs Mack and Nighttown, he does not find them loathsome.

To pursue this matter further, it may be helpful to consider the way Joyce and Gogarty handled their fellow student, John Elwood, when they depicted him in their works. It has been suggested that Gogarty perhaps romanticised Elwood's attractiveness;[2] but Elwood Temple in the *Portrait* is an exotic and the Citizen Elwood in *Tumbling in the Hay* is immensely attractive to women—or at least to the ladies of the Kips. In both works Elwood—enigmatic, cryptic, elliptical, and startling—is a striking figure. In the *Portrait*, however, Temple functions as a grotesque parody of Stephen Dedalus. He is the outsider, the unbeliever, the cynic, who cannot be taken seriously. Polar opposite of the bird-like, soaring 'artificer' Stephen wishes to be, he is a 'cod', the 'artist'—Elwood's own word for Joyce[3]—as fake; he is dismissed by Cranly, who despises him, with the 'Whoosh' appropriate to a barnyard fowl. In effect, the sole significance of Elwood-Temple in the *Portrait* is that in Stephen's consciousness Temple is a horrible example of what Stephen might become. Outside of Stephen's mind, Temple has no importance whatsoever. Even if one were to argue that in *Tumbling in the Hay*, Elwood is someone that Ouseley-Gogarty wishes to be, one would have to admit that he has an independent significance beyond the consciousness of that *persona*:

> His dancing eyes regarded me, while his beautiful mouth was hardly touched by his slow enigmatical smile. A companionable hour with him was impossible, not to mention a continuous or even a coherent conversation. He appeared to think in flashes from some deep uncommunicable life. He had a way of shooting out a word as if it contained a secret message or revealed to you some secret with which he held you to be concerned in some mysterious way of which he had a quizzical knowledge.

The 'Circe' chapter in *Ulysses*, the expressionistic Nighttown sequence, is, at moments, particularly in the apotheosis of Leopold Bloom, uproariously funny; yet Nighttown as it emerges from the phantasmagoria of the chapter is utterly repellent and degrading. Of course, Joyce makes no pretence of giving an objective reality in the episode. Particular moments in the whole do convey an external reality; yet the 'Circe' for the most part expresses the conflicts in the deeps of the character's psyches, and it does so through the fantasy of the novel's supposedly invisible author. In short, Nighttown is the consciousness of James Joyce and its expressionist symbolic details are a means of making exterior his aberrations and obsessions. No more than Temple-Elwood of the *Portrait* does Nighttown have a significance in and for itself.

On the one hand, then, Joyce regards the world he creates as inseparable from himself. Probing into the most shameful and aberrant depths of his own soul, he is able to express the conflicts, perversions, and neuroses of Stephen and Bloom: of all men, in fact. On the other hand, Gogarty-Ouseley looks out upon a Dublin Nighttown that is external to the self, and upon a widely varied assortment of people, all of whom have a substantiality about them. He is clearly not naïve about what may happen and is happening in that world. He takes a good look at the worst, but his eye does not linger there for long because there are other things to divert him. On the whole, he is not repelled by what he sees, even if he judges it, for he does not participate in all that he sees.

Furthermore, there is cleansing laughter and always something more to be seen.

It could certainly be argued that the distinction here is between a profound artist and a superficial one, between one who plunges into the very depths of being and another who skirts reality. I think I would want to view the matter somewhat differently. Joyce's achievement is unquestioned; his was the ultimate triumph of Romantic egoism. But compelling as *Ulysses* happens to be—and it and the *Wake* may constitute the modern world's 'philosophic poem' which Santayana called for in *Three Philosophical Poets*—it does not exhaust the possible responses to existence nor is its vision all-inclusive. Neither as readers nor as sensibilities can we afford to reject other visions and other responses, or to exist at a single level of experience. *Tumbling in the Hay* can be esteemed for what it achieves on its own level of intensity. The Ouseley-Gogarty vision of the Kips has its own comic integrity.

There is a comic moment early in the book when Ouseley spots his ineffective tutor crossing the Trinity yard, 'clear-eyed, rushing into the past'. The direction of the book and of its youthful protagonist is the opposite one; and the image of a clear-eyed Ouseley racing his bicycle to some anticipated victory dominates the early chapters. If the myth of a return to a garden state lies in the deeps of *As I Was Going Down Sackville Street* (only to be repudiated by its final vignette), the myth of the untested hero's quest lies below the surface of *Tumbling in the Hay*, though, paradoxically, one of its stages is a vision of a more innocent past. Indeed, in Gogarty's best work there is always much more going on below the apparently chaotic surface than has customarily been recognised. The structure of *Tumbling in the Hay* is entirely episodic, though chronological. Continuity is provided by the various stages, in lecture hall, examination room, laboratory and hospital, of the medical student's education; focus is gained by the frequent returns to Golly's pub, where Ouseley and his friends gather; variety is achieved by the students' encounters with various Dublin grotesques, these from apothecaries, pawn shops, and pubs, from the circus, the racing world, the lawcourts, and the kips. Although disguised by turn-of-the-century Dublin trappings, there are here too many of the elements of what Joseph Campbell has called the monomyth of the hero to be ignored. Indeed, education being an initiation, it is probably the case that any account of a young man's education would reveal the archetypal pattern. The pattern is there in *Tumbling in the Hay*, and it satisfies by its presence. Ouseley who, like other disguised heroes, often sees himself as a bit of a churl, is transported by his mother in a carriage to the threshold of his adventure. There she defeats the guardian presence: two university Registrars! Past the threshold, Gideon, now freeing himself from the maternal influence but assisted by various benevolent forces—Golly, Tyrrell, Macran, Sir Thomas Myles—encounters a series of combats (playful rivalries with his brother medicals, the menacing bicycle race in Belfast) and tests of increasing intensity (the examinations in Biology, Anatomy, Midwifery, Surgery, and Medicine). Ouseley has his encounter with the goddess-mother: deliveries at the lying-in hospital. He descends into the Underworld, Dublin's red light district. He encounters there the goddess as temptress in the form of the tumbling ladies of the Hay Hotel. Gideon has also his discovery of a 'secret' that makes him 'wise': medical specialisation under Sir Robert Wood at the Ear, Throat, and Nose Dispensary! He experiences recognition by the father-creator through a series of events—the climactic speech by a doctor of Medicine who 'Small as he was bulked very largely'; legal independence of his mother by a 'deed of gift' he makes her; and finally 'qualification', which sets him free. If the monomythic hero succeeds, he returns from 'the kingdom of the dead' with a restorative power. Ouseley turns to self mockery at the close of the following passage on the book's last page, but the purport of his own ironic recognition of cycle and paradox is inescapable:

> I thought of the first cab-drive six years ago, and of this preposterous journey at the end. It began in a cab and it ends, appropriately enough, in a pathological cab. Tomorrow to fresh Woods— How far I have travelled in all of these years from cab to cab! All I have learned! All that stuff about philosophy— that there is a dialectic of death in life and life in death. I would like to believe that, even though, if I did believe it, I wouldn't know exactly what it meant. An Irishman believes best in what he knows to be untrue.

No matter how self-deprecating his manner, Ouseley has travelled far on this 'preposterous journey'. The frankness of his self-depreciation should not mislead us as to the difficulties of the journey or its distance—or its purpose.

From his mother's point of view, that purpose is certainly associated with family status. Prepared to enter Gideon in the Royal School of Anatomy (Irish and Catholic), she is so offended by the Registrar's rudeness and indifference when she mentions her late husband, that she whisks her son off to Trinity (Anglo-Irish and Protestant), where the manners are better. Neither mother nor aunt (who also invokes the proprieties) approves of Ouseley's friends, as he well knows. Lacking cuff links (which his friends have pawned for drinking money) when he registers, he enters Golly's with 'a sense of degradation. My friends repelled me. If my mother knew! . . . But it was not her fault. It was mine, to degrade a family heirloom.' Mocked by his Catholic medical pals for 'Trinity swank', Ouseley makes no effort to introduce his Trinity friend Birrell to Weary Mac and Silly Barney. 'Birrell was well brought up, so was I; but he was Protestant and might think that my friends were low. Being a Catholic, I didn't, so I got more value out of life. I may be a bit of a snob, but you cannot mix "Varsities".' A candid admission such as this, particularly taken in conjunction with equally candid admissions elsewhere (such as *Sackville Street*'s 'I dearly love a Lord'), may easily be misinterpreted. There are conflicts in Ouseley (as there were in Gogarty) of a complex nature. Eventually and amusingly, Ouseley introduces Birrell to the Citizen, Weary, and Barney at Golly's and they hit it off splendidly, the Trinity 'medical' recounting to the Royals his discovery of 'Agamalgia, "Engaged Man's Gonad", or Birrell's Disease'. In fact, when Ouseley describes the attitude of mother and aunt, he indulges the same kind of satiric impulse. He tells us that the friendship of Charlie Pease is important to him inasmuch as Charlie lends some respectability to Ouseley's cycling, a sport the ladies at home feel to be entirely lacking in tone:

> The fact that Charlie indulged in such an unaristocratic game as cycling saved me. He looked so like an infantry officer . . . and he dressed and behaved so mannerly and won such lovely cups on his shining bicycle that he was an exemplar and an excuse.

The very tones of mother and aunt are heard in criticism of the rest of the cycling world:

> For the rest, were they not all tradesmen? Could I point at one, with the exceptions mentioned, who was not engaged in some

trade or other, and did I expect my aunt or my mother to recognise the plumber?

Ouseley then observes:

It sounds like snobbery; and why shouldn't it? It was. But when a fellow has an aunt who knows all about the Royal Family and half the Almanach de Gotha by heart, and when we have turkey, goose or gurnard for dinner, calls the stuffing 'the concealment', what is a fellow to do?

Ouseley satirises the family's gentility here, and its consciousness of status, just as he mocked his own assumption that Birrell and the Catholic medicals would not mix.

At the same time, there is, in Ouseley's comments, a realistic knowledge of men and society. His 'snobbery' is of a very different kind from that of mother and aunt. If Birrell and the Citizen do mix, Varsities don't always. At the Bailey, Arthur Griffith clearly will not mix with a Silly Barney intoxicated to the point of song by taking Honours in Anatomy: 'Silly's attitude appeared to Arthur to continue the tradition of the stage Irishman.' No more does another friend, Kinch (James Joyce), mix well with the medicals: 'It's a great thing to get rid of Kinch,' said John.

What distinguished Ouseley's 'snobbery' from that of his ladies is that, while conscious of special and religious differences, he will not be limited by them. At Macran's salon, he looks around the room, and it occurs to him 'that with the exception of the benign Doctor and myself all were from the North'. Yet while more than aware that he is a well-brought-up Catholic, he also knows that he enjoys *more* social levels than do his family, his friends, and associates, and thus gets more value out of life. As a prosperous Catholic at Trinity with low Catholic friends, Ascendancy associates, and a mother and aunt with distinct social notions, Gideon Ouseley is a social and cultural anomaly, unless, of course, he can manage to contain or control these diversities. Ouseley wants to 'bring the Muse into Medicine, or rather, bring Medicine . . . back to Phoebus'; he wants to claim large tracts of English literature but also to support the politics of Sinn Fein. But he does not want to be Protestant, even if his Catholic orthodoxy is more than suspect. During a tutorial—and drinking—session with Macran on the dialectic, he gives a bit of a lecture on the Reformation. 'What', he asks rhetorically of the English,

> has pinched and darkened their faces and taken from them the Falstaffian fulness which was the face of Merrie England? And we all know that Falstaff was a typical Englishman until Luther treated him as scurvily as Prince Hal. What are the English people taking so seriously? Can they not find any more people to forgive for the wrongs they themselves have inflicted? Can it be that when Luther came in, mirth went out?

Ouseley prefers Hegel's desire to live beside a Catholic Church and drink good beer, to Luther and Protestantism, and he is opting for the Renaissance, Humanism, Hellenism (particularly as opposed to Hebraism), and inclusiveness.

The essential quest of *Tumbling in the Hay* is Ouseley's attempt to live in as many worlds as possible, to contain within himself as much as he possibly can. Undertaking medical study at Trinity, he must repeat his two years at the Royal. Victimised, as he feels, by the dour McNought, who resents his cycling and fails him repeatedly at Anatomy, he is taken up by Tyrrell, who awards him a ten for a paper: 'So you are the young man who admires Tennyson and remembers so many lines?' Discoursing on Aristophanes over port, Ouseley so pleases the benign Epicurean that he is invited to Jammet's for prawns and ale. At *An Stad*, a centre for Gaelic enthuiasts and Sinn Feiners that he begins to visit, he admires the athlete Michael Cusack for his calves, the Gael Cathal McGarvey for his poetry, and Arthur Griffith for his forehead. Ouseley would be athlete, poet, and political leader. Following on a low-life and comic triumph as a cyclist 'up North'—'someone was meant to win and it wasn't supposed to be me'—and another defeat by McNought, Ouseley has his session with Trinity's Professor of Moral Philosophy on Hegel. And following on revels with his friends in Midwifery at the Holles Street Hospital, he sups with the gods—not only Tyrrell and Macran but J. P. Mahaffy, Provost of Trinity. Somewhat discomfited by the Master's allusions to 'Nero's predeliction . . . for tavern company', Ouseley is still able to bask in talk of Chrysippus and Diogenes Laertius, of Seneca and Gallio. With Chopin in the background, epigrams in the air, playfulness in the conversation, except when Tyrrell losing his Stoic detachment insults Mahaffy, Ouseley again assumes the guise of naïf and insists upon his own ignorance. But he is plainly at home here too.

Tumbling in the Hay is filled with comic detail—the rhymes and barbs at the expense of the venereal Sinbad, for instance—that are characteristic both of medical students, whose callousness is a defence mechanism, and of the Irish comic sense, with its unique awareness of the grotesquery of physical decay. Yet at the climax of the book, as Ouseley and his friends are about to be qualified, Gogarty introduces a speech of four pages, in direct response to the student's clownishness. According to Ulick O'Connor, the speaker was an actual Richmond Hospital physician, Jock O'Carroll,[4] but, unlike the other examiners who figure in the book, the small doctor is not named—and appropriately not—for it is really Gideon Ouseley's moment. The entire speech is a moving one. Even some brief excerpts may suggest its force:

> There has been, one might almost say, a good deal of merriment, suppressed and expressed, this morning. That is no harm; it is better, I must admit, than profound gloom.
>
> . . . .
>
> You will see that sightless forces, the pull of the grave that never lets up for one moment, draw down the cheeks and the corners of the mouth and bend the back until you behold beauty abashed and looking down on the sod as if to find a grave. These are no delightful thoughts, but they will inevitably be yours and your recompense for them is that your work for a short space may ease pain and baulk, if only for a year or two, the forces of annihilation and decay.
>
> . . . .
>
> It is by Charity that this miracle is wrought. By Charity.
>
> . . . .
>
> For this you must be prepared to sacrifice more than your lives. You must sacrifice your delight in Beauty; for, as you gaze on it, your knowledge tempts you to see beneath the bloom the intimations of decay. That is the price that you must pay for this knowledge. That is the sacrifice you must make. . . . Your joy in life must be exchanged for devotion to the service of mankind.

The point at which Ouseley would part company with the eloquent physician is that at which he sacrifices 'delight in Beauty' and 'joy in life'; indeed, following the lecture, Gideon launches another verbal attack on the Reformation: 'Luther had a discharging ear and he suffered from subjective noises, one of which he thought was the voice of the Devil.' Ouseley will have medicine and Charity; but he will have Beauty and joy as well.

The last four chapters of *Tumbling in the Hay* are, for comic energy and colour, perhaps the best prose Oliver Gogarty ever produced. It is in them that he leads us from the dingy establishment of Mrs Mack, where he has gone to seek the Citizen, to the superb disorder of the Hay Hotel. There, as Maria the cook prepares such gusty dishes as Tripe and Onions and Skate's roe, the hotel seems to teem with women enamoured of Citizen Elwood. The tumbling begins. On an impulse Jenny Greeks, widow and partner of a circus acrobat, balances herself upside-down amongst the crockery on the table, revealing the briefest of drawers. Not to be outdone, a very tall grey-haired woman fastens up her skirts, stands on her head on another table, and revolves, until she falls backward among the plates of tripe. In an adjacent chamber, Mercedes, the Shakespearian manqué, attempts suicide by gas out of jealous pique. Nearby, Mrs Adrian, 'the well-known and popular epileptic', has a fit. Challenged by the tall grey-haired woman, Jenny has leapt to the hotelier's shoulders, turning herself upside down once again. For Ouseley, who has travelled far for this vision of a world un-Reformed, untouched by the grim spectre of Puritanism, there is elation:

> Her agility gave the sordid place the atmosphere of a little village in France where one might see balancing women and contortionists in the booth of a travelling circus. I felt transformed out of place and time. The abandon and elan of medieval life filled me full.

Independent now of his mother, since he has signed away any claim on his father's estate, Ouseley knows there are other things for him to see and do. Most of the fabulous people of Dublin's underworld—Jenny and her fancy man, Rasher Doyle, Piano Mary (none other than Mercedes), Liverpool Kate (Mrs Adrian herself)—whose names have echoed through the book, have been shown to him. But Jack Lalor the barber, whose name is ever on Mr Golly's lips running through the book as a comic motif, is yet unmet. The fabulous remains, in the very midst of the mundane.

And Gideon knows, as he reflects on the choice of medical practices open to him, that 'none of these things was sufficient. Freedom was the chief advantage; whatever knowledge I possessed I could give. I could afford to be no man's man.' If Ouseley is a snob, he is an experience snob. He might be Faustian, were he not so Epicurean and so cheerfully ironic. At the end of his journey, he has only begun. He knows though that if he is to be his own man propriety cannot restrain him. Somehow he will have to range from the witty banter of the salon to the vital abandon of his vision at the Hay. He will define himself not by what he will negate but by what he will contain.

In choosing to narrate *Tumbling in the Hay* through the *persona* of Gideon Ouseley rather than *in propria persona* (and in ascribing, this time, his own verses to others), Gogarty was moving closer to the fictional mode of the romance and a little away from the confession. In doing so, he did not gain perfect control over 'point of view'. There is a noticeable lurch in the opening chapter as Gogarty shifts from omniscience to the first person. He makes this shift throughout the book though elsewhere far less obviously and with more justification because he does so in discrete chapters. If, except for his youthfulness, the Gideon Ouseley of *Tumbling in the Hay* is not terribly different from the Oliver Gogarty who talks all the way through *Sackville Street* and *I Follow Saint Patrick*, it is not because Gogarty fails to objectify him as a *persona*. The speakers in all three of the works see themselves objectively in comic and ironic terms. No more than Oliver Gogarty does Gideon Ouseley indulge in subjective brooding; he is too interested in all the lively things going on around him. Certainly the conflicts of the young Ouseley were those of the young and the mature Gogarty—a desire for social eminence, even swank, coupled with a love of the vulgar tongue and common life, a desire to give of himself to others coupled with an intense need to be unique, his own man, a servant only of Beauty. *Tumbling in the Hay* is itself a measure of the success with which he resolves his conflicts. Apparently not political at all as both of its predecessors had been and certainly—in its picture of Dublin as an extended slum—not exhibiting an ideal community, *Tumbling in the Hay* is implicitly political in depicting a world in which there is freedom and space. Despite the flaw in the handling of point of view in the opening chapter, the book is unique in so many ways—as social history, as a doctor's testimony to his profession, as a rendering of the comic language of turn-of-the-century Dublin, as the revelation of an exuberant relish for life, as an archetypical quest and initiation—that it must surely be recognised, along with *Sackville Street*, as one of the liveliest works of the Irish Literary Renaissance.

New Forms, New Forms!

Going Native, published in 1940, was the first of a series of prose works in which Gogarty gradually departed from the fictive modes he had mastered at the end of the thirties. Like the works that followed it, *Going Native* was the product of new circumstances and of his effort to try his hand at new things. It opens with a scene in which Gideon Ouseley is persuaded by William Butler Yeats—the latter on the threshold of death—that he should leave the Ireland of de Valera, at least for a time. The rest of the book is concerned with a stay of six weeks that Ouseley makes in England, following that visit to Yeats. Gogarty was actually sixty-one at the time *Going Native* was finished, but the Ouseley *persona* acts and thinks like a man twenty years younger. Moreover, the world with which *Going Native* deals is the world of the later twenties and the early thirties rather than England under the shadow of World War II; and the book is the fruit of Gogarty's experiences in English social circles during those earlier years. The book has so many interesting qualities and remains so readable that one can only regret it is not of the same imaginative order as its three predecessors of the thirties, though it is closer to them in its conventions than the two works that immediately followed it.

Sackville Street, I Follow St Patrick, and *Tumbling in the Hay* are anything but 'pure' examples of a genre. Indeed, they are books that doubtless horrify the more simple-minded practitioners of generic definition; yet each of the books is a fiction, each is distinctive, and all emerge from ancient and vigorous traditions of prose forms. The problem with *Going Native* is not that it is a mixed form, but that, this time, the mixed elements somehow clash with one another.

The loquacious Ouseley has no difficulty in holding one's attention throughout the book; his eyes and his wit are bright enough to probe both the absurdities and the charms of the aristocratic set he enters. Moreover, his digressions are varied and entertaining. The range of allusion and subject is extraordinary. One finds here the description of the aged Yeats, a terse cultural analysis of the civilisation of the Mediterranean basin, a lovingly detailed contrast between the Liffey and the Thames, an analysis of the sound qualities of the first Idyll of Theocritus, and a discourse on the relationship between sensibility and landscape. One finds amusing passages on Scotland Yard, country houses, clubs, and divorces, on Rabelais' Abbey of Theleme, on the English cult of the dog and its relation to birth control, on Yorkshiremen, on the difference between England and America, and on man's idealisation of woman. There is even a disquisition on the female orgasm that finds Gogarty, though from a medical perspective, close to D. H. Lawrence!

Much of this material has a value and interest independent of the merit of the entire work. The Yeats description, for instance, follows on a badly overwritten opening passage, 'The immemorial hills of Ireland, that were melted and moulded in the crucible of primal fire out of which they were poured undulating into rotundity . . . glowed again from within. . . . It was almost two thousand years ago that Finn and his companions ranged these hills and the father of Oisin sang the first spring song.' The very strain one senses in the prose of these opening paragraphs is the saddest indication one could have that an age was over, that the spirit of the Irish Renaissance could not be rekindled. But as Gogarty gets closer to Yeats and their conversation, the chapter comes alive: 'He kept his head bowed, maintaining silence while his jewelled hand moved gently; then he said sorrowfully, "Grandeur is gone, Ouseley, Grandeur is gone." ' And in the passage that follows, one begins to see the significance Gogarty had for the old Master. For that matter, one also see the disillusionment of the leaders of the Literary Revival with the new society that had formed:

You must leave this country! You cannot go on filled with bitterness or chilled with contempt for little office-seekers and rude civil servants which is all that Ireland, left to itself, has made of its freedom. The Anglo-Irish are the salt of the earth. They are being persecuted. You must fly with the wild geese. You must go. To stand still is to sink in the bog.

Impossible as it is to determine whether we are getting an accurate report of a conversation, it is possible to assert that Yeats's words to Gogarty-Ouseley coincide with the attitude he expressed towards the doctor in his Preface to the *Oxford Book*, his BBC *Lecture on Modern Poetry*, and in the poem 'High Talk':

> 'I am old and ill,' he said. 'You are younger and stronger. You must go to where there is reality and material beauty and where there is a zest for life and where people stand firmly on their feet.'

For Gogarty, Yeats plays in *Going Native* a role comparable to that he played in *Sackville Street*. To be sure, 'it was evident that the great poet was about to set sail upon the Shadowy Waters'. And it was tragic that 'the golden dreamer awakened from the creative dream of his that turned his country into faery land, a land of the Ever Young, to be confronted with the worthlessness and worldliness of his countrymen'. Still, Yeats's response to his disappointment, says the *persona*, quoting the epigraph 'Cast a cold eye,' is Stoicism. Gogarty-Ouseley knows that he is 'losing' the only hero 'I had ever met in the flesh'.

Leaving behind the island of poetry and dream, Ouseley finds himself deeply immersed in the unheroic prose of English life. One of the main episodes of the book deals with the Vicar of Mea Culpa's decision to celebrate the feast day of St Roche, patron of dogs, by blessing dogs (pedigreed only) at the lych-gate of the Church. At once aberrant and humdrum, the Blessing of the Dogs provokes a short satirical essay on cultural decadence:

> Whenever I see a dog, I see in it a prevented family. The dog is the wagging symbol of birth control, of the sex sublimation of the race. A glance at the sentences of cruelty to children compared with those for cruelty to dogs makes the dog 102 times as precious as the child. If a dog is worth 102 children and if there are (and there are) 400,000 of these substitutes for families in London alone, how many unconceived children do these dogs represent?

The 'Blessing of the Dogs' is a conceit worthy of Huxley or Waugh. The Vicar, we learn, 'preached ever so well . . . only when he hesitated for a word . . . the barking was renewed and the leashes grew tight'. The sting here punctures both empty institutional religion and organised sentimentalism.

As did those satirists of the thirties, Huxley and Waugh, Gogarty also reacted to the disintegration of the family and of marriage among the fashionable. The characters of *Going Native*, mostly caricatures, and the episodic events, largely farcical, are concerned with a series of amorous debacles. Doubtless the book might be read as a *roman à clef*. (Indeed, Gogarty indicated to a correspondent that the Rector upon whom he modelled a central character 'had informed his parishioners that he and they were in a novel and asked them to read it!'.) More to the point, however, are the traces of English satiric novelists that one discerns. The bizarre names of the characters—Vavasour Vennel, Vicar of Mea Culpa, Lady Constance Marygold, Sir Chalfont St Gules, Lady Bumfrei-Bumphrey, Parmenis Innes—the extreme contrasts of their ages, their marital and extra-marital relations, evoke Ronald Firbank and his more accomplished heir, Evelyn Waugh. So do the ridiculous or banal place names—Mea Culpa Rectory, Twitchings, Glos., Nether Wallop—but these gathering places, which permit the characters to do almost anything so long as it is not socially productive, and the intellectual concerns of Ouseley also evoke the early Huxley. And Gogarty, like Firbank, Waugh, and Huxley, even if he has an eye on a real person, also has an eye on satiric techniques of distortion and exaggeration in his depiction of the sexual mores of the English aristocracy in the twenties and thirties.

Divorce, rest homes for the 'mildly mental', and sado-masochism are comic motifs throughout the book. The Vicar decides to divorce his wife, when her nervous breakdown carries her off to a rest home. He admits that he knew of her first husband, but that 'it would never have done to have married a divorced woman'. His neice, Parmenis, with whom Ouseley falls in love, has had a miscarriage and a divorce. Sir Chalfont is trying to divorce his wife, who has deserted him after a week of marriage. Lady Bumfrei-Bumphrey need not divorce Lord Bumphrey, since they are 'living in sin'; but she does need to stay at a rest home before she marries 'Warts', who bruises but satisfies. 'Hurdles' provides details on the rest of the cast:

Then Malkyn, that lovely kid, can hardly turn round, her husband's so damn jealous, and she'd sleep with anyone in England. And she dare not be divorced for her mother is a

Roman Catholic, and rolling in it, and doesn't believe in divorce
—Cut her off, don't you know? Then what about Baby Eyes
with the long eye-lashes? . . . She's in love with a doctor who
beats her and wears a gardenia—extraordinary chap! Any way
she likes it. . . . She's got a husband somewhere, but she dare
not have a divorce for the sake of the doctor—ruin him and all
that. And lastly there's me. I'm hoping for custody of the kiddie
even for half of the year.

All the women in *Going Native*, even when like Lady Bumfrei-
Bumphrey and Baby Eyes they enjoy a good beating, are sexually
aggressive—from the elegant and face-lifted Lady Marygold, who
tries to seduce Ouseley in the blackberry bushes, to the sallow tart
who picks up the Vicar at Shottery Fair, and complains of her
husband, 'I never get the least thrill with that man.' Parmenis,
Ouseley's mistress, who strikes him in the eye at their first meeting,
then insults, bullies, and seduces him before she rejects, deserts,
and commits him to a rest home, is best described by the psychia-
trist who attends Ouseley: 'She is a man.' Ouseley feels 'physically
sick but psychically cured'.

It is at this point, when *Going Native* begins to explore the
relation of the sexes in modern society, that it is most provocative,
and, I suppose in contemporary terms, most 'sexist'. Reflecting on
the sallow tart's dissatisfaction with her husband, Ouseley observes:

If the girls and women who talk so up-to-date and glibly about
thrills, when they mean orgasms, realised to what the inter-
mittent disturbances which they call 'nervous breakdowns' were
due, they would ration their thrills a little. . . . I asked:
'When had you your last nervous breakdown?'
She eyed me with a mixture of suspicion and wonder:
'You're a bit of a fortune-teller, all right! I gets awful pains
twice or three times a year and the doctor doesn't know what
to make of them.'
—It would be just as unavailing if he did, I thought.

Tantalising as this interrupted conversation is, no less so is one
Ouseley has with Bumphrey in the rest home. Sensing that the
only thing comparable to the transcendentalism of the Celt that
can be found in modern England is the *affaire de coeur*, Ouseley
is also beginning to suspect his own error in the affair with

Parmenis. He tells Bumphrey, therefore, 'We have hung our dreams on women . . . and it is not fair to them. Some of them are beginning to resent being heroines and beauties kept in the harems of men's imaginations. Give them a chance to express themselves.' Tantalising all this is, but not quite resolved, inasmuch as an independent Parmenis will still be a 'man'—with awful pains two or three times a year. Indeed, not until *Rolling Down the Lea,* written a decade later, would Gogarty find the means—a myth— that would integrate the idealised woman of his earlier poetry and the destructive female of *Going Native.*

To say that these passages of Ouseley's analysis intrigue but do not satisfy the imagination is another way of saying that there is a formal defect in *Going Native,* that the continuous present and continuous presence of Ouseley do not work here as the Gogarty and Ouseley *personae* work in *Sackville Street, I Follow St Patrick,* and *Tumbling in the Hay.* In the earlier works anatomy, con- fession, and romance, even a touch of the novel in *Tumbling in the Hay,* fuse effectively; in *Going Native,* anatomy and confes- sion, which are the medium of Ouseley, jostle the comedy of manners to which the other characters belong. Both the early Huxley Peacockian novel of conversation and the Evelyn Waugh oblique satires of the thirties are more successful with the element of satire in fiction; the one by making the discussions of the various characters representing divergent points of view absolutely central by gathering intellectual 'types' in a setting such as Twitching and permitting all to talk out the theme of the work; the other by permitting scarcely any satiric point to be scored directly and by embodying nearly all meanings in character, detail, action, and symbol. In *Going Native,* we have, on the one hand, the voice of the Irish Ouseley, always living in the present and interpreting on the spot; on the other, we have the ridiculous behaviour of his English friends. Ouseley is prevented from following his most interesting perceptions through to a conclusion by the demands of the comic action; the action is prevented from effectively expres- sing the intellectual conflicts at work in the book by the insistent observations of the narrator. Gogarty's hope for *Going Native* was that it would succeed both as farce and as idea. 'There is farce enough in the book but not in the idea behind it which is hinted at in the quotation from Renan—viz. the deep and radical differ- ence between the Celtic and Teutonic, or Anglo-Saxon natures—

always inimical, always opposed, and the results from one impinging on the other.' Had he written the book in the manner of *Sackville Street*—that is, dominantly as anatomy-confession—or gone much further in the direction of the romance-novel than he did, even abandoning the Ouseley *persona*—Gogarty might have succeeded better than he did with the unstable combination he produced.

Even if the Ouseley *persona* clashes with the comedy of manners, anatomy with novel, in *Going Native*, one might yet wish that the liveliness and quirkiness of the Ouseley voice were heard in the pages of Gogarty's next book, *Mad Grandeur* (1941). The circumstances of Gogarty's life had changed radically when he wrote this historical romance in the New Jersey country house of a friend. On lecture tour in the United States when World War II began, he was persuaded that it would be madness to return to Ireland; by October, 1940, he was convinced that he should take out First Papers and become a citizen of the United States. Indeed, that decision was foreshadowed in the closing pages of *Going Native*, where Gogarty, in effect, bids farewell to England, and indicates that his aspiring Celtic psyche must look elsewhere, if anywhere, for its home:

> In America they are adolescent still and they are still 'going places' with the fresh interest and zest of children. The Englishman has been places. He has seen all the pictures. ('He has been here since Julius Caesar.') He has arrived long ago. His is a state of being. America is a state of becoming. America is forever straining forwards.

Committing himself to this culture of becoming, at the age of sixty-two, Gogarty was joining the flock of Wild Geese, the Irish in exile. He was also setting out to earn his living by his writing. Quite cut off now from his profession by his concentration on political and literary activities in the thirties, as well as by American medical requirements that he was now too old to satisfy, suffering from a series of financial reverses—a sharp reduction of income in the thirties,[2] the loss of the *Sackville Street* libel suit, the isolation of Renvyle House (rebuilt, after its burning, as a hotel) from the tourist trade by the war—a writer who had known affluence was forced, at an age when many men retire, to depend almost entirely upon his literary talent for his income.

Thus, *Mad Grandeur* was a frankly commercial effort, the first of Gogarty's career, inasmuch as other more important motives had impelled him to the extraordinary output of the late thirties. It is not that *Mad Grandeur* is shabby or cheap, nor that it is totally without interest, but it lacks both the wit and the seriousness of the four weeks that preceded it, and, above all, their thematic strengths.

Set in the Ireland of 1798, against the background of the Revolutionary and Republican currents that led to such risings as that in Wexford, drawing on Gogarty's storehouse of legend, anecdote, and traditional street songs, the novel depicts the involvement of Hyacinth Martin-Lynch and his family in this atmosphere and in an abortive rising in County Mayo. We enter, in a series of colourful scenes—the best in the novel—the world of the prizefight ring, the horse race, the duelling field, the Dublin underworld. Most of these scenes take place at or near a series of great country houses, based on ones known to Gogarty, his own Renvyle, Lady Gregory's Coole, the Gore-Booths' Lissadell, Moore Hall and others; and these, as Lisadill, Martyn Hall, and Attymon House, are rendered in elaborate detail. There is a huge cast of characters, drawn from most levels of Irish society. The landed if threatened Catholic aristocracy is here, their fugitive aristocratic relatives from France, their servants and retainers. There are also the 'Bucks' of the Hell Fire Club (a noted gaming and sporting club of the eighteenth century). There are English officers and officials, conniving English estate managers and magistrates. There are portraits of native Irish involved in the rising: Roddy, the uneducated but intellectual agitator; Myles, the blacksmith leader of the rising; Father Colyer, the parish priest who opposes revolutionary thought but dies alongside his parishioners in the rising. The book is crowded with excitement and event: the secret landing of fugitives from France, the cottager's celebration of Hyacinth's wedding, Hyacinth's encounter with a highwayman, his swim across the Shannon by night, sword-play on the streets of Dublin, secret meetings and ambushes, a hanging at Newgate Gaol, the looting and burning of Martyn House.

Yet for all this amplitude of detail and character and for all of Gogarty's knowledge of and enthusiasm for the period, *Mad Grandeur* never quite comes alive. The central action—Hyacinth's efforts to preserve his family and estate when they are threatened both by English rulers and native rebels—is carefully varied. Romantic subplots and distinctly spaced set pieces—the prize fight between the Irish boxer Deaf Burke and an English fighter, the horse race won by Hyacinth's 'Green Glint', the duel of honour between a gouty and seated Sir Richard and the caddish Fosdyke: these are almost *too* well disposed for the sake of the balance they achieve. One cannot help but think of the impact at the close of the thirties of *Gone With The Wind* and of the formulae of dozens of other historical romances that made their way to the screen. (The sale of film rights to this book would have gone a long way towards transforming Gogarty's situation.) But not only is Ouseley not here; neither are Scarlett and Rhett. We have an octet of lovers and successful matches, to be sure. The novel opens with the honeymoon of Hyacinth Martyn-Lynch and Ninon; it records the reunion and eventual union of two more mature lovers, Le Chevalier Constant d'Estournelles and the widowed Ellice St George and the betrothal of Sir Richard de Vesey and La Baronne Clement de Ronquerolles; it closes with the anticipated marriage of two very young lovers, Ninon's sister, Mabs, and Ellice's son, Denis St George. Nearly all of these figures are one-dimensional and curiously stilted, their names even suggesting a certain un-reality in their conception. Of the women, only Mabs, the tom-boy who disguises herself as a youth to attend the prize fight between Deaf Burke and his English opponent at the Hell Fire Club and as a jockey to win an important race at the Curragh, seems to touch upon reality. Of the men, only Hyacinth is convincing, and he only when he reflects Gogarty's own experience of political upheaval in modern Ireland. It is striking that Gogarty, who had moved in aristocratic circles for years and created elsewhere the zaniness of peers and their peers, was no more successful at bringing his upper-class characters to life than was Liam O'Flaherty in his late historical romance, *Land* (1946), and that both of these vigorous writers seem to turn staid and conventional as they attempt to recreate the manners and dialogue of an earlier century.

Among the minor characters, and particularly among those of the lower reaches of the society, there is much more liveliness. Toucher Plant, a racing tout, who serves the Buck Tiger Roche and his Society for Aiding Order, may owe his origins to the clever likeable rogues of Boucicault but he is real, as is his language. Indeed, the Toucher, though considerably chastened, appears in the novel that followed *Mad Grandeur.* So apparently this *picaro* took on such life in the first book that he insisted upon appearing in the next. Perhaps it is an inherent flaw of the idealised historical romance that its grotesques and minor figures have more life than its central and straight characters, but there is no gainsaying the compelling vividness of such low-life scenes as that in a late chapter of the work, 'The Night Before Larry Was Stretched'. Taking its title and hint from a traditional, earthy, and cheerfully cynical Dublin street-song, the chapter recounts how Toucher Plant, seeking information, insinuates himself into the 'clamorous, merry pit' of Newgate on the eve of a highwayman's execution. There criminals, bawds, whores, jailor, and informer roister:

> In the midst of the din and shouting the Toucher was assuring Larry, mouth to ear:
> 'There's a doctor friend of mine who says he will give you a snick in the jugular when ye're dead. It relieves congestion and has saved many a half-hanged man, he says.' Larry was not now drunk enough to give this credence.
> 'You may ax him to snick me—'
> 'And make a Jewman of ye, is it?' Becky called out, leering.
> The Toucher tried again:
> 'Ye might pay the sojers to cut you down soon, as they would be sure to do if there was anyone waiting to be stretched after ye. Bumleigh has lots of coin. And, by the way, what did he want?'
> 'He axed me where the pocketbook was I took from him with his watch.'
> 'Where is it?'
> 'Ye must ax Harris, the jeweller, who takes the swag he buys from us to London every month. There was nothing but names in it.'
> From out of the hurley the young whores, hysterical with drink, were starting up a bawdy old Dublin catch, when the granite hand of the warder seized one of them by the throat.
> 'In the name of Jayshus, cannot ye have common decency?'
> Having silenced them, he withdrew his hand and picked up the cards on the coffin with short, quick, busy jerks.
> 'Yes, indeed,' said Becky Cooper, 'and him going to his God.'
> 'And you shut your gue as well,' the warder commanded.

Earthy and macabre as the episode and the language are, they have, like most of the other scenes of low-life, a richness one does not find in the central action of the four love affairs. It is interesting to find Gogarty in a letter of January 1941 complaining that *Mad Grandeur* was heavily cut by the publisher,[3] and in another letter of August 1941, protesting that Lippincott had a man 'stream-lining' the work. Indeed, Gogarty resented the bowdlerisation of the novel and mentioned by way of illustration this prison scene, from which was deleted a song sung by a drab:

> I gave her inches one
> And, sez she, it's going on.
> Keep your belly close to mine,
> Stick it in: Send it home!
>
> I gave her inches two etc.

That song, a variant of one that became almost universally known during World War II, does not seem in the least out of keep-ing with 'The Night That Larry Was Stretched'. So it is under-standable that Gogarty should protest: 'You see how my style loses vigour and, what is worse, the contemporariness with that lewd and gallopin' century.'[4] A copy-edited manuscript of the novel has survived, and does, in fact, reveal extensive deletions, but no editorial responsibility for the saccharine quality of characters like Ninon, Ellice, and Clemente or the woodenness of the Chevalier and Denis. Possibly Gogarty sensed that *Mad Grandeur* was stronger in such scenes as he mentioned in his letter of August 1940, than in its central characters and action, and compensated for his own dissatisfaction by overstating the damage done by his editor.

As I earlier suggested, the improbably named hero of the novel is most interesting when he is closest to his creator, when, to put matters differently, Gogarty's own political experiences are seen in all their 'contemporariness with that lewd and gallopin' century'. For Hyacinth Martyn-Lynch's predicament is that he is entirely sympathetic with his people's desire to be free of English rule and prosperous, at the same time that he recognises the inevitable destructiveness of their aroused appetites. And he comes to despise not only such English types as Crosbie and Weld who have made a good thing out of the improvidence of Irish landlords and the degradation of Irish peasants but also such types as the 'small, dark, rat-eyed little Dubliner', who seizes upon the legitimate grievances of the masses and leads them and the Catholic aristocracy to a common ruin. In effect, Hyacinth's situation is that of a Yeats, an AE, a Gogarty, even a Frank O'Connor, of those Irish artists who dreamed of freedom and then came to feel that freedom was betrayed by demagogues, climbers, and trimmers. Moreover, the futile destruction that is wreaked by the peasants at the climax of *Mad Grandeur* is comparable to the destruction of life and property that Gogarty himself witnessed and suffered during the Civil War and its aftermath. The destruction of Gogarty's Renvyle and of other country houses, even the levelling of Lady Gregory's Coole and its woods lie behind Hyacinth's reflection :

> Gone was that ash wood with its grassy floor so clean and free from undergrowth. The soft small grass that had carpeted their feet when he and Ninon first explored the great demesne had enriched the clean boles of the silver trees closely and trimly. When you turned you could see far through many bright groves, for the trees stood far apart from each other, each keeping its distance and respecting the presence of its neighbours—aristocrats among trees, now fallen and destroyed, never to rise again and winnow the tremulous tides of light.
>
> . . . .
>
> It was strange how the loss of his wood went deeper into his heart than the loss of his home. The dull, obstinate, persistent peasant hatred was never manifested worse than here. You would think that these infesters of the land had seen into your mind with demoniacal cunning and destroyed all that you held dear and appreciated for its beauty. If the beauty and grandeur that were a part of him were reft, Hyacinth thought, was it not a sign that he too should go?

That summons to 'Fresh Woods' which Hyacinth, like Ouseley-Gogarty, answers has an emotional force and an imaginative validity. At its best, *Mad Grandeur* realises the rising of '98 in terms of the 'Troubles' as Gogarty knew them, and realises the language and vulgarity of the Curragh and the Gaol in terms of the track and the Kips as Gogarty knew them at the turn of the century. At its worst, the romance suffers from the limitations of its conventions, conventions that did not suit Gogarty's talents and that he was unable to transform or transcend—probably because of the public at which the novel was aimed.

Mr. Petunia, completed in 1944, and published in 1946, is another historical romance, slightly longer than a novella. Set in Virginia at the opening of the third decade of the nineteenth century, *Mr. Petunia* is as economical as possible, and its concern is with close psychological observation rather than with panoramic sweep, with character rather than with action or event, though in summary the plot cannot help but sound melodramatic. It depicts how Mr Petunia, his advances repulsed by the heroine, sets out to blackmail her and then by an act of arson to eliminate the only person who can expose him. In language and in characterisation it is a far more vigorous and believable book than *Mad Grandeur*.

Throughout the novel, Gogarty calls attention to the language of the characters. Thus, in the last lines of the novel, the genteel Belinda is shocked that the Toucher should describe his father as 'auld fellow', and she stuffily criticises his disrespect. Toucher is incorrigible : 'I haven't a thing against him; he was a decent "auld bags" and he knew how to make a cow hold a bull. . . . Whoever heard of larupping a mare with a shovel?' It is the chilling and negative Petunia, however, who constantly makes an effort to drain the vitality from language. Thus, in one instance, when Toucher whose language is always quick observes, 'You ought to be hairy enough by this time not to get robbed,' Petunia, offended, replies : 'When you mean "experienced enough" don't say "hairy enough". It's not done in polite society.' Never does Petunia, unlike such vital and likeable characters as Ann, the Toucher, and a number of minor characters, hazard a metaphor, a bit of slang, a rhythm that catches the spirit of life. When we first encounter Petunia, Farrell, an Irishman, exclaims of the season : 'Sure the trees is flaming. I never seen such pink and white. There'll be a bumper crop and no mistake. The bees is about already and the air is roaring with flies. Them crab apples over there is for pollen. Bumper crop! Aye, indeed, and bushels of it and tuns of cider, enough to tangle your toes.' In response to this vision of amplitude, Mr Petunia, suspecting an 'enthusiast', exudes coldness and murders language with sterile jargon : 'Wait till the June fall . . . You will then be in a better position to judge and assess the orchard's yield.' In view of Gogarty's lament about the editorial devitalisation of *Mad Grandeur*, it seems quite possible that he shaped *Mr. Petunia* both in form and language not only to escape the fate of its predecessor but to rebut the arguments and methods of an earlier editor.

Like *Mad Grandeur, Mr. Petunia* depicts contrasting pairs of lovers, but now the relationships are handled ironically, disparities rather than harmonies being emphasised. There are no innocent or inexperienced lovers here and no important unions. The heroine, Ann, daughter of an English craftsman, marries Mr Pendleton, the ageing master of Oakenhurst, a substantial estate; despite Pendleton's desire for an heir and Ann's passionate sexuality, she remains barren until, on an impulse, she spends the night with her husband's younger brother, Halmar. Pendleton lies dying, when the male 'heir' to his estate is christened. Yet upon Mr Pendleton's death, Halmar's offer of marriage is rejected by Ann; he returns to the West, exiled in consequence of a brief amatory encounter and disinherited by his own son. The sixteen-year-old Gaby, who has been seduced into a perverse relationship with Petunia, marries at the close of the novel the One-Eyed Man, Tommy Corcoran, realising full well that her life as the wife of an inn-keeper will not be at all easy. Possibly the happiest of the unions, then, is that of a now respectable Toucher Plant and Mr Pendleton's feather-brained and flighty sister, the widowed Belinda Bellocq; and this marriage is based on Belinda's total misapprehension of the Toucher's character and past. (She takes him to be in direct descent from the House of Plantagenet!)

By contrast to the pasteboard ladies of *Mad Grandeur*, moreover, the women of this novel are flesh and blood, even the victimised Gaby and the silly Belinda. Ann, the most complex of Gogarty's women, passionate, intelligent, humorous, is both very feminine and very physical. She comes fully alive in the novel as soon as she appears and sits down to a lunch of fried oysters with the apologetic Gaby:

> 'I am very sorry I cannot give them to you fresh. They have to be fried, for my uncle says that sea-food will not stand a journey. The only safeguard from all sorts of diseases is to cook them. He never gets stomach trouble since he made that rule. He knows an awful lot about medicine.'
> 'It is to be hoped that he doesn't,' Ann said. 'I hate men who go in for health. What is it for, but to be taken for granted?'

She filled her mouth with succulent food and chewed, making a noise as she put in some celery, probably in order to masticate the oysters all the better.

Gazing about the board she asked where the pepper was.

'Oh, the pepper!' Gaby exclaimed. 'It has to be ground daily. I will fetch the little pepper mill and you can grind it for yourself.'

'Does it also grow dangerous in two and a half days?' Ann asked, bending her head over her plate as she ate. With her mouth full she looked up for an answer to her question. Her eyes smiled with good-humoured mockery.

Gaby's admiration for her visitor was growing. She envied a spirit as emancipated as Ann's.

Ann surveyed the room. 'Clocks, clocks, clocks!' she said. Gaby evaded an answer.

'Won't you drink something?' Gaby inquired, remembering the long journey of her guest.

'Well, just to burn up any infection that might still be lurking in the oysters, and has escaped my gastric juice, a tumbler of Bourbon would be the very thing.'

As independent as she is appetitive and mocking, Ann rejects Halmar at the novel's end, not out of any sense of guilt or penitence certainly, but, as she puts it, because, 'I was someone else that night, someone I have never been before or since, someone I will never be again.' In this characterisation, though his own sexual attitudes were formed in the Edwardian age, Gogarty is revealing his insight into a later modern feminist sensibility. 'I'm sick of eating celery and prunes and taking cold baths,' Ann acidly responds to Pendleton's suggestion that she see a doctor about her barrenness. 'How can I tell a strange man about how many times you wakened me and how long I had to stay in bed with the damned bed nearly upside down. Why there's not a mare in the stables that Plant would treat as I have been treated, and yet it is I who have to take the blame.' At the same time, Gogarty associates Ann with an earlier age and sensibility than that of the novel's setting. When she enters the starved atmosphere of Petunia's household, the house itself seems to Gaby,

filled by the glowing and confident spirit of Ann which made her as free and admirable as some great lady from the Court of

Love or some heroic spirit from the sudden and exultant sphere into which you feel yourself immediately transported on reading a single Shakespearean line. There was something of the bravery and bustling grandeur of the spacious days about her, something of that haughty, disdainful and dangerous world.

Even the neurotic Petunia senses that Ann belongs to a world 'bustling with adventure . . . a world without meanness, of moving accidents and gay audacity.'

While Ann is associated with the expansiveness of the Renaissance, Petunia, the delicate and ingenious craftsman, is associated with the manner of the eighteenth century. We learn that 'in his own particular way', Petunia admired poetry:

To him it was a matter of meticulous writing. In detailed exactness and design carried out with preciseness he found a *curiosa felicitas* which acted upon him like an inspiration. Precision was poetry to Mr Petunia, as it was in another craft to Alexander Pope. It engaged his thought and provided a world which, being microscopic, could all the more appropriately be made his own.

Certainly in depicting Petunia, his secretiveness, egoism, self-righteousness, and destructiveness, Gogarty was conscious of contemporary diagnoses of paranoia; indeed, he may have based this psychological portrait on a well-known engraver of his acquantance.[5] It is also possible that certain aspects of Joyce's character and work were in Gogarty's mind when he observed of the watchmaker Petunia, who is blind to visual beauty but in love with system, that 'By cunning he would revenge himself on an unappreciative world.' Yet any specific sources for details of the characterisation are secondary to the fundamental symbolic and cultural contrasts that are developed in the clash between Ann and Petunia: between the Renaissance sensibility and the Augustan; between the healthy and the outward-going and the introverted and perverse; between impulse and calculation; between the will to self-fulfilment and the destructive will to power; between the clockwork and paranoid world-view of those who would

pull the whole world through the little round window of their eye, which cannot help but mould and round it into a unity of sorts and thus reduce it apparently to a system and those who can boldly accept the chaotic ungermane liberty of Creation, limitless in scope, self-sufficing in simplicity, indifferent to all human adjustments and limitations.

In the light of these thematic contrasts, the role and function of Toucher Plant can be understood better. Early in the novel, the Toucher is discovered to be in secret relation to Petunia, a characteristically dependent role for him, even though he has grown prosperous. Yet Mr Petunia rides a horse to Oakenhurst that has been sold to him by the Toucher, and the horse is very nearly blind and quite unsure of its direction, particularly when ridden by a horseman as poor as Petunia. In a balancing scene at the close of the novel, the disinherited Halmar purchases a mare from Toucher Plant, now fully assimilated to respectability and wealth. The Toucher, despite his newly achieved respectability, has sold a mare he knows to be 'as barren as a mule'. These ironically conceived episodes certainly represent an artistic ordering. Yet the implication of the ironic balancing is that experience itself is 'open'. It is as if Gogarty deliberately set out to criticise the neat series of marriages in *Mad Grandeur* by refusing to satisfy the expectations of his readers that Ann will marry Halmar and share in his family inheritance. Furthermore, we move from a situation in which Petunia appears to control Plant but controls neither him nor the horse to one in which the apparently resourceful, sexually vigorous, and independent Halmar can anticipate nothing from the future. Gogarty makes his meaning and his irony too obvious when he reflects that 'Belinda and the Toucher remained alone, unaffected by the machinations of Petunia. For only the good and the merry are unscathed by evil in this life.' The situation and its implications, though, are compelling despite the obviousness of the reflection. Only the *picaro*, Toucher, who anticipates no order and assumes no morality, and Ann, a Nietzschian heroine surely since she wills her freedom despite what she suffers from Petunia's sick plots, are in tune with the impulse of existence itself.

Period details and historical colour are subordinate in *Mr. Petunia* to the psychological interests and to these main symbolic contrasts. Still, by the time he wrote *Mr. Petunia*, Gogarty had seen and read enough about America to be able to imagine himself back from the contemporary scene into the rural and still feudal old Dominion. Unburdened by period detail the book may be, but it is also the product of a sharp social intelligence. Consider this passage describing Mr Pendleton and his level of culture:

> He was a well-bred but not a well-read man. The traditions of scholarship had been left behind. For all its fertility Virginia did not flower into the arts. True, many of the great planters had the feeling for family rooted deeply enough to make them wish for an ancestral record, a sketch, a cameo, or a portrait in oil of their parents or of themselves. This they held in common with the rest of America. But libraries and scholarship were not part of the equipment of all the mansions in the Old Dominion. Mr Pendleton was more of a naturalist than a bookman. . . . Yet for all that he was a man of taste. . . . He had more taste than many of his class in England or Ireland who, situated in somewhat similarly leisurely circumstances, had suffered the stable to invade the study and more attention to be given to the raising of blood stock than to the cultivation of the mind and the care of heirlooms and objects of art. His drawing room displayed two large Chinese screens, some oak and pearwood from the days of the Second Charles and a few pieces of walnut with the design of the period of Queen Anne. These he appreciated and prized. He had a clock by Graham.

Gogarty's lecture tours throughout the United States and his visits to upper-class American homes certainly lie behind such a passage, but his capacity for imaginative historical projection is also there. Not to be classed with his three best books of the thirties in which anatomy and confession are dominant and the ancient modes release his originality, *Mr. Petunia* would nevertheless seem to be Gogarty's demonstration that he could write a conventional historical romance, designed for popular consumption, and even invest it with thematic significance.

The Eternal Return

NOT for a decade after *Sackville Street*, *I Follow St Patrick*, and *Tumbling in the Hay* did Gogarty write comparable work in prose; and, when he did, he published another account of a saunter in Dublin and a journey across the island. *Rolling Down the Lea* (1949) was occasioned by a return visit to Ireland in 1945 and, more particularly, by political events that excited his imagination— the defeat of Fianna Fail (de Valera's party) and the formation of a coalition government under John A. Costello, a Fine Gael politician in the tradition of Gogarty's friends William Cosgrave and Arthur Griffith. Looked at merely in terms of its resemblances to earlier books, *Rolling Down the Lea* might be said to repeat what had been done already and with sufficient intensity in *Sackville Street* and to reiterate a metaphor that might seem to have been exhausted in the book on *St Patrick*. The first six chapters of *Rolling Down the Lea* (nearly a third of the book) are a record of conversations on the streets of Dublin, the burden of which is a satiric attack on aspects of modern society in general and in particular on modern Ireland, de Valera, and Sean T. O'Kelly, who had been elevated to the ceremonial Presidency. Furthermore the metaphor of stream and pool pervades the book. Like the Liffey as Spenser described it, Gogarty goes rolling down the lea, and, at the climax of the book, discovers a pool that has haunted his imagination since childhood. One might go further in considering this passage and point out that it resembles the conclusion of *Sackville Street* in that it depicts a childhood moment recaptured.

An old man's exhausted attempt to repeat earlier successes? Scarcely that. For *Rolling Down the Lea*, if not as original as the earlier books, is a necessary complement to them. Into this pool, furthermore, one must gaze. It is true that in its depths lurks once again the heroic quest motif and the universal archetype of the search for self-realisation. Yet the insistent metaphor of pool and stream is fresh and different as Gogarty handles it, even when he mocks Freud with it, and the surface details are also new and lively. Gogarty seems (like Flann O'Brien in his private correspondence) never to have run out of fresh invective on the subject of de Valera.[1] More importantly, the mythic and psychic patterns which are a source of the book's vitality are more completely resolved than in the earlier works. Oliver St John Gogarty had to be seventy-one in order to write this book, which, like all his best prose works, is deceptive in its apparent simplicity and guilelessness.

Read casually, *Rolling Down the Lea* probably seems almost formless. On Merrion Square, the Gogarty *persona* encounters an acquaintance who gleefully mentions the banning of the doctor's novel *Mr. Petunia* and thus provokes a discussion of censorship. In the chapter that follows, a car ride (apparently across the countryside and into Dublin) with a friend provokes a discussion, among other subjects, of the sexual, emotional, and cultural differences between Catholic South and Protestant North. Encounters near Trinity first with MacGlornan, next with the charming pink and white Dulcie, and then with the 'Senator', all provide occasion for a devastating exploration of the foibles of de Valera and the failures of his government. This onslaught starts off at an appropriate pitch of satiric invective with the words of McGlornan that open a chapter: 'Because he's a huer and a bastard!' Subsequently a glimpse of the Loop Line Bridge that mars the narrator's view of the Liffey provokes an attack on modern civic defacement by the vulgar and the tawdry, the quotation of a recent speech by a high-court judge on political climbing and place-seeking, and a catalogue of the destruction wrought by the present state. A series of pleasurable visits offers relief from the sustained social criticism. We are taken to the Dolphin (formerly one of Dublin's best restaurants) where a horsey set has gathered and the Gogarty *persona* offers an inspired account of the social significance of racing horses' names; to the Provost's House at Trinity; to the Lodge in Phoenix Park—residence then of the American ambassador; to the house of Richard Best, where the conversation—which is of the best—turns easily from reflections on death to a bit of lively gossip about George Moore and James Joyce. Dublin is left behind as the narrator entrains for Galway, reporting what he

G

sees and hears on the way, as well as giving us an account of his visit in Galway, where what he hears of the local sexual mores convinces him that a favourite city has become 'a Cytherea, a shrine where Venus was worshipped'. A bus ride, a stay at a cottage on Tully Lake, another visit to a peasant's cottage where tales are told, a return to Dublin, and a visit to Dunsany Castle that lauds another teller of tales precede a lively account of a horse race that celebrates the new government and prepares for the book's climax.

One might be tempted to believe that Gogarty had simply and haphazardly pulled together remembered conversations, vivid moments, striking incidents that occurred during his return visit, and memories of earlier days. And possibly it is the case that we are getting—not certainly any slice of life—but slices of this and that. It may be instructive then to examine one passage of the work in the light of the information we have of the actual facts behind it.

When Gogarty meets his 'sharp-nosed acquaintance' who announces the banning of *Mr. Petunia*, anyone who has a memory of the 1929 Senate debates or has read the record of the Seanad Eireann, must be startled to hear Gogarty state, 'Try to remember this. When I voted for the Censor Bill, I did so eagerly because I realised that, during the periods that censorship was most astringent, literature was most remarkable.' Now, Gogarty's memory later in his life certainly could be inaccurate as it is here. For in the course of the Senate debate on the Censorship Bill, beginning with reservations about the Bill and concern for its effects on serious literature, he began to stiffen his opposition and to sharpen the sting of his satire, referring to this 'lamentable bill', as the debate continued. Soon he was warning of the danger of 'a Ku Klux Klan' to suppress thought; and mocking that 'each village in Ireland' would have a 'literary pimp' or 'Holy Willie' to suppress significant literary work. On the third reading of the Bill, the doctor was doing even better, insisting that there should be no such bill at all and exclaiming, 'I think it is high time that the people of this country found some other way of loving God than by hating women.'[2]

What Gogarty has to say in *Rolling Down the Lea* on the subject of censorship is thus *not* accurate memory. On the other hand, what matters in *Rolling Down the Lea* is the perversely mocking rhetoric of the outrageous argument he is pursuing with his friend. Wishing to demonstrate the pettiness and prudery of the censorship in Ireland, he points out that 'The inquisition produced some of the greatest geniuses of Europe,' and then bounds on to the impertinent irony that he who (in fiction at least) supported censorship is one of the first to be banned. Bounding off in another direction, he insists that he is distressed about the banning, because having hoped to be banned in Boston and thus to increase his sales in the United States, he has now had his hopes dashed. Not even Boston would stoop to ban what has been prohibited in Dublin. 'No one asks a eunuch for an opinion on divorce.' It is inescapable I think, that what we are getting here and elsewhere in the book is what this quirky sensibility has chosen to give us and how he has chosen to shape and form it. All the episodes are as discontinuous as they are varied; but the form of the anatomy-confession is so direct an extension of the *persona*'s interest and comic sense that any striking or amusing notion may be pursued, any intriguing fantasy elaborated. In the second chapter, for instance, Gogarty's driver alludes to a famous 'queen of Cootehill', a Dublin neighbourhood whore so noted for her 'perennial innocence' that she was known throughout the district as 'What's That?' Springing to her defence, Gogarty asks 'Would you have her shameless? There is nothing so revolting and demoralising as an immodest woman'; he contrasts her favourably with 'devil-may-care Mary Anne' celebrated in Dublin song for not caring a damn. When he learns that 'What's That', Lysistrata-like, went on strike when she learned her soubriquet, he begins to vary his theme for he has the hint he needs to spin sense from nonsense:

> There are many Orangemen, too, on Cootehill; and you know how those rugged and illiberal men refused to yield an inch of their artificial Ulster and their slogan, 'Not an inch'. Therefore, What's That may be considered with her abnegation, an embodiment of the Orange North. 'Not an inch.'
>
> While good old Mary Anne with all her liberality and large discourse and 'There's a belly that never bore a bastard', becomes a worthy symbol of the South. Our problem, or rather the politician's problem, resolves itself into a merger of 'What's That' with Mary Anne, North with South. Intangibility on the one part; illimitable invitation on the other. 'Not an inch' with 'Let them all come!'

Starting with the absurd, the tag-name of Cootehill's whore, Gogarty leads us to the ridiculous—which also happens to score a serious cultural point. So do most of the apparently witty, comic, or humorous asides with which the book is filled. A casual reference to a chap who, in the midst of the Gaelic Revival walked on the quays of Cork in a silk hat and answered a fishwife's greeting, 'Laun braw' with 'Law braw, by Jove!' is something more than an incongruity: it is a declaration of belief in Western culture. An anecdote about Mrs Dunne, mother of eight, who listens for a minute to a sermon on Holy Matrimony, and 'then said fervently as she turned to go: "I wish to God I knew as little about it as that fellow"' is a telling comment on marriage and attitudes towards birth control in Ireland. Funny even as isolated specimens, these and other anecdotes like them, are part of a sustained attack on the aberrations of institutions, on cultural shibboleths, and on social hypocrisy.

Discontinuous as the episodes may seem and inclined as the author may appear to be to pursue almost any association of thought, the episodes are in focus, and there is almost always a method in the digressions. One of the objects of Gogarty's ridicule throughout the book is the notion of 'the Stream of Consciousness', which would appear to be 'a stream with no banks, in which modern novelists flounder in default of a current or an estuary'. In *Rolling Down the Lea*, the Stream of Consciousness is consciously channelled, however freely it may seem to roll. The six opening chapters have as a satiric object everything that is 'cultureless, cheerless, songless' in the political and social life of Ireland; the successive visits that lead to the climax of the book redress the balance revealing that which is vital, imaginative, individual, and creative. Throughout both sections apparently casual details form patterns of comic meaning. At the Dolphin, Gogarty is offended by an intrusive citizen's response—'Dan Chaucer me arse'—to a whispered tip on a horse. (It is to be feared that Gogarty's Senatorial friend has already identified de Valera and Sean T. O'Kelly with a line from 'Lillibullero': 'That we should be ruled by an ass and a dog.') Inflicting the satirist's punishment on folly, Gogarty picks up a manufacturer's name from the urinal, attaches it to a non-existent horse, and passes a tip on 'Shank's Pat' to the intruder. Later, on the train to Galway, he overhears a passenger passing on a tip he picked up at the Dolphin: 'The horse is Pat, Pat something.' As the rumour spreads, in effect it disintegrates among those who are not true devotees of the cult of the horse. On the other hand, at the races, when he finds himself among true votaries of the cult who are 'orgiastic and unrestrained' in their rite, who have even grown to resemble the object of their worship, he is startled to hear that Shank's Mare is a winner. Casual and comic as these details are, they are leading us away from the emptiness represented by the pushy eavesdropper at the Dolphin and from everything in Dublin that is destructive and empty and into the vital world of myth, where the accidental has meaning. When Gogarty hears the announcement of Shank's Mare's victory he is in the company of a horsey Marchioness, whose 'nose was blunt like the nose of a horse'. As the Marchioness discourses upon the relation of breast feeding to the fitness, strength, and speed of the horse and to the physical strength of her own children, Gogarty begins to associate her with the Mare-headed Demeter, with the fertility principle itself.

Chapter twenty-one, 'Once Only', which provides the climax of *Rolling Down the Lea*, was first written as an autonomous piece and may be found among Gogarty's late manuscripts under the same title.[3] As free and episodic as the tradition in which it is written permits it to be and drawing upon three other essays in addition to 'Once Only', *Rolling Down the Lea* was, nevertheless, then shaped in detail and incident to lead to this climax; it is as far from being a work in which independent elements are artificially related to one another so as to produce a book as it can be while yet retaining the disarming casualness of its conventions. In short, beginning with an ending that somehow mattered to him very much (and for psychic reasons that we shall explore), Gogarty then contrived through episode, encounter, detail, and allusion, to foreshadow all the key elements of the climactic chapter. Mocking at the modern novelist's conception of the stream of consciousness (a stream without banks or direction as he saw it) throughout the book, Gogarty was bent upon suggesting that consciousness could be both coherent and psychically profound, that flux could be both perpetual and meaningful. As he puts it, ironically, 'I take very little credit for being conscious.' Change is the subject of the work, change as it is embodied in central and archetypal myths, the myth of the god-hero who must die and of the triple goddess who is giver of life, preserver, and destroyer,

Sensing change and its inevitability as he traverses the streets of Dublin from the moment when he notes that 'The One-Eyed Man had changed hands—most taverns do,' he laments but accepts, despising only that change which is debasement and hypocrisy. O'Connell Street (formerly Sackville) touched by 'the phosphorescent decay of Broadway', the Temple in the grounds of Delville, with all of its associations with Dean Swift, demolished because it stood in the roadway to a new hospital: these are forms of debasement. Inextricably linked to them are the hypocritical pomp of the President receiving the ex-Prime Minister in the Vice-Regal Lodge, a bit of mummery that mocks the myth of the king's necessary death and rebirth:

> It was a miracle play like 'Everyman'; but it had in addition another aspect of a miracle, the chief character 'Bad Conscience' (black soft hat and black double-breasted coat), was received by one of his own creatures in a black tall hat. It was as if a medium was to shake hands with his own ectoplasm. . . . Nobody asked how came it that, by shaking hands with himself, so to speak, an honour was bestowed on Bad Conscience. Above all, nobody asked of what the President was President.

If one were to ask that embarrassing question, one would have to answer—as Gogarty sees it—not of the Republic for which de Valera, here received by Sean T. O'Kelly, had precipitated a murderous civil war, since Ireland had not yet been declared a republic.

Shortly before the climactic chapters of *Rolling Down the Lea*, Gogarty pauses to observe that the hero of the narrative is not the writer, but the land itself. 'The country is the hero, the landscape if you like to call it that, or the *genus loci*, the spirit of the place. . . . And, this being so, the history of the hero's vicissitudes is not out of place.' As confusing on this point as myths of hero-victims and triple-goddess—both associated with the land itself—are apt to be, Gogarty is nevertheless helping us to see that the neon on O'Connell Street and the bogus ritual in the Vice Regal Lodge are temporary vicissitudes, negligible in terms of the fundamental rhythms of the earth itself. Throughout the book he is apt to identify the land with woman. In the opening Dublin sequence, in the midst of all the political railing, he encounters the 'one serene mind in this passionate maelstrom', 'pink and white' Dulcie, the mistress, one takes it, of a dead friend: 'And yet she has one characteristic of the Saints, that is, of some of them: she has fragrance.' Not surprisingly following this encounter, he asks, ' "How is poor old Ireland and how does she stand?" ' For Dulcie, like the Cytherean matrons of Galway, like 'What's That' (virgin and whore), like Mrs Dunne, who mocks the sermon on Matrimony delivered by a celibate, is an emanation of Kathleen Ni Houlihan. So is the horse-faced Marchioness, who is associated with the real triumph of Shank's Mare, which contrasts so ironically with the false rumour of the victory of Shank's Pat. 'One of the aspects of Demeter was that of a mare. Under the appearance of the Mare-Headed, she was worshipped in Arcadia, and may she not have appeared in this Western Arcadia to us?' Though he does not mention the Celtic horse-goddess Macha, in emphasising the immemorial cult of the horse in Ireland and in asserting that 'Like the Earth of the Marchioness, Ireland is a Mare-headed goddess,' the narrator is answering his question. If the horse-goddess of fertility presides over the races, it is the hero who sports there. The new Prime Minister arrives: Costello, who *has* proclaimed the Republic, for which his opposition fought a Civil War. Looking out over the fluxional 'sea of heads', Gogarty imagines them passing to give way to other generations. Only a few, he senses, will be remembered—men like his friend William Cosgrave and his successor as leader of Fine Gael, the present Prime Minister, John Costello 'not because he is in a series that is historical, but for the quality of his statesmanship.'

But at the moment of fulfilment—for which the first third of the book, for all its funniness, cries out desperately—there is a startling recognition to which the myth he evokes, national experience (the legend of Parnell), and personal experience (the untimely death of Griffith) lead him. Costello's government, whatever its accomplishments, will perish. Like the mare-headed Goddess of fertility, like Earth herself, Ireland 'is also a goddess of death'; and the hero is a scapegoat. No Irishman, no man, 'can endure being himself for long'. In consequence, he has chosen to be 'represented by a hero who, like the victim king of primitive times, perished after a little reign'. Whatever a man's accomplishment, the cycle is there. In another passage of ingenious argument, comparable in sleight of mind to his discourse on censorship, Gogarty carries us in a series of logical leaps to the climactic

Chapter twenty, 'Once Only'. He must leave the racecourse, leave Ireland. Otherwise he might become the hero-victim. Not that he is conceited. 'Just look at the heroes we have had! After all, very few people know me. That's what makes me so eligible. And once you become a trash can for the soul of Ireland, the Marchioness, the Mare-headed, will get you surely.'

By these outrageous and abrupt leaps of mind, Gogarty brings us to his journey's moment of transformation. He returns to Roundwood to search for the little mountain pool and stream that have haunted him, he asserts, in dream or vision, since childhood and throughout this journey. He finds the pool; he gazes into its crystal basin; he climbs the stream. The narrator of *Rolling Down the Lea* steps suddenly into another time, into a nineteeth-century village.

Dream vision or another dimension of reality, what happens there is linked by numerous correspondences to what has gone before: the best of Dublin's squares to the eighteenth-century buildings of the village; the tales the narrator heard from peasants about enchanted isles to the experience he has of an enchanted village; his own capacity for an 'ecstasy' or waking vision manifested in the midst of a conversation on the street in Dublin to this escape from time. There are other correspondences too. The gossip he heard of the sexual mores of Galway finds a parallel in the *ménage à trois* existing in the home of Dr Purefoy. The account he heard from his driver of the filming of Henry V at the Powerscourt demesne prepares him to view the village as a perfectly constructed film set. The procession of the Lord Mayor through the village has its analogue in the arrival of the Irish Prime Minister at the racecourse. The wine merchant named Sir George Brent he finds in the village is a curious and cinematic transmutation of Lord Dunsany's wine merchant, Sir George Brooke—discussed at a dinner with the Lord. Even Dunsany's explanation of the wonderful names of his fictions is pertinent to the events of this chapter: 'They flowed into his brain.' And the photograph Gogarty examines of a boy holding a fishing net, surely this image is related to his memory of a pool and a trout he once gazed upon as a child. Even a fake comic account he has had from his driver of the local population's resentment that in the filming of Agincourt the English won every day is reflected—as is the entire heroic motif—in his decision to rescue Miss Orr from Dr Purefoy.

One of the pleasures of 'discovering' Gogarty is to learn how a certain recklessness enables him to carry off, in his best works, literary stunts that ought to be impossible. 'Once Only' is a perfect demonstration of literary bravado. On the surface it is the entirely characteristic dream or vision of an age of cinema. Climbing the stream from the pool, the *persona* happens upon what appears to him to be a completely realistic film set. He encounters Mrs Purefoy, her son, and Miss Orr, the governess; he is invited into the Purefoy house when doused with water by the boy, joins the Purefoys at dinner, learns that Miss Orr is, in effect, their prisoner and promises to 'save' her. At the stream once again, awaiting the arrival of 'Evangeline', he turns back to the village. 'There was no town!' The whole situation is a perfect cinema convention, a cliché, in fact.

Yet in its context the episode raises so many insistent questions that it is impossible to ignore it. What, after all, does any of it have to do with the myth of the mare-headed goddess and the hero-victim? What is the function of the Purefoy boy in the episode, and, more specifically, why is his photograph described in such detail? Why is the narrator so puzzled that Evangeline should identify him as half the age of Dr Purefoy? And why is it necessary to imply that, in the episode, the *persona* is perhaps twenty-five and Dr Purefoy is fifty? Why, indeed, in a work that mocks Freud, even hint at a meaning in dreams? Furthermore, why does Gogarty evoke associations extrinsic to the text? Why has he used the name Purefoy for the apparently gracious but sinister doctor, the name of an actual Dublin doctor at the turn of the century, a Professor of Midwifery who is depicted in his own *Tumbling in the Hay* and whose name James Joyce had usurped for the insignificant clerk and archetypal father whose wife gives birth to a child in the Holles Street Hospital scene of *Ulysses*? Calling our attention, as he has, to the most central of man's myths and mocking the materialism of Freud, Gogarty has really compelled us to look at the pattern these events compose, beneath the accidental and external details of the cinematic treatment.

And a pattern one cannot help but discern, for it is there to be seen. In the episode there are three different simulacra of Gogarty: the mature narrator, the twenty-five-year-old wooer of Evangeline and conqueror of Dr Purefoy, and the child who had once gazed at a trout in a crystal pool and appears now dowsing a stranger with water and, in a photograph, carrying a fishing net. The triple-goddess is here too, disguised a bit by the trappings of film melodrama but insistent in her appeal. ' "Take me out of this," she moaned. "Oh, take me away." ' and later, ' "Promise," she implored.' The goddess has tempted, and, as Robert Graves has asked and answered, 'When with her right she crooks a finger smiling, / How may the King hold back? / Royally then he barters life for love.' It does not matter that Evangeline disappears with the scene, for the promise is made; the 'hero' will free her from Dr and Mrs Purefoy. A pattern known to Freud—and to the literature that preceded him by hundreds of years—is here too, though with a difference. The narrator of the book in effect experiences the moment when the father is overthrown, the parents eluded, the goddess as mother replaced by the goddess as bride. These intrinsic meanings are perhaps as far as one need go in responding to *Rolling Down the Lea* as literary work. In regarding it as a psychological document, one cannot help but note that, in a displacement characteristic of dream, the Victorian Dr Purefoy corresponds to Gogarty's own father, a Dublin doctor who died in 1887, and that at the age of six Gogarty was, like the Purefoys' child, given into the hands of a governess, as the goddess shifted shape for him for the first time.

In keeping with the mixed form of the anatomy, Gogarty quotes poetry often in *Rolling Down the Lea*, quotes two of his own poems in full. 'Anglers' (*Selected Poems*, 1933) is the first of these. It praises,

> That pleasant Chinese poet, Chin Chi Ho,
> Who spent his time in fishing with no bait,
> . . . .
> Sitting beside the water with his line.

'Recalled at last from exile,' the Chinese poet refuses to go, preferring to 'catch his rhythms half asleep, / Watching below the lilies fishes shine.' The poem, appropriate in a work that recounts a return from exile, alludes to Gogarty's Senatorial duties and concludes:

> There's not a roof now on the courts whose schemes
> Kept men awake and anxious all night long
> Distracted by their working out; but dreams

He dreamt in idleness and turned to song
Can still delight his people. As for me,
I, who must daily at enactments look
To make men happy by legality,
Envy the poet of the baitless hook.

It is a poem perfectly related to the governing theme and metaphor of the book, for pool and stream are implicit in it and suggest a reality that transcends the distracting changes of society. The second poem, a hundred and sixty-four lines, and one of the few poetic successes of Gogarty's later career, is one he came to call 'The Dublin-Galway Train'; it constitutes the sixteenth chapter of the book, and it celebrates in rollicking rhythms the journey by rail, the spectacle of station and stop, the colour of life glimpsed from the train, and the variety of the land itself:

It strains at first, then settles down and smoothly rolls along
Past villages with Gaelic names that sweeten on the tongue:
Clonsilla, Lucan, and Maynooth beside the long canal,
Where yellow-centred lilies float and no one comes at all,
The long canal that idle lies from Dublin to Athlone,
To Luan's ford: but no one knows who may have been Luan
The Royal Canal that joins two towns and makes of him a dunce
Who holds that nothing can be found in two places at once;
A long clear lane of water clean by flags and rushes brimmed,
Where crimson-striped, the roaches steer, and, by the lilies
                                                          dimmed,
The greenish pikes suspended lurk with fins that hardly stir
Until the Galway train comes on and shakes each ambusher.

Closing with lines that are sharply satiric, because this marvellous train has been cancelled by the Government in an emergency measure, 'The Dublin-Galway Train' treats with disdain the packed 'reasty bus' that has replaced it. In the bus there is 'A crowd that stinks and the air befouls, / And children puke as the full bus rolls.' 'Anglers' and 'The Dublin-Galway Train' complement one another, despite their contrast in mood, in that each of them expresses a contrast between the fundamental natural rhythms of process and change and the clumsy 'enactments' of man which are not necessarily in harmony with them.

Pool and streams are emblems in *Rolling Down The Lea*,

emblems of metaphysical states, of the psyche as it may be known in the flux of being. Like D. H. Lawrence, Gogarty would protest against what he felt to be mechanical in Freudianism, scoffing that 'the seat of the spiritual impulses of man is placed in the lower bowel by a quack like Freud'. Impossible as it is to accept his observation literally, one can see what he means. The psychic enactment of the dream-vision of this book has to be seen as universally human, healthy, and immemorially ancient. The psyche, as Gogarty renders it, may be known as the repository of significant truth about experience; it is also the pool into which flows meaning from beyond the self. When Lord Dunsany tells the narrator that the wonderful names of his creation 'flowed into his brain,' the latter reflects 'I should have guessed as much. For that which is breathed into us is "inspiration".' And when he records the composition of a poem at his cottage on the island, he affirms, 'The comforting thing about poetry is that it requires no effort. It is one of the few things that will come if you leave it alone.' Not to be taken as a comment on the craft of poetry but on its originating impulse, this perception is very close to that of Yeats, who could also conceive of consciousness as both material and transcendent:

> So great a sweetness flows into the breast
> We must laugh and we must sing,
> We are blessed by everything,
> Everything we look upon is blest.

Rolling Down the Lea cannot end at the moment when the narrator steps back into the present, for the full cycle of the hero-victim's round has not been completed; the goddess, Earth herself, has not exacted her penalty. She does, in the final chapter, as the journey through Ireland is being completed. Gogarty visits a branch bank to cash a cheque on his American bank. The manager, a friend of his youth, a sprinter who can remember Gogarty as a cyclist, exclaims, 'It must be over fifty years ago,' and then explains that this is his last day of service. 'He would make way for younger blood: give the boys a chance.' The King must die. To this inevitability, to every aspect of its universality, Gogarty wryly reconciles himself in the closing pages of the book. Going through customs, in the very midst of the most offensive of modern enactments, the red tape of travel, he encounters 'a little fellow with an insignificant head', and learns that the fellow's 'mother always said that I was the dead spit of you, and here you are!' Once again, only paradox will express the nature of experience. Freed by the agent's identification with him from the prospect of becoming a national hero, he also sees that he 'must bear in mind that I am like a clerk in a clearing house'. So this, the last of Gogarty's hero-quests ends with the sharp irony of discovery. The hero-victim is, indeed, universal: he is all men. And even the man who railed for decades against the commonness of modern experience has something in common with the most ordinary of fellows. Hero-victim the narrator of *Rolling Down the Lea* may be. Still he no longer need hesitate to accept all the implications of the universal cycle he has imagined: 'There will always be new and original characters in Dublin and, relying on that, I would not have the Liffey change in bed or cease from rolling down the lea.' *Rolling Down the Lea* is thus not only one of Gogarty's most delightful books; it is also the conclusion to the quest he began in *Sackville Street* to reconcile his individual life to a cycle of Being more comprehensive than the self.

The Bloody Illuminated Coal Scuttle

WHEN the American edition of *Elbow Room* appeared, in 1942, Oliver Gogarty was sixty-four years old. Soon after the death of Yeats, he had written to his friend Horace Reynolds, 'I have not yet recovered from the loss of the Archpoet. I never shall.'¹ Whatever personal and political motives (and both were important) may have entered into Gogarty's decision to settle in the United States, he certainly was conscious that the death of Yeats marked the end of that yeasty burgeoning of talent we have come to speak of as the Irish Literary Revival. Indeed, by writing *Sackville Street* and *Tumbling in the Hay*, he had already indicated that he sensed the time for memorials was at hand. Gogarty himself had survived into a new age. It was not simply that Yeats was no longer there to encourage and to criticise. The associations, the friendships, the cultural atmosphere that had nurtured Gogarty's talent were all fading from a Dublin itself a dim shadow of what it had been. In a quatrain that Yeats had admired and included in the *Oxford Book* ('Colophon'), Gogarty had written:

> While the tragedy's afoot,
> Let us play in the high boot;
> Once the trumpet's notes are gone,
> Off, before the Fool comes on!

As if in response to this stoic imperative, Gogarty had gutsily departed the city he loved, and settled in New York.

A new imperative made itself felt during Gogarty's American years: the need to earn money from his writings. An income America did provide and, as Gogarty often pointed out, the freedom to say what he pleased.² Still, for an ageing man—even one like Gogarty who always seemed to his friends a decade younger than he actually was—and for a man disinclined to be provident and disdainful of prudence, the demands of the literary marketplace must have been exacting. Between 1941 and the year of his death, while lecturing frequently, Gogarty produced eight volumes of prose, three volumes of poetry and the *Collected Poems*, not to mention numerous incidental pieces of prose and verse that were journalistic in nature: an astonishing production that suggests the energy of the man and also the pressure under which he was working. When the work of Gogarty's last years was weak or disappointing, it was so in part because of the commercial nature of his enterprise. By the spring of 1944, he found himself churning out material in which he had no interest, hoping to place it in a popular magazine, a task for which he lacked the formulaic skill.[3] A few weeks later, engaged in the same kind of work, he burst out to one of his New York associates, 'Damn potboiling. When can I write as I like?'[4] But the later work, though much of it was ephemeral, was not always disappointing or commercial. *Rolling Down the Lea* is one of Gogarty's most engaging works: On his own turf once again and writing out of powerful imaginative and psychic forces, he wrote a book so unique that it was apparently regarded as too uncommercial to be issued by an American publisher.

Yet the fact remains that New York City in the forties and fifties was not Dublin. Its suburban fringes were anything but the Wicklow Hills; its cocktail lounges and bars, even when the bartenders were Irish, were not comparable to the pubs of Gogarty's loved city. The structure of American intellectual and cultural life was light years away from the intimate and loquacious atmosphere in which he had flourished. 'I had not realised how distributed life is over here,' he wrote in 1942. 'No centre but half the world.'[5] Whereas Gogarty had been close to the centre of the Irish Literary Revival, he was discovering that in the United States there *was* no centre at all. He was active in New York among those associated with the American Poetry Society—mostly poets hostile to modernism, but not really constituting a circle and peripheral to the dominant cultural tendencies. Though Gogarty had many friends at American universities and was amused, in the spring of 1948, to find himself offering a course at New York University,[6] the academic world's poetic establishment was dominated by an Eliot-Pound experimentalist orthodoxy that had routed the traditionalists; Gogarty might lecture frequently at American universities but none could have permanently attracted him. AE, cognisant of Gogarty's need for a certain kind of criticism, once observed that he needed a committee of fellow poets to select for him.[7] Fortuitously he did find a sympathetic listener—or sounding board—in Mary Owings Miller who launched a little magazine, *Contemporary Poetry*, in Baltimore in 1941. Though Gogarty was to meet Mrs Miller only once and only briefly, he joined the advisory board of her magazine, published *Perennial* and *Unselected Poems* in a series Mrs Miller sponsored, sent her poems for publication, promoted her magazine whenever he could, urged her to publish some of his old friends—Lord Dunsany, Shane Leslie, Hugh MacDiarmid—and carried on an extensive correspondence with her. It was no longer possible for him to chafe under the 'censorship' of Yeats or to pass his poems around in the snug of a Dublin pub to a circle of friends and rivals. By one of the strangest ironies of fate, he found that he could write to a Baltimore lady, mock his recent poems as 'doggerel', ask her of a new poem, 'Tell me if it is any good,' even request her opinion of a word-image in one of his most successful late poems.[8] Nothing could more sharply define the circumstances of his American years.

Gogarty himself was entirely conscious of the consequence of his residence in America, particularly to his poetry. Writing from the Ritz Tower in the summer of 1940 he noted, 'I am attempting an elegy on Yeats but this is no country for poems on death.'[9] A little more than a year later, he was writing of his 'Elegy on the Archpoet', 'I wish the thing were better but for that I should have to resume the Dublin Hills.'[10] To another correspondent he observed, 'Since the miraculous medley of Lycidas there was never such a gallimaufry. It badly needs melody and sublimity.'[11] For years, though he had certainly not spared Yeats from his wit, Gogarty had seen 'the Archpoet' as a heroic being. And certainly his admiration for the man he called 'the greatest guardian of the English language in our time'[12] is apparent in the poem. 'You brought the Brave among us here, / And high above the tinsel scene / Strode with the old heroic mien. . . .' Yet this elegy is simply not comparable to 'Aeterne Lucis Redditor', his tribute to Tyrrell. A 'sequence' like so many of Yeats's major later poems, the 'Elegy on the Archpoet' gets off to a laboured start. Only in its last three sections does it rise above the conventional and develop a sustaining imagery to support the structure. In these last three sections Gogarty develops most of the precise details as well as a governing and expanding metaphor of spring, though even in its spring imagery the Elegy does not achieve the precise, delicate, and evanescent visual qualities of his best work. Yeats, improvising on his visionary 'system', does come alive:

> . . . in that orchard house of mine,—
> The firelight glancing in the wine
> Or on your ring that Dulac made—
> How merrily your fancy played
> With the lost egg that Leda laid,
> The lost, third egg, Herodotus
> In Sparta said he came across;
> Or broached a problem more absurd:
> In the beginning was the Word,
> Since there was none to hear, unheard?
> Or linking stranger mysteries,
> The Spring with dates of the decease
> Of Caesar, Christ and Socrates . . .

Praising Yeats's imaginative capacity to explore the 'exultant and perverse' resources of the mind, Gogarty laments that he himself has been left 'Where April comes new-drenched in green'. He achieves a resolution to the poem when he recognises that death gives meaning to life. 'For who could bear the loveliest Springs / Touched by the thought that he must keep / A watch eternal without sleep?' A memorial poem in every sense of the word, this elegy draws to a close mourning the death of Yeats—and of Gogarty's world. Its catalogue of the extraordinary men who helped to shape Gogarty is both simple and moving though flawed by a bad couplet (dreams/meseems):

> Tyrrell, Mahaffy and Macran,
> The last the gentlest gentleman,
> And golden Russell—all were gone,
> Still I could turn to you alone.
> Now you have turned away
> Into the land of sleep or dreams
> (If dreams you rule them yet meseems).
> With clowns in tragedy,

Here solitary, I, bereft
Of all impulse of praise, am left
Without authority or deft
Examples in a rhyme.

Would the eighteenth-century squares—Fitzwilliam or Merrion,
where he had known Yeats—have evoked for Gogarty not only
memories of his friend and mentor but the architectonic the elegy
lacks? Or a drive past 'Riversdale', where he saw Yeats in his
final days, and on into the Dublin Hills have evoked intenser
imagery? The mourner of the 'Elegy' 'Whose hand you held,
whose line you filled', recognises the loss of Yeats to be immeasur-
able. The Gogarty of the letters to Horace Reynolds recognises
fully the consequences of exile; it is no accident that the metaphor
of 'Colophon' returned to him as he worked on the poem. He had
left behind the Dublin stage, only to find himself, 'With clowns
in tragedy . . . bereft'.

The actor Richard Aherne, in one of W. R. Rodgers' BBC
broadcasts, described an occasion in a Third Avenue Bar, when
Gogarty was telling 'many of his wonderful stories' to a group of
five or six:

> We were about to move off but he said, 'now I want to tell you
> this.' So he proceeded to tell another story and when he was
> about to come to the point, a young man, sitting at the bar,
> went over and placed a coin in a jukebox. All hell broke loose.
> The expression on Gogarty's face changed; he became very sad,
> a combination of sadness and anger and he said, 'Oh dear God
> in Heaven, that I should find myself thousands of miles from
> home, an old man, at the mercy of every retarded son of a bitch
> who has a nickel to drop in that bloody illuminated coal-
> scuttle.'[13]

America provided a refuge for the ageing Irish man of letters, an
income (usually adequate), a circle of generous friends, the freedom of expression he sought. But the World of Wurlitzer was too
far from Ely Place and Renvyle. Had he not been so ebullient and
plucky, the later years of this man who lived beyond his literary
time and place might have been very sad. But he *was* plucky.

Between 1948 and 1957, Gogarty published four collections of
prose pieces, many of which had appeared first in American

magazines. None of these collections of essays, portraits, stories, autobiographical narratives, and anecdotes is without interest, but many of the individual pieces belong properly to the realm of journalism. *Start from Somewhere Else* (1955) reads something like a commonplace book of jokes and anecdotes, something like a disorganised assortment of remnants from other books. Subtitled 'An Exposition of Wit and Humour Polite and Perilous', it neither defines nor illuminates either wit or humour, even though it cites some good instances of both. One can only regret that Gogarty was not dissuaded from publishing it—except for two appreciative passages, one on the poetry of George Redding, the other on Scots poetry, ancient and modern. Both of these might better have graced another one of his collections. *Mourning Becomes Mrs Spendlove* (1948) and *Intimations* (1950), though aimed at the same audience of casual readers, are far more satisfactory books.

The first of these, a group of 'Portraits, Grave and Gay', combines essays with various kinds of narratives and short stories. It ranges in subject from the title piece about the bizarre career and costume of a Victorian prostitute, to an account of a Vermont dowser, or water diviner, to essays on Joyce, Yeats, and the film maker Robert Flaherty. There is an elaborate comic story, set in a Vermont vacation spot, depicting the amusing consequences of a series of artificial inseminations ('The Vicarious Fulfilment of the Vicar of Dumbleton Centre'); and there is an ironic story that depicts the accidental 'betrothal' of a Franco-American to his cousin, during a visit to a village in the Pyrenees ('Museum Piece').

But Gogarty was most readable when he dealt with Irish materials and memories. Such stories as 'Missed by a Mark', the saga of a chronic medical student, and 'Mr. Pirrie, Pyrophile', an account of a lodger who finally proposes to a widow so as to acquire the regalia of the late Fire Captain Ryan, give freer play to his delight in Dublin eccentrics. But the best piece in the book is 'the Hero in Man', a 'fictionalised' narrative that shows us AE, identified only as the Organiser, as he breathes spirit into an Irish farm community in the course of promoting the Irish farm cooperative movement. It is no accident that this truly moving 'portrait' of the mystic George Russell using all the power of his eloquence to summon up a vision of the Irish heroic past—of Cuchulain, Finn, and Oisin—is followed by three autobiographical narratives, 'Dublin Revisited I: the Town', 'Dublin Revisited II: The Country', and 'The Merriman'. At the close of 'The Hero in Man', stirred by AE's eloquence to memories they cannot even understand, a number of the villagers have determined to free themselves from the rapacity of the local gombeen man and to establish a local co-operative. 'The Hero in man had not altogether gone in the early morning train,' reads the closing line of the piece. Clearly this theme, of the exceptional nature of the hero and the commonplace heroism of Everyman, filled Gogarty's imagination at this time. It became the subject of *Rolling Down the Lea*, which incorporated much of the material, transformed by its reworking, found in the two Dublin essays and 'The Merriman'.

Just as varied in its concerns and subjects and somewhat more uneven was *Intimations*. In this collection there are no short stories or tales, but rather essays of various degrees of formality. Some of these are among Gogarty's best; others are very slight indeed. In the first group of essays, 'Dubliners and Others', wherein Moore, Joyce, and Mahaffy appear again, there are also pieces on Wilde, Swift, and the Bullyns in Ireland, and there is one on the necessity of praising famous men. These last are uninspired, as are all the essays in the USA section, excepting the closing piece, 'American Patrons and Irish Poets', a much deserved tribute to a group of men who played an important role for both Yeats and himself. In the group entitled 'Intimations', there are several admirable essays—leisurely, appreciative, highly individual, the product of wide reading and generous impulse rather than of meticulous scholarship. Both 'Intimations', the title essay, and 'Green Thoughts' are essential, if we are to understand Gogarty's poetic sensibility and metaphysical impulses; and, like 'The Wonder in the Word', 'Poets and Little Children', 'How the Poets Praised Women', and 'I Like to Remember', they are a pleasure to read, even when idiosyncratic in their critical assumptions, for they embody a response to poetry and language which is not that of either an academic, a literary critic, or a professional reviewer, but of a breed of literary men of whom Gogarty may well have been the last. Dated they certainly were, even when composed, and often questionable in their judgments. 'Loveliness', Gogarty writes in one of them, 'is on the wing, and this club-car in which we find ourselves is running fast to a silent destination. Therefore not a moment should be lost in giving praise to the beautiful (praise helps to increase their beauty), even though the beauty seems untranslatable.' The literary appreciations of *Intimations*, Gogarty's testaments to beauties he had discerned, are cultural documents and also historical guides to the social and intellectual world—Dublin, Trinity, Oxford, the Edwardians—that Gogarty embodied.

The best piece in the entire collection, however, is the second of two essays on Moore, 'George Moore's Ultimate Joke'. Here we find Gogarty at the top of his form, witty, irreverent, commemorative. The essay opens with a series of outrageous sallies which remind us that Gogarty as well as Wilde knew Mahaffy:

> Most funerals are boring and uneventful—at least in this world. The mind refuses to cherish them and dismisses them as gloomy and unproductive memories. Some funerals can be tragic when they touch our affections. On the other hand, there are desirable funerals such as those I would willingly stand one or two people I have met through no fault of my own, though the cortege were expensive and the catafalque beyond my means.

Moore's funeral, he then asserts, 'is one which I will always remember with pleasure, not because I was not sorry for its subject, but because of the diversion it provided and because I had a shrewd idea that the principal intended it, as he had intended so many actions of his life, to be an embarrassing jest.' According to the specifications of Moore's will, he was cremated and his ashes were to be 'spread over Hampstead Heath where the donkeys graze'. Doubtless Moore's behest was designed to horrify his devoutly Catholic brother and sister, Colonel Maurice Moore and Mrs Kilkelly; it provides Gogarty with the occasion for an irresistible wordplay:

> So George had done it again, I said to myself. 'Even in our ashes. . .' He knew quite well that his family would never permit his ashes to be scattered among the donkeys. The newspapers would be full of scandal. No. Ashes to asses would never do.

Fearing the disapprobation of the Church and the country people's hostility to so pagan a rite, the Moores make careful arrangements to bury George's remains on Castle Island in Lough Carra, Moore Hall having been burned down during the Civil War. Although Gogarty claims that 'on the whole' he 'enjoyed' Moore's funeral 'more than any other funeral I ever attended,' 'on the whole' cannot be taken to include his passage of Lough Carra, with a disapproving Mrs Kilkelly, bearer of the urn. The heat is stifling:

> Forgetting my passenger, I took off my frock coat. I pulled in silence in my shirt-sleeves. My hands were peeling. Foolishly I dipped them in water to cool them. It made them worse. I blamed the heat for most of my troubles and I removed my waistcoat. . . .
> 'I trust you will not think it necessary to divest yourself of any more apparel.'

Suddenly, Gogarty thinks, in mock-heroic delight, of how Moore must be enjoying his ultimate joke:

> Charon, by gad! . . . He has turned me into a Charon to row his shade across this Lethean lake. How he must laugh at me now. Perspiring and in pain, without even an obol to pay for the ferrying.

The distinction of 'George Moore's Ultimate Joke', however, is that Gogarty recognises Moore the artist as well as Moore the joker and manages brilliantly to vary the tone of the essay. At the moment of interment, Richard Best reads the oration written by AE, who was unable to attend. Russell's words superbly transform the implicitly comic into a rich and dignified irony, and then into a moving tribute:

> It would be unseemly that the ashes of George Moore should be interred here and the ritual of any orthodoxy spoken over him; but I think that he who exercised so fantastic an imagination in his life would have been pleased at the fantasy which led his family and his friends to give him an urn burial in this lake island which was familiar to him from childhood.
> . . . .
> His ironic spirit would have been pleased at this urn burial in this lonely lake island, so that he might be to Ireland in death what he had been in life, remote and defiant of its faith and movements.
> . . . .

If his ashes have any sentience, they will feel at home here, for the colours of Carra Lake remained in his memory. . . . It is possible that the artist's love of earth, rock, water, and sky is an act of worship.

His paper 'flashing till it looked like the sword of some Homeric hero', Colonel Moore then evokes pre-Christian Ireland and the period to which the burial urn belongs. Balancing the mock-heroic and the elevated, Gogarty observes, 'I was so filled with admiration that I looked around for an Englishman to fight,' and then describes the scene of the return journey from the island:

I spent the time of the return journey gazing in rapture at the waters of the lake. Liquid gold, liquid ecstasy! . . . the waters of Lough Carra were more wonderful because I little expected a miracle, a miracle of beauty at a pagan funeral. Moore Hall took the sun now and again over the mile of wine-light water. Its cremated walls rose dark against the darker circle of its woods.

The absurd gesture of Moore, the eloquent language of AE, the Colonel's celebration of a heroic past: all these are brought to focus in the person of the narrator. He adds his own sensitivity to landscape, his own unique juxtaposition of the comic and the ecstatic:

The funeral had been a great success. Nobody had dropped dead to cast a gloom on the proceedings. It had touched the two pinnacles of life, beauty and excitement. I returned to the city 'smiling that things had gone so well'.

With its ironic recognition of the way experience moves between poles of farce and ecstasy, with its extraordinary cast of the dead, the living, and the absent, 'George Moore's Ultimate Joke' encapsulates the spirit of a great age in Ireland and Gogarty's role in it.

The last of these collections of Gogarty's incidental work was the posthumous *A Week End in the Middle of the Week* (1958), which like *Mrs. Spendlove* includes a range of fictional forms. The most uneven of the three collections, it was the one most in need of an editor who could have distinguished between what Gogarty churned out for bread and butter and what was more lasting. Some of the pieces appear elsewhere, under somewhat different guises or titles. Both 'They Carried Caesar' and 'The Rehabilitation of Abington Talmey' are episodes found in his autobiography; and 'Who Was Dean Swift' is the same as 'The Enigma of Dean Swift' which had appeared in *Intimations*. 'One Way of Improving Morale', a cursory treatment of the diamond, and 'Are All Americans Morons?' which is so lacking in specificity that it quite misfires, were not worthy of inclusion. A number of other slight pieces desperately needed editorial attention; others are little more than anecdotes. Yet there are good things almost lost in the confused jumble. Gogarty's one-act farce, *Incurables* is found here—and only here. 'The Romance of the Tree', 'The Romance of the Horse', 'Swords and Singers', all permit Gogarty to range from Greek poetry to the life and literature of the present in the kind of sprightly but casual display of enthusiasm and learning at which he excelled. 'The Most Haunted House of Them All', an account of his personal investigation of the ghost of Leap castle, is a fitting companion piece to *Intimations'* 'An Amazing Coincidence', which details the malign influence exerted by two great statues from Lord Granard's Castleforbes. One can only conclude of *A Weekend in the Middle of the Week* that it is an extreme instance of the confusion of occasional pieces of journalism with more substantial works that one finds in all of these compilations. Or, to put matters somewhat differently, however *Mourning Becomes Mrs Spendlove, Intimations, Start From Somewhere Else*, and *A Weekend in the Middle of the Week* may have served Gogarty's career in the literary marketplace, a single volume including the best of these short works would have served his reputation better.

Among the late prose works, in addition to *Rolling Down the Lea* only *It Isn't This Time of Year at All!*, which is subtitled *An Unpremeditated Autobiography* may be said to rank with the three prose works that appeared at the end of the thirties. In one respect, *It Isn't This Time of Year at All* (1954) is a very disappointing book; it is not really an autobiography at all. The Gogarty *persona*, loquacious and 'inconsequent', is the centre of the book, to be sure, but he is there telling us more about others than about himself, indifferent to date and sequence, always ready for an excursion into some satirical aside, lively fact, or cherished opinion. In effect, the unpremeditated autobiography is another blend of anatomy and confession, filled with portraits, remembered encounters, and colourful bits of gossip. At one point, Gogarty typed out a scheme for thirty-two of the forty-two chapters of the book, which would reveal his lack of interest in deliberate sequence, if the book itself did not make that point emphatically enough! There is, of course, a general chronological progression in the book; but this once established, Gogarty was prepared within a particular group of chapters to move from 1904 to 1902 and 1905 and thence back to 1904.[14] Furthermore, except for a brief excursion to 1930 when Augustus John and Yeats were at Renvyle, rebuilt as a hotel, the book does not move much beyond the mid-twenties. We look in vain for any detailed account of Gogarty's years of medical practice, domestic life, or Senatorial service; and there is nothing of the American years at all. At points, Gogarty touches episodes, situations, lines or details he had used elsewhere. 'Fugax Erythema' actually repeats an amusing episode of his medical training found in *Tumbling in the Hay.* 'The Divine Doctor', which recounts the difficulties Tyrrell ran into when he fell asleep at a Trinity Board meeting and how Gogarty and Jan McCabe came to his rescue, is found as 'The Rehabilitation of Abington Talmey' in *A Week End in the Middle of the Week.* 'You Carry Caesar', which tells of his kidnapping by the IRA is the same as 'They Carried Caesar' in the same collection. The attack on de Valera and his role in the Civil War is resumed, certainly as vehemently as ever. And yet there are new details on Griffith and the Bailey Circle, a fresh account of Gogarty's own response to the Easter Rising, fresh insights into the social background of the Treaty negotiations. Yeats, Joyce, AE, Moore, Tyrrell, Mahaffy, Dunsany, Augustus John, Griffith and others appear again in this book; a number of Tyrrell's and Mahaffy's better lines, used elsewhere, are quoted again. Yet there is remarkably little duplication or reworking of whole episodes, with the exception of 'Fugax Erythema,' and the witty lines of the famous that crop up here are found mostly in the later collections—legitimate source books—rather than in the earlier books. There is, furthermore, new and interesting material about Gogarty's infancy and boyhood, about his medical training and his association with Joyce.

Seen as what it is, not really an autobiography at all, but a Gogartian excursion in time, *It Isn't This Time of Year at All!* is a far more satisfying book. The style is conversational, provocative, pulsing with Gogarty's still volatile personality. In short, it is everything that the later collections of short pieces are not. Consider the following passage and the relation it establishes with the reader:

> They [melancholics] equate goodness with unhappiness, as some ladies in great cities equate culture with seriousness. To these snouts you will always be bad; and it's no use trying to appease them. They are all paranoids and there is no bottom to their private hell. Have nothing to do with them if you want to lead a good life that is a merry one: 'For only the good are merry.' I prefer to think of life's great optimist, Brian O'Lynn who, when he fell into a river exclaimed hopefully, 'There's land at the bottom!' Tell that to the bluenoses.

There could be only one inspiration for the tone and manner of that passage: Maître François Rabelais, a lifelong enthusiasm for Gogarty who reflects that other doctor's disdain for humbug and his healthy optimism throughout this book. Now no less certain that perspective is everything than when, around the turn of the century, he jotted down, 'The world stinks? Your standpoint is a dunghill.'[15] Gogarty claimed himself lucky:

> My nurse used to say that good luck was poured on me at my birth. She did not make me lucky or happy-go-lucky, but she foretold it, and she was right; to be lucky means to have a cheerful temperament.

Though Gogarty implies that he will 'record only sunny hours' in this work, it is not the case that in *It Isn't This Time of Year at All!* he averts his eyes from conflict and disappointment but that he will not be downed by them. His optimism is not that of Polyanna but of Pantagruel. Describing a summer at Garranban House in Connemara bathing with his sons and teaching them how to swim, Gogarty reflects:

> Looking back, I realise that those were the happiest days of my life. Did I realise it then? From what I know of myself I must have done so, but not as much as I do in retrospect.
>
> This retrospectful look is what makes a Golden Age. That age was mine and it was contemporary. I had attained the greatest happiness that men can reach. I had dwelt in the Golden Age. Who can realise it fully until he leaves it, or it leaves him?

That passage works in two directions: to typify the moment, and to remind us that there were many moments that differed from it. Moreover, throughout this work, in episode and detail, he manifests the difference between a healthy optimism and naïveté, as well as between a vital enthusiasm for experience and negation. A case in point is the episode at the Bailey Tavern in which he contrasts his own attitude with that of Seumas O'Sullivan (disguised as 'Neil'). During the course of the book, Gogarty himself has had plenty to say that is harsh, even bitter. But O'Sullivan is sunk in bitterness. When James Stephens leaves the group, Gogarty quotes from Lord Gray's description of how as a boy the impoverished Stephens slept in parks and fought with the swans for a scrap of food:

> As far as my quotation went, it only bored the company. Neil was the first to show resentment.
> 'Oh, for God's sake!' he implored. 'It used to be dogs: now it is swans.' Neil was getting to his acerb state.
> 'There's a magnificent portrait of Stephens by Tuohy,' I remarked.
> 'I understand that the painter committed suicide,' Neil shot out.

Leaving then with Monty (James Montgomery), Gogarty discusses O'Sullivan's attitudes and remembers the latter's hostility to Arthur Griffith and the Treaty with England; he repeats the gentle AE's devastating, satirical quatrain on his disciple. His reflection on the episode then demonstrates the sophisticated nature of his optimism: 'Why is it that I like something imperfect even in a bar? . . . My Eden requires a serpent.' It would seem to be possible, Gogarty is implying, to regard men as imperfect without indulging in a religion of suffering. Accepting Joyce's mock-heroic identification of him with Mercury, Messenger of the Gods, he exclaims at the opening of the book, 'Why should my winged ankles be thrust into a pair of jack boots? I did not come down from Olympus for that.' Later he describes how when he was competing as a cyclist for Trinity, he saw a poster in the window of Clery's shop advertising a race to be held at Ballsbridge. ' "Gogarty V Time", it announced.' Refusing to be defeated by Time in this book, he rules it through imagination, mercurially changing the subject when he wishes, and refusing to be ruled by sequence. Though he claims that his autobiography will deal more 'with the good and the brave than with evil men,' it is not without mountebanks, fools, and knaves; and it has as villains an odd trinity of de Valera, Einstein, and Freud! If it is not immediately comprehensible why these three should be associated with one another and cast in the role of tripartite villain, Gogarty nevertheless has his 'reasons'. Once past the shock of his initial attacks on them, one can perhaps understand why he would confine all three in an open-air asylum. It is because they are for him symbolic of system-making, of the Hebraic rather than the Hellenic impulse in our civilisation. Obscurantists inasmuch as they render the simple and the apparent unclear by an elaborate jargon, they also abstract from the complex richness that is life a distorting formula which is an over-simplification. 'I am bringing the Cosmos into an equation,' are the words Gogarty puts into Einstein's mouth. 'I achieve freedom by restricting it,' might be de Valera's, as Gogarty sees him; 'The psyche is a machine,' Freud's. All 'seek', as he puts it elsewhere, 'to impose a rule and regimen on life'. In a dream he relates, in which both Einstein and de Valera figure, the line, 'The swifter the river, the nearer the bridge,' came to him. Though he says he cannot explain it—and the metaphor is ambiguous—it depends upon a contrast between fixity and flux and implies the advantage of giving oneself to the flow.

Gogarty's effects, often disarmingly casual, are, as we have seen, anything but that. He records early in *It Isn't This Time of Year at All!* that as a schoolboy with an essay assignment to write he had a kind of vision in which he saw a plain with banners and pennons and tents, perhaps dimly associated with a tavern sign depicting Brian Boru, the warrior hero. Reminding us that the Greek word for knowing is the same word as that for having seen, he observes that unconsciously he learned that 'all writing depends on seeing'. At the close of this book, the themes of time, luck, and vision, all of which seem most accidentally disposed throughout, are drawn together. One evening, he writes, as he was driving along Lough Corrib, in the autumn of the year, suddenly 'the land seemed to open out, light shone on a fresh earth and bright grass; all figures moved in beauty.' Quoting Yeats's uncollected and then unpublished poem 'Crazy Jane and the King'—a vision of the Tuatha de Danaan—and alluding for the second time to the line 'Saw the lucky eyeball shine,' he identifies the 'magic' of Ireland's

West with luck and with a capacity for supernal vision. He had seen the Delightful Plain, Tír na nOg, the Land of Youth, a preternatural correspondence of the Edenic garden of Fairfield House upon which his eyes had gazed in infancy and the Golden Age he knew during the happiest days of his life, teaching his sons to swim in Connemara. How literally are we to take this vision of Tír na nOg with which *It Isn't This Time of Year at All!* closes? Not at all, probably. And yet there should be no doubt at all about the validity of the metaphor as a rendering of a visionary capacity that we *are* to take literally. The Pantagruellian optimism of the book rests on Gogarty's belief not only that the psyche may be free within the moment but that at any moment the psyche may experience release into a transcendent freedom, as it will ultimately. 'Some day, on the first of November perhaps,' he reflects in the closing words of a book that is less a record of events than a description of a way of looking at them, 'the earth will be opened and I shall enter into no stranger realm but the realm of earth renewed, Boys! O Boys!'

A Few Wild Leaves of Laurel

THE failure of the Yeats elegy and Gogarty's consciousness of it, the severing of his taproot into Irish soil, the demands of the literary marketplace, the sheer quantity of the prose he produced while in the United States, all of these might seem to indicate that not much should be expected of the poetry Gogarty published during his American years. Earlier, towards the close of the thirties, when the prose impulse and the emotional forces behind it had become dominant, there had been a falling off in Gogarty's poetic productivity and poetic control. In the United States he did write a quantity of poetry but much of it was, as he wrote, 'hardly up to standard as I guess.'¹ Indeed, when one turns to his last published volume, *Unselected Poems* (1954), one finds, with the exception of a single ballad-elegy, poems that are pretty much on the same level as the journalism of the period. Though Gogarty wanted intensely to publish this small volume, he also concluded that 'the book is hardly worth dedicating to anyone'.² Only two of the unselected poems were carried over to the *Collected Poems,* and only the ballad-elegy, 'Farrell O'Reilly', deserved to be. 'Job's Healer', which was but should not have been, is in the style that typifies most of the nine poems of the small collection, and that was close to the smart commercial accent of certain of the more sophisticated American magazines. In the one poem of the group where Gogarty attempts a serious theme, 'The Phoenix and the Unicorn', there is a serious conflict of styles, informal, comic efforts clashing with poetic diction ('ere'), and all being put to shame by two splendid closing lines in his old classical manner: 'The Unicorn's anfractuous tine, / The Phoenix fledged with fire.' But 'Adam and Eve' is characteristic of most of the work in the collection. In it, as in most of these poems, Gogarty depended on comic rhyme effects and irreverent contemporary references; he manages to be funny, spinning lines out as far as he can, and his satire is also amusing, but there are simply not the spontaneous high spirits and allusiveness of his early *facetiae* :

In an unlocated Garden
Our First Parents used to roam
While a most assertive Warden
Ran their happy, houseless home.
They had vegetarian menus,
Nothing then was poisonous,
No one thought of cooking sinews
For they hadn't got a house;
And they wore not even sporrans,
For they hadn't got a kilt;
Our First Parents lived like morons
Or like nudists—in their pelt. . . .

Even in verse as slight as this, there are touches of the old Gogarty bite. One cannot help but appreciate his characterisation of the God of the *Old Testament* :

Happiness might have been boring
Had they not been kept in awe
By a cross between Hermann Goering
And falutin' Bernard Shaw.

Yet turning to the poetry Gogarty produced between 1940 and 1945, to the additional poems he added to the American edition of *Elbow Room* (1942) one finds some rather interesting develop-ments. Of this small group of poems, all of which appear in the *Collected Poems*, only two are specifically linked to American places. 'High Above Ohio', attempts to embrace the landscape in tetrameter quatrains, but the language of the poem is prosaic, discursive, abstract. On the other hand, 'To A Friend in the Country (Wyckoff, New Jersey)', though in the sonnet form that is always too constraining for Gogarty, is far more successful, particularly in the sestet. Here the season—spring—a particular setting—a house, its gardens—elicit a far more intense and felt experience. The octave creates the conflict, New York's 'mad bombardment of the brains'. Longing to escape this, the poet finds resolution in his image of an envisioned moment (nicely rendered in the detail of the grass and the oak leaves) and a sense of transcendence :

> My God, I would give anything to reach
> Your old house standing in the misty rain,
> And turn my thoughts to things that do not pass,
> While gazing through a window at the grass
> And wet young oak leaves fingering the pane.

In most of the other poems of this group Gogarty appears to be turning back towards the epigrammatic and terse manner of the twenties. Time and transiency, spring in the cycle of existence, the modest and prayerful acceptance of what is allotted to man : these are the themes and concerns of 'A Prayer for his Lady', 'For a Birthday', 'To an Old Lady' and 'The Eternal Recurrence'. And as the expectations of the poet narrow and his subjects are restricted to simple but timeless things of most immediate concern, his control over the whole poem returns. 'The Eternal Recurrence' can illustrate one of the modes of expression in Gogarty's poetry during these few years :

> I thank the gods who gave to me
> The yearly privilege to see,
> Under the orchard's galaxy,
> April reveal her new-drenched skin;
> And for the timeless touch within
> Whereby I recognise my kin.

In short, although he produced only a handful of poems comparable to his earlier work during the American years and though I think the last poems, those that appeared in *Unselected Poetry*, cannot be taken seriously, for a half decade in the forties, when he was well into his sixties, Gogarty's muse returned to him and is manifest in the shorter poems of the American *Elbow Room* and in several of the poems in the two editions of *Perennial*.

There were uninspired poems in *Perennial* (1944): a sonnet writer's tribute to a friend and patron, some memorial stanzas for a friend's son, killed in the service. And the volume also contained a number of poems from *Elbow Room* and earlier collections. All the success of the volume, therefore, is in 'Perennial', 'Croker of Ballinagarde', 'Suburban Spring', 'Leave Taking', and 'Between Brielle and Manasquan', and in the variety of comic styles that we find in them. If nature and the metaphysical states of which it is emblematic is more important in the later Gogarty than love and if *Elbow Room* (1942) seemed to dwell upon woman touched by time, 'Leave Taking' revealed that Gogarty could still catalogue the fragile charms he admired in women:

> From some rush-hidden spring
> A stream in little trebles
> Tinkled from pools of pebbles
> And gurgled, preluding
> Each laughing, liquid note,
> Coiled in a woman's throat.
> I said, 'I hear her laughter';
> And then, a moment after,
> The stream began to sing.

Woman, nature, and spiritual state become one in the conclusion to this lyric:

> The bank I rested on
> Was gently curved and warm,
> I dreamt about her form.
> I said, 'she has withdrawn
> Into herself delight
> And joy from every sight.'
> The wind that dusks the grasses
> Tells when a spirit passes—
> I felt that she was gone.

Girl, nymph, muse, or anima, her fleeting presence is caught for a moment in the lines.

But Gogarty had done things like 'Leave Taking' before. The American scene itself—not from a plane over Ohio but in amusing human and local detail—he catches in 'Suburban Spring' and 'Between Brielle and Manasquan'. The first of these opens with evocative and delicate images; yet ones more universal than particular:

> Now the delicious air
> Persuades the lovely trees
> To loose their golden hair

H

From old embroideries
And make an airy screen
Of gold that turns to green.

Gradually the mood of the poem becomes less tentative, the
trimeter lines more boisterous and detailed:

A soft, green, maple rain
Has paved the little lane,
The lane behind the rill
That runs down to the mill;
And every little gully
Gushes replenished fully;
And in the fields beyond
Are dipping, scooting, ducking;
Foals, calves and lambs are sucking,
(A thing I would not mention
But for the pastoral convention) . . .

The poem moves on, its line now crowded with comic detail and
homely suburban activity:

And Peggy's out, not caring
To ask how Dick is faring:
The Miller, where no breeze is
(It's dust or sinus) sneezes;
And men in sleeveless shirts
Are plying little squirts,
Or making rainbow mists
With a kind of hose that twists;
And all the world's agog
Like a seedsman's catalogue.

This poem rests on a comic paradox. All the vital details it
amasses result from the fact that the globe is 'out of plom'.
  'Between Brielle and Manasquan', even more particularised than
'Suburban Spring' by its coastal New Jersey place names, renders
in sharpest detail the atmosphere of a place and its history, a place
where 'The old sea captains, when their work / Was done on the
eternal sea / Came each ashore and built a house.' Those houses,
'painted white / With shutters gay and pointed gables'; the
builders themselves, 'some stocky men with beards / And some . . .
tawny blue-eyed men'; the loot they have left behind, 'Weapons

with silver work inlaid / . . . . Carved shells and bits of Chinese jade / . . . /A figurehead called Spumy Nancy': these seem almost to be Gogarty's sole concern. A perfect rendering, on one level at least, of the 'quaintness' of a certain kind of Eastern seaboard town, the poem moves, slyly enough, onto another level of perception. Beyond the charming gimcrackery and tidy houses is the redoubtable and long deserted sea. This vast force, never comprehended, almost forgotten now by those who have filled the town with her emblems, is vengeful:

> She swished her tides resentfully
>   And tons and tons of sand collected
> And silted up the narrow way
> That leads to Barnegat's still Bay.

The meaning of the poem is implicit in its vivid comic details, and these delicately convey both man's absurd creation of an illusion and his failure to grasp the vast inhuman force over which he has so little control. These are the last lines of the poem:

> They could not sail now if they hankered;
> You'd think, to see their homes festooned,
>   A fleet was in the Bay and anchored,
> So gaily grew the creepers mounting,
> So gaily flew the flagstaffs' bunting.

Gogarty's irony here is not qualified by his clear sympathy but comprehends it. He both admires the pluck with which the landlocked town presents itself as a cheerful harbour and also recognises the charming unreality of everything about the place.

More broadly comic than any other of the new poems in *Perennial*, 'Croker of Ballinagarde's tetrameter stanza and rhymed couplets provide a gusty accompaniment to the narrative:

> Ballinagarde was a house to be sure
> With windows that went from the ceiling to flure,
> And fish in the river and hens in the yard
> And Croker was master of Ballinagarde.
>
> He bought his own whiskey and brewed his own ale
> That foamed up like beastings that thicken the pail.

Randy as the rhythms and the language are, they are in keeping with the provincial setting and the zesty hedonism of Croker, who both enjoys and shares his plenty. When Croker suffers a fatal accident and the parson is summoned to his bedside, the latter offers conventional wisdom:

> He tried to persuade him and make him resigned,
> On heavenly mansions to fasten his mind.
> 'There's a Land that is Fairer than this,' he declared.
> 'I doubt it!' said Croker of Ballinagarde.

Croker's scepticism is his way of celebrating the fullness of life. And though often comic, even homely, in tone and mood, these late poems of Gogarty's may all be said to be celebratory of Becoming.

In one group of new poems added to the English *Perennial* (1946), Gogarty's senses were as sharp as ever and his sensibility still attuned to the world of process but seen as a manifestation of pure Being. 'The Water Lily', for instance, opens with this sensuous apostrophe:

> Between two elements you float
> O white and golden melilote,
> Emerging by a cyprian birth
> The loveliest flower asoiled of earth!

As the poem progresses, the flower is seen as 'ineffable . . . word', 'one perfect syllable'; it is meaning without explanation. A word itself and a world, the flower is suspended on the water between the 'immemorial mud' and the sky. Uttering only itself, it is neither 'mystery' nor 'answer'. Yet the discursive elements in the poem seem crude by comparison to the delicate sensuousness of the opening or lines like these:

> There is no sound. Your golden glow—
> A sky above, a sky below—
> Is now the centre of a sphere.

In a related poem, 'The Dragon Fly', the insect, an insubstantial flashing of light, paradoxically suggests the liberated spirit within a moment of time. Once again the rendering of the particular, the insect—'Just a Swift ephemeris / Fashioned to keep up with bliss'—is more effective than the prosaic elements: 'In instantene- ity / Slumbers an eternity.'

The kind of ecstatic response to nature and natural things that lies behind these poems is suggested in Gogarty's essay 'Intimations'. He confesses:

> I shouted with joy last spring, when, in a little wood in Maryland, I came upon a tree all white with bloom in the middle of the wood's fresh green. There was no one there to hear me. Had there been, I might have been taken away to be psychoanalysed by one of those maddening mechanics who dissect the mind as if it were a material thing. From them is the vision withheld. I wonder to what they would attribute the joy I felt when I saw beside the wood a mist of light blue flowers lying like a little lake of Azure in a yellow field.
>
> . . . .
>
> And the effect of these intimations is ecstasy, an extension of oneself to become merged in divinity. Saints, poets and certain philosophers have experienced it. Plotinus called it 'achieving the term'.

Gogarty goes on to allude to 'a great poet'—it is, of course, Yeats and the experience he depicts in 'Vacillation'—who experienced 'More than intimations . . . the actual experience of immortality.' I think the burden of these remarks is that while he himself has not had so complete an experience of transcendence as Yeats, he has had 'intimations' akin to that experience. The joyous lyric 'The Apple Tree' carries even further the implications of 'The Water Lily' and 'The Dragon Fly'; and it very much suggests the experience described in 'Intimations'. Like the water lily, the blooming tree is seen as word, a shout, 'The Logos itself, the Creative Word'. But in this poem, image and theme are not separable. The cycle of growth in the tree is an enactment of the creation and an analogue of cosmic process as well:

> Each rosy globe is as red as Mars
> And all the tree is a branch of stars.
> What can we say but, 'Glory be!'
> When God breaks out in an apple tree?

Nothing so naïve as a Pantheist, like Yeats and like AE, for that matter, Gogarty could not help but conceive of antinomies of matter and spirit interpenetrating one another. Probably the most satisfying of these late poems of vision, to the extent that it is rendered entirely as experience, 'The Ho Ho Bird' was added to the *Collected Poems* (1951). Imaginary rather than observed in nature, the mythic oriental bird enters the mind of the poem's speaker, leaving 'a path of amethystine flame' and evoking a mental landscape that responds to it:

> Mountains and trees and rocks and springs
> Answer the waving of its wings:
> When, suddenly, to my surprise,
> My mind becomes a Paradise.

But none of these visionary poems can be said to achieve what 'Fresh Fields' had done in a few lines of the utmost simplicity and precision. To find poems in which Gogarty does something he had not done before, one has to look at a group in Constable's *Perennial*, poems that quite eschew anything like a high style. The least of these is 'Bill Baveler', a comic ballad turned to the purpose of elegy. Its subject, an American tavern keeper, a rustic wag, is fittingly mourned in comic rhymes, as his awful jokes are remembered:

> He was too old to go to war,
> His heart was bad, he could not march hard,
> He hoped he was not 'steering for'—
> He'd look churchwards—'the marble orchard'.

> His rustic mind would entertain
> His simple guests whose minds were simple.
> It took no zephyr from the brain
> To make their round cheeks 'cream and dimple'.

> 'What are those great big things with guns
> That on the enemy like hell come,
> Like great big trucks, big iron ones?'
> If you said 'Tanks,' he'd say 'You're welcome!'

The ballad form is supple enough to permit a rapid shifting of tone, and even an uncharacteristic bit of confessionalism on Gogarty's part:

> His soul was sound and free from harm:
> A gentleman whose ways were gentle
> He'd take me gently by the arm
> At dawn when I was growing mental.

And it can turn to tenderness, too:

Ah, Death you always take the best
And time alone makes you the leveller.
You might have taken any guest—
You might have spared the good Bill Baveler.

There was also among these *Perennial* poems a turning back to
Ireland through memories, not sentimental in the least, but joyous,
even sharply realistic. And handling Irish subjects in the simplest
and most traditional of forms, Gogarty achieved the best effects
of his later poetry. An early draft of 'Oughterard', for instance,
reveals a poem of three stanzas, clumsy in its combination of
trimeter and tetrameter lines with heptameters, indifferent and
banal in most of its language. Here are two stanzas of the draft,
'Old Oughterard':

Old Oughterard where I drank all night with Sweeney
Till he brought out the 'special'
That was hid behind the bed.
Old Oughterard where the policemen are leaning
Gazing at the gosling from the old gray bridge's head.

Old Oughterard, I am going with your river
Down to brim Lough Corrib
By the walls of Auchnanure.
Old Oughterard, I could live in you forever
If I could find a way to make the stream of life secure.

The original opening line, 'Old Oughterard, with the black stream
sliding through it' becomes the more immediate and lively, 'Do
ye know Oughterard with the stream running through it' of the
finished poem. Four quatrains, a free tetrameter, Irish colloquial-
isms, even the accent—clearly not Gogarty's—transform the draft
version into an earthy street song, vigorous in its specificity:

God be with the night when I drank there wid Sweeney
Till he brought the 'special' from under the floor
And dawn came in square through the bar-parlour window;
And 'Jaze us!' sez Sweeney 'It's twenty past four!'

In old Oughterard I could get on quite nicely,
For there I know decent, remarkable men:
Jim Sweeney, the Sergeant, and Fr McNulty
Who took the first prize with his running dog 'Finn'.

Bad cess to the seas and bad cess to the causeways
That keep me from goin' back homeward once more
To lean on the bridge and gaze down at the goslings,
And get a 'Good Morrow' from black Morty Mor.

Gogarty's final elegy—and his very best—was 'Farrell O'Reilly'.
While he is not using a ballad stanza here, the narrative is essentially ballad-like, the longer stanza being needed for the rich
accumulation of remembered detail. This superior poem of childhood remembered and perhaps of anticipated death ('So maybe,
because I am nearing the ground / The days of my youth and my
childhood are here.') is addressed to a most unprepossessing figure:

You, Farrell O'Reilly, I feared as a boy
With your thin riding legs and your turned-in toes;
I feared the sharp gimlet-like look in your eye,
Your rumbling brown beard and your pocketed nose.

Vigorous and fresh in diction, the poem creates not only the
Master of the Hunt, but a whole end-of-the-century Irish hunting
world and a child's sense of the awesomeness of the adult:

Like everyone else who was in his employ,
Alert, lest, surprised, I be taken in error,
In spite of foreboding, I snatched at my joy,
For joy is a pleasance surrounded by terror.
Wood, river and well—to maid and to man
Sharp Farrell O'Reilly appeared as god Pan.

A triumph of tone in its mingling of classical allusion and rustic
detail, the poem does not falter as it leads to a gnomic climax. The
speaker himself makes a discovery when the intimidating and
larger-than-life O'Reilly senses his fatigue at the end of the hunt:
'And Farrell said nothing, but looked at my Father; / Then carried
me home; and I found, for a truth, / There's sometimes great
kindness behind the uncouth.' The poem ends simply and superbly,
with the traditional elegiac gesture, a convention truly in this
context revived and entirely in keeping with the gnarled and
homely quality of the poem: '. . . now everything yields / To the
breath I drew first from the winds of my morn: / So Farrell
O'Reilly, in token from me, / Accept this wild leaf from your
own twisted tree.' One can understand why Philip Larkin selected

this poem, along with 'Ringsend', for inclusion in his recent
Oxford Book of Twentieth Century English Verse.

One other poem of Gogarty's American years stands out, too,
as belonging among any selection of his best. It is the title poem
to *Perennial* and seems to me one of those poems by which he
makes a claim upon our attention. Less perfect in utterance than
Housman's 'Loveliest of trees, the Cherry Now', to which it frankly
alludes, 'Perennial' has an emotional and tonal range far beyond
the other modern 'classicist' and a reality in its dwelling upon the
imperfect that Housman never touched. Its tetrameter couplets
could not be more conventional, but neither beat nor rhyme is as
insistent as in some of the less successful later poems nor as homely
as in one like 'Farrell O'Reilly'. Here the sense stress and phrasing
counterpoint the carrying beat and rhyme:

> The other day I chanced to see
> By an old lot a cherry tree,
> An old wild cherry blooming brightly,
> A sight of joy in the unsightly.
> It sprayed the air with April snow
> As merrily as long ago
> When every little wind that blew
> Could bend it, and with blossoms strew
> The garden or the shaven lawn.
> The lot was bare, the house was gone;
> And yet the brave old tree bloomed on.

A less vigorous and joyous poet than Gogarty might have considered that paragraph stanza the poem, for the traditional contrast
of youth and age has been suggested; the classical convention has
been, as it were, satisfied. But the Irish exile had something fuller
and more moving to do with the traditional symbol:

> Bravo! I cried. You make me think
> Of some old Roman soused in drink
> His wreath awry upon his head,
> For all that, primely chapleted;
> Or that gowned man who loved to foster
> My waking wits, Tyrellus noster.
> I like the rings upon your rind

Suggesting hoops. They bring to mind
Barrels and kilderkins enough
To stillion the Septembral stuff.

Anything but orderly, the tree is associated with a Bacchic Roman, with Trinity's bibulous classicist, Tyrrell, with a whole harvest of alcoholic essences. The wild cherry is a symbol of the *persona*'s desire—and, we may note in passing, of the dilemma of Gogarty's later years and of his triumph in this poem:

How do you keep your sap so young?
If I could only break in song
As you in bloom, and disregard
Ruin around this old back yard,
I'd raise such foison of sweet sound
That trees would jig it on the ground;
Kettles and garbage cans would swirl;
You'd think that Orpheus found his girl;
Or that this old daft heart of mine
Improved, as it grew old, like wine.

Gogarty's love of the classical tradition and his Irishness come together to create the fantasy of a jig that transforms a wasteland. In 'A Dialogue of Self and Soul', the very passage to which Gogarty alludes in 'Intimations', in fact, Yeats wrote:

I am content to follow to its source
Every event in action or in thought
Measure the lot; forgive myself the lot!
When such as I cast out remorse
So great a sweetness flows into the breast
We must laugh and we must sing,
We are blest by everything,
Everything we look upon is blest.

Gogarty never composed on that level of inspiration, any more than he in *his* 'intimations' experienced, as he felt Yeats had, 'immortality'. But from the rowdy, roistering climax of 'Perennial' he leads us on to concluding lines that have, without violation of the essential comedy of the poem, their own dignity and passion. Remorseless, he embraces the waste-lot itself, the very wasteland, not only growth but loss, decay, and death:

By God, I'm grateful for the Spring
That makes all fading seem illusion;
The foam, the fullness, the profusion;
For every lovely thing misplaced;
The bloom, the brightness and the waste!

Evoking once more the thought of Heraclitus that had stirred him since early manhood and in a voice that could be his alone, in those lines Gogarty affirms the flux of existence, the eternal cycle of life and death, the mythos of recurrence, indeed, every triumph and defeat of his own crowded life. In his own way, Yeats's friend had a vision of the unity of being—a vision surpassing wit itself.

Conclusion:
To Laugh as All Men Laughed

A FEW years after its publication, W. H. Auden described Yeats's *Oxford Book of Modern Verse* as 'the most deplorable volume ever issued from' the Clarendon Press.[1] Indeed, from the moment of its publication, Yeats's anthology was violently attacked. Even today the anthology is apt to be regarded as a monument of perverse judgment and prejudice. Certainly if one goes on the assumption that Yeats was attempting to offer a neutral record of modern poetry from the death of Tennyson to 1935, one can only conclude that his *Oxford Book* was a catastrophe. In the first section of his long 'Introduction', Yeats reveals that he has drastically edited Oscar Wilde's *The Ballad of Reading Gaol*, has 'plucked out even famous lines', and, doing so, has brought 'into the light a great, or almost great, poem.' 'My work', Yeats says, 'gave me that privilege.' Arrogant the action and the words may have been, but they point to the fact that Yeats never regarded the *Oxford Book* as a detached historical record or as the reflection of a critical consensus. Indeed, in 1935, a dominant consensus cannot be said to have existed—though it was just beginning to take shape.

Oliver Gogarty's private correspondence contemporaneous with the *Oxford Book* suggests to me that he had better understood the anthology than those who were infuriated by it—and, in particular, by Yeats's generous selection from Gogarty's own poetry. 'What right have I to figure so bulkily?' Gogarty asked in November 1936. 'None from a poetical point of view. . . . Sappho could not have made a more subjective anthology.'[2] Surely that response of Gogarty's helps to put in perspective what Yeats had actually done in editing his anthology. It is worth noting that Lascelles Abercrombie, who first undertook the editorial task for Oxford, soon concluded that he could not possibly exercise judicious choices, would alienate his friends and possibly destroy his own reputation if he continued with the project. Finally, he pleaded with Oxford to release him from his contract.[3] Yeats, by contrast, once he had accepted his task, did not swerve from his conception of it. And his Introduction, in which he sharply distinguished himself from such modernists as Pound and Eliot, continues to grow in importance as a critical document. That Introduction makes very clear the premise on which Yeats was working: that he was exercising a personal prerogative. He was offering to the public those poets who had mattered to *him* from the nineties on. The *Oxford Book* was *his* history of modern poetry, *his* critical perspective on past and present.

In another letter of November 1936, Oliver Gogarty returned to the subject of the anthology. Once more, what he has to say is illuminating, if more partisan:

> The English critics who have never forgiven Yeats for taking the Nobel Prize from their despairing poets, or rather poets of despair, are hard on his heels over the anthology. . . . Yeats always set his face against poetic diction and never confused it, as these critics do, with poetry. . . . Praise above all the consistency of the old man Yeats who never trimmed or set his jib to the prevailing gales of fashion or popularity. . . . God only knows why I am given such undeserved prominence. Possibly because I set my face against the revival of 'folk' poetry and Padraic Columism; and insisted that there were better things to hear and still finer things to see in Ireland than turf smoke and cottage songs.[4]

That passage from Gogarty's letter is worth reflecting upon, not merely because it is a defence of Yeats's integrity, but because it reminds us that the Irish poet Yeats rewarded by inclusion in the *Oxford Book* more than any other was no flea upon the coat of Yeats's genius. As wit and poet, Gogarty had spent a lifetime rejecting most of the tenets of the literary revival Yeats had generated and all the mannerisms of Yeats's imitators.

In making as generous a selection from Gogarty as he did, Yeats was once again expressing poetic principles manifest throughout the anthology. He was also attempting to promote the reputation of a friend. 'I am asking for a lot,' he wrote to Gogarty, and, conscious of the limited budget Oxford had provided him as well as of the good he might do Gogarty, he added, 'but don't charge me much. I can get you a thousand readers for every one your publisher can get you.'[5] He offered praise to Gogarty in the same note, too, indicating that he regarded him as a very special and rare talent: 'I think you are perhaps the greatest master of the pure lyric now writing in English.' Yeats was not, of course, saying that he regarded Gogarty as a greater poet than himself but that in a special kind of poem—a poem not dominated by dramatic effects, philosophical theme, or contemporary issues—he considered Gogarty to be greatly accomplished. A subsequent letter leaves no doubt as to the kind of response he elicited from Gogarty: 'I thank you for your . . . nobility in omitting the "jingle of the guinea".' Nor does it leave any doubt as to how he viewed his own endeavour as anthologist or the pressures applied by the press. 'The publishers [sic] circular is stressing Hopkins because they have a bad poet in the office with a topical mind.'[6]

In Yeats's introduction to the *Oxford Book* Gogarty plays a symbolic role. He is the very opposite of the topical mind. Yeats sees him as the heir of those men on stilts, Lionel Johnson and Ernest Dowson, but without the self-destructive impulses of their 'tragic generation'. 'His poetry', Yeats writes, 'is gay, stoical—no, I will not withhold the word—heroic song.' The seventeen Gogarty poems chosen for the anthology, mostly brief lyrics—none are addresses or mock-heroic narratives—demonstrate again that the Gogarty Yeats admired was the singer, the poet closest to the Renaissance lyrists, or the epigrammatist approaching the lyrical, in the classical tradition of economy and restraint. The effect of Yeats's Introduction and of his selection from Gogarty was the opposite of the one intended, for though it enlarged Gogarty's public, it seemed to suggest that Yeats was exaggerating Gogarty's importance and that of a number of Irish poets at the expense of Eliot, Pound, Owen and other war poets, and the Auden group. In fact, Yeats *was* declaring a personal preference, one in keeping with the commitments of a lifetime.

In the two decades following the publication of Yeats's *Oxford Book*, the reputation of T. S. Eliot grew steadily. Eliot emerged as the commanding figure in Anglo-American literature, and, at the time, schools of literary criticism responsive to his work and that of other 'difficult' modernists rose to a position of dominance among the literary intelligentsia. Our universities became centres where the criticism and writing of poetry was practised and taught, to which poets themselves gravitated, and from which streams of influence began to flow. Educated tastes in poetry came inevitably to be dominated by those qualities most admired in the universities. Though the poetry of Oliver St John Gogarty always has had a small band of admirers, even among those responsive to modernism, it cannot be said that the taste of readers shaped by modernist orthodoxies have been particularly attuned to the 'classicism' of Gogarty. Until approximately a decade ago, when a turning of the tide of Eliot's reputation became detectable, his 'classicism' was, by contrast, almost irresistibly attractive. Now, though it is understood that Eliot's poetry is suffused with classical allusions, the better we get his work in perspective, the less possible it is to accept the once orthodox notion of him as a 'classical' and impersonal artist. Fifteen years ago, when Eliot was still almost as sacrosanct as a cathedral, it would have seemed a public sacrilege to contrast Eliot with Gogarty; now it seems no more than a permissible irreverence to demonstrate essential aspects of the work of each. Probably any modern classicist, including Gogarty, is a Romantic, as he himself knew well; and the chiselled, marmorean lyric is not the only kind of poem that may demonstrate classical influences, as it was not Gogarty's only kind of 'classical' poem. But distinctions can be made as to radically different kinds of poetic expression by pursuing so *outré* a contrast as one between Eliot and Gogarty. Let us first consider Gogarty's 'Portrait', 1928 (later retitled 'I Tremble to Think'), the opening of which is a direct first person utterance: 'I tremble to think that soon / Darkness shall close my sight.' As the lyric continues, clouds come to symbolise not only all the 'Beautiful shadows and forms' of nature that the speaker hopes to preserve but also 'dreams' he has dreamt of a beautiful woman. Ironically, the clouds of natural forms are transient but enduring, while the lady's beauty can only endure if he has time to preserve it:

> But I whom the nets of the years
> Surely at last shall enmesh
> Before I can save in verse
> The timeless traits of the flesh,
> Shall have no peace till the cloud
> Of thought takes definite shape,

And bodies you forth unbowed,
Tall, on a bare landscape,
Where earth the stone upthrusts—
Holding your exquisite frock
Against the morning gusts,
And light is on half the rock.

The image of the woman is realised here by a language that is spare, highly selective, and yet emotionally intense in its implications. It would be impossible to say whether the woman was wife, mother, mistress, daughter, friend, or painting; and about her cling no discernible subjective or private significances. In fact, it matters not at all from what particular circumstances of the poet's life the poem may have emerged; whether real or imagined, the beautiful woman has taken her place in a structure that the poet has—in the best sense—impersonalised and generalised. By contrast—and it must be clear that I am not concerned with aesthetic valuation, which would be preposterous, but with aesthetic distinction—the lady of Eliot's 'Ash Wednesday', 'Who walked between the violet and the violet / Who walked between / The various ranks of varied green / Going in white and blue, in Mary's colour' is at once public and private in what she suggests. Associated with the Virgin and with Beatrice, and thus with God's prevenient grace, she is public and Anglo-Catholic; yet as 'one who moves in the time between sleep and waking, wearing / White light folded, sheathed about her, folded' and in the total context of the poem she is more elusive, more special, and finally private in her implications. The distinction being made is not simply between works of different degrees of complexity—though that *is* one difference—but between works that are different in kind. To put matters in a somewhat different way, the beautiful woman of 'Portrait' regarded in the context of all of Gogarty's poetry may be seen as part of a pattern in the carpet of his *oeuvre*. She is the *anima*; she emerges from deep and personal concerns of the poet, as he himself well knew. 'Women', he wrote in another poem, 'are our sub-conscious selves / Materialisations from our souls' / Regions where fairy queens and elves / Disport beyond Reason's controls.' But, in 'Portrait', Gogarty's lady emerges from the irrational underworld, she is detached from its special circumstances and becomes public. On the other hand, the 'hyacinth girl'

of Eliot's *Waste Land*, 'her arms full, and . . . hair wet,' is part of
the public theme of rebirth rejected but also of private and obsessive concerns of a sexual nature. In the larger context of Eliot's
work, she is related to images in 'Ash Wednesday' ('Blown hair
is sweet . . . Lilac and brown hair') that are transcended by the
Beatrice figure, but also to a persistent concern with the transcend-
ing of desire, to inescapably subjective psychological pressures. In
short, Gogarty's women emerge from the private into the public
realm; Eliot's consistently lead us from the private into the public
and back into the private again. To invoke the dictum of 'Tradition
and the Individual Talent', in Gogarty's poetry 'personality' is
more nearly escaped than in Eliot's; and in him, as a traditional
poet, the man who experiences and enjoys is quite separate from
the mind which creates. Even those lyrics of Gogarty's that deal
with a vision beyond the visual, that spring from unique aspects
of his nature, that, in effect come closest to Romantic subjectivism,
are realised through natural images accessible to any man and
public in their implications.

In his BBC lecture, 'Modern Poetry', Yeats complained of the
generation of English poets that followed Eliot that 'they were
too near their subject matter to do, as I think, work of permanent
importance'. Throughout his career Yeats used the word 'personality' in a special way; indeed, for him the terms personality
and impersonality held perhaps the reverse meaning from that
they held in Eliot's criticism. It is interesting to note that while he
believed that about the time of *The Waste Land* English poetry
'gave way to an impersonal philosophical poetry', he believed that
Irish poets, unable 'to get it out of their heads that they themselves . . . will be remembered by the common people, instead of
turning to impersonal philosophy . . . have hardened and deepened
their personalities'. Following that observation, he began to talk
about the poetry of Senator Gogarty.

Consistently and insistently Yeats argued the superiority of an
art that depended upon popular tradition to the 'very highly
individualised' and urban art of the *avant garde*. (His own record
of a debate on this subject with the young James Joyce is a classic
statement of his attitude.)[7] At the very close of his career, he
insisted that he had always 'hated and still hate with an ever
growing hatred the literature of the point of view,' which he
'compared to the web a spider draws out of its bowels'. Yeats

began the 'General Introduction for My Work' in which he con-
fessed this hatred by asserting that 'A poet writes always of his
personal life. . . ; he never speaks directly as to someone at the
breakfast table, there is always a phantasmagoria.' In regarding
The Waste Land as 'impersonal, philosophical' poetry and the
Cantos of Pound as formless, brilliant improvisation, betokening
a loss of 'self-control', Yeats was anticipating the arguments of
recent critics that despite the apparent importance of *personae* to
these American poets, neither of them effectively moved beyond
the subjective self, beyond, in Yeats's terms, the literature of the
point of view, beyond the web drawn from the spider's bowels.
And in arguing that such poets as Gogarty, Stephens, and Synge
(and, implicitly, he also) had disdained 'impersonal philosophy'
but had 'deepened their personalities', he meant to suggest that
they had moved beyond the subjective self, had tapped the general
imagination of man. 'I wanted . . . to get back to Homer, to those
that fed at his table,' Yeats wrote in his 'General Introduction',
'I wanted to cry as all men cried, to laugh as all men laughed.'[8]
When he observed of Gogarty's poetry that it was 'heroic song',
he was suggesting not only that it seemed to him to differ in mood
and attitude from much contemporary English poetry but that it
had an objective quality, that it had 'personality'—that is, that it
touched the deeps of universal rather than idiosyncratic experience. The extent to which Gogarty and Yeats shared a common
frame of reference is illustrated by Gogarty's words of praise for
Yeats's *A Woman Young and Old* : 'Great stuff and you'll live to
hear it grimly like Dante in the popular mouth.'[9] No prophet
certainly in that observation, Gogarty nevertheless reveals his
understanding of Yeats's belief that poetry should emerge from a
culture rather than from an isolated individual, express something
more universal than the self, and be accessible to a people as well.
Not an admirer of the folk, Gogarty must have seemed to Yeats
to have found in the mask of the Renaissance singer, in the mask
of the Roman Stoic, in Dublin street song and ballad, the means
to deepen his personality.

When the American publicist who originally urged Gogarty to
prepare a memoir wrote to him in 1935, he argued that the book
'should in all ways constitute your *apologia*. And don't be reluctant
to talk about yourself,' he advised. 'What did you think about up
on the Martello Tower?'[10] Since Gogarty was noted as a colourful

character and as a highly individual conversationalist, these suggestions were perhaps inevitable ones. But, of course, not even in his autobiography did Gogarty attempt an *apologia* and the last thing he would have considered doing was to recount what subjective thoughts or feelings came to him while resident in the Martello Tower. Gogarty's best prose works—*Sackville Street, Tumbling in the Hay, I Follow Saint Patrick, Rolling Down the Lea* and *It Isn't This Time of Year at All!*—are ones in which the talkative *persona* is either some dimension of Gogarty or his surrogate, Gideon Ouseley. They are books in which the *persona* is far more interested in others, in scenes and situations, in ideas, books, and poems than in the exploitation of his own ego. It was not the interior of his own psyche that Gogarty sought to depict but the point at which his most significant or amusing perceptions intersected with what he regarded as most vital, telling, ludicrous, or dreadful in experience. Thus it is that *Sackville Street, Tumbling in the Hay,* and *Rolling Down the Lea* are both individual and archetypal and *Saint Patrick* and the autobiography as much cultural as personal in their emphases. In the opening pages of the last of these, Gogarty advises his readers that making himself the hero of a book is 'no congenial task to me'. He then explains how it is that his autobiography tells far more about others than about himself: 'As "I am part of all that I have met" you can judge me on the principle of "show me your company and I'll tell who you are." Show you my company, that I will gladly do; and if I cannot keep myself altogether out of the picture the blame will be on you, for I am satisfied to sit in the proscenium . . . while my company is acting.' Years earlier, in a review of a new biography of Tom Moore, Gogarty drew attention to Moore's love of Ireland and his disdain for Dublin; he judged Moore's dislike of Dublin to have been 'short-sighted and ungrateful' and asked 'What was it gave him his multi-sidedness and power of being all things to all men, but that he met all types in Dublin and sucked in its sympathy with his mother's milk?' To be all things to all men ordinarily has pejorative connotations, but it does not as Gogarty uses it here; it implies no abnegation of the self but rather the capacity to make a universal appeal in particular situations, because the sympathetic wholeness of a culture has become part of one's flesh and bones. This is the capacity Gogarty praises in Moore and Robert Burns, for him two of the greatest singers of song in all of English poetry. 'Who except Burns', he asks us, 'reaches deeper in the general heart of man than Tom Moore?'[11]

Gogarty issued few pronouncements on the subject of poetry and made no boasts about his own. In letters to American friends in 1934 he did, however, make some observations that give us an insight into the quality of 'impersonality' (in Eliot's sense) or deepened 'personality' (in Yeats's sense) in his own work. 'If I could write poetry,' he observed in one letter, 'it would be smooth and dateless so that it might provide a means of escape from petty concerns and transient enthusiasms.'[12] His comment, particularly in the context of the thirties, might be taken as the justification for a trivial escapist art, and there is no question but that his thinking was diametrically opposed to that of such younger poets as Auden and Spender, as to attitudes that have dominated much of modern poetry. Yet the escape Gogarty describes is from the petty and the transient, from the ephemeral catch-cries of the town, from those contemporary distractions he would regard as an evasion of the lasting realities. Several months later, he returned to the issue in another letter. 'Poetry is a way of singing ourselves out of our trivial time with the best that mocks our planning'. And here he is quite explicit about his attitude towards the contemporary scene and its rhetoric, for he advises against 'mixing period with poetry', citing Homer's example in putting his actions 'out of time and memory'.[13] There is no reason at all to think that Gogarty adopted a *persona* in his major prose works or sang impersonally in his poetry because he had adopted a programme that committed him to a certain kind of literary performance. What he did as a maker of fictions and poems was almost surely the product of his own character and impulses and inclinations and of the Dublin atmosphere, as well as of an ideal of an art to which he aspired. He himself did not always escape 'period'. Among the poems he was gathering together for a new volume at the time of his death in 1957 is a ballad-like narrative of six stanzas, 'The Changeling'. Though published in 1954, the poem might have been written at any time from the turn of the century on. But this uncollected poem is an exception among his works in that it is distinctly of the Irish Literary Revival, being based on an Irish folk belief according to which the spirit of a newly born child is carried off by the fairies, who leave behind a withered replacement. An earlier draft of 'The Changeling' has also survived. In reworking the original, Gogarty not only compressed sixty-one lines into twenty-four, but introduced one particularly interesting revision. The original version of the poem was inescapably auto-biographical: it is in the first person, alludes to Gogarty's actual birthplace, and implies the separation of his real spirit from the conventional world. This draft version opened: 'They ought to have guarded my cradle better / In number five Rutland Square East; / In Dublin they thought that it need not be done; / My Father was talking about his prize setter, / My Mother preparing my baptismal feast.' In the final version all the personal elements have disappeared—both the pronoun and the Dublin address—though the particular details of father and mother have been retained. The poem opens: 'All for the want of the crimson berries / Of the mountain ash on his chamber door'. Not a very important poem in itself, 'The Changeling' strikingly demonstrates Gogarty's disposition to objectify his work and to impersonalise subjective concerns.[14]

'Verse', a poem found in *Wild Apples* (1929) expresses both in its matter and its manner many of these essential attitudes of Gogarty. Transparent, spare in language, and rhythmical, the lyric rests on paradox, for it succinctly defines both an occasional and a memorialising role for poetry. The subjects to which it alludes are timeless and universal; but they must be preserved from time, being of it, by poetry:

> What should we know,
> For better or worse,
> Of the Long Ago,
> Were it not for Verse:
> What ships went down;
> What walls were razed;
> Who won the crown;
> What lads were praised?
> A fallen stone,
> Or a waste of sands;
> And all is known
> Of Art-less lands.
> But you need not delve
> By the sea-side hills
> Where the Muse herself

All Time fulfils
Who cuts with his scythe
All things but hers;
All but the blithe
Hexameters.

Lady Gregory wrote to Gogarty that she had copied down those lines when they first appeared and thought them 'almost your most beautiful',[15] and, within their chosen limits, the lines are fine ones. Independent of a particular speaker, they obliquely allude to Housman's 'To an Athlete Dying Young' and to Shelley's 'Ozymandias'. But they are so direct and so simple that they are apt to reach only a reader whose tastes are catholic enough to appreciate the rhythmic technique by which Gogarty varies the beat and the 'weight' of his dimeter lines or to appreciate the triumph of 'blithe' followed by the isolated 'hexameters' in a context where every other word is toned down to prepare for them. In Gogarty's association of mirth and gaiety with the epic hexameter one can discern the grounds for Yeats's admiration for him as one of the 'swift indifferent men' and for the epithet with which he characterised him : 'gay adventurer'.

It may be that the Oxford University Press now has made amends for Yeats's anthology and for all of its shocking aspects, including the space given to Gogarty. In 1973 it issued Philip Larkin's *Oxford Book of Twentieth Century English Verse*. Larkin, a poet of distinctive gifts but nothing like the commanding figure Yeats was when he edited the *Oxford Book*, has righted all of Yeats's wrongs to Owen, Auden, and Eliot. He has dismissed one of Yeats's enthusiasms, W. J. Turner, altogether and reduced another, Dorothy Wellesley, to a single selection. He has written the tersest and most non-committal of prefatory statements, little more than a page. Possibly in an effort to avoid being charged with favouritism, as Yeats was, he has opted for inclusiveness. He has drastically reduced the selections from Yeats's Dublin friends, putting those Irishmen in their place. Oliver St John Gogarty is represented by two poems, well-chosen ones certainly. Thus he is better off than flocks of obscure English poets who are represented by a single poem. He is on the same level as Sir John Squire, Gerald Gould, Richard Church, Stella Benson, Colin Ellis, Michael Roberts, and many others, including certain Irishmen whose names somehow have a more familiar ring—J. M. Synge, James Joyce, and Austin Clarke. He is thus not so well treated as John Meade Falkner, Charlotte Mew, Andrew Young, Francis Cornford, Ruth Pitter, Basil Bunting and others rather more celebrated who are represented by three or more poems. I should mention that I have cited only figures from the earlier part of Larkin's anthology, those roughly contemporaneous with Yeats and Gogarty, but that I cannot help but begin to wonder if Larkin's inclusiveness is to be preferred to Yeats's selectiveness and exclusiveness.

One distinct superiority of Yeats's anthology to Larkin's is that though Yeats's Introduction is an argument for a particular critical view of the development of modern English poetry up to 1935, it is nevertheless *a* perspective on poetic changes and developments. In his exiguous prefatory remarks, Larkin entirely avoids perspective. On the other hand, he seems to reflect a contemporary censensus view of the major poets of the century, excepting that Hardy is given more prominence than Yeats. Once past those figures, he is indisposed to leave anyone out, and yet, on the basis of the number of poems he selects, he does make judgments. In the particular case of Gogarty, who is not represented at all in the most recent and crowded of American anthologies of modern British and American poetry, Larkin at least has been able to indicate that if not so substantial a figure as John Meade Falkner or Charlotte Mew, Gogarty is at least as significant as Sir John Squire.

Crudely interpreted, Yeats claimed a place for Gogarty among the major poets of the first part of the century. Understood, he sought to bring Gogarty's work to the attention of a larger audience and claimed a place for Gogarty's poetry 'among the greatest lyric poetry of our time'.[16] It may be that Yeats's definition of the lyrical—which led him to deny the applicability of the term to Eliot—was too special to be acceptable; and it may be argued also that the connotations of his words of praise for his friend were excessively honorific. But the context in which Oliver Gogarty is found in Larkin's anthology is surely not the place for him. In the whole body of Gogarty's poetry, published and unpublished, there are perhaps a hundred poems by which he will live. Of these, at the very least, some two dozen shorter lyrics and a dozen longer poems are exceptional enough to hold their own in the diverse body of modern poetry. Uneven at times and sometimes careless,

as Yeats noted, Gogarty could also carry off whole poems flaw-
lessly and achieve effects of unequalled lightness, delicacy, and
wit. Never departing from conventional forms, rhythms, and
rhymes, Gogarty was indifferent to the romantic impulse constantly
to devise new modes of expression, to re-invent, as it were, poetic
language and forms. So to the *avant-garde*, whether real or
imagined, he is not apt to appeal. Moreover, one of the ironies of
his poetic and his practice (as of Yeats's) was that he wrote a
poetry that will never have a wide popular appeal. But just as, over
the decades, readers have turned from, say, Donne to Herrick or
from Wordsworth to Landor to find pleasure in a very different
kind and intensity of expression, one can hazard the opinion that,
in the future, readers will turn from Yeats to Gogarty and understand what Yeats found to admire in him—and other pleasures
too in poems Yeats did not quote or anthologise.

Horace Reynolds's early prophecy of the difficulty 'all the
publicity about stately plump Dr Gogarty' would create for those
seeking to characterise Oliver Gogarty has proven only too true.[17]
Decades later, regrettably, it is possible to see that the spectre of
Buck Mulligan and the myth of Gogarty-the-personality have also
stood in the way of any proper understanding of Gogarty the
writer. One still encounters innumerable members of the intelligentsia who find it possible to have an opinion of Gogarty's
talent without ever having looked into what is going on in either
his poems or his prose works. After all, did not Gogarty describe
Joyce as a schizophrenic? Was he not anti-Semitic? Did he not
have a vicious tongue? Was he not a snob? Did he not castigate
de Valera in the Senate? Was he not rude to people who bored
him? Was he *serious* enough to be taken seriously? In these pages
I have sought to move beyond these tiresome stock responses, to
examine the works Gogarty left behind him and the development
of his talent, to engage only those issues the works seemed to me
to present. In fact, in emphasising the works rather than the life
of the writer, I have not been able to forget some words in a note
Oliver Gogarty wrote to a reviewer of a volume of his poetry:
'I am very grateful to you. You wrote about my poetry and not
about my Mercedes.'[18]

Considered from a historical point of view, two of Gogarty's
works, the play *Blight* and the memoir *Sackville Street*, must
survive as documents, for the first played a role in the develop-

ment of the Abbey Theatre, the second records first-hand impressions of a great cultural epoch in Irish history. But if my efforts to explore the interior of Gogarty's works have been in any way successful they should have demonstrated that, like the best of the poetry, *Sackville Street* is something considerably more than a piece of historical source material, that both it and *Tumbling in the Hay* are among the most impressive books to have been inspired by the Irish Literary Renaissance. Copious, highly individual as literary forms though belonging to a unique tradition of the fictive, thematically and imaginatively complex, these two works in themselves, had not Gogarty also been a poet or produced three lesser but also memorable prose works—*I Follow Saint Patrick, Rolling Down the Lea*, and *It Isn't This Time of Year at All!*—would ensure him his proper place in the history of modern Irish literature and modern literature in English. No doubt that was a condition to which he aspired from early manhood on, chafing against the demands and restrictions of convention, profession, and modern civilisation. But there was another hope he had for what he produced, and for that we can be grateful. 'I cannot deceive myself,' he said in light-hearted disparagement of one of his books, 'but when it comes to anything that hearkens back to "All the charm of all the Muses", then I let myself regard my book, as Falstaff did himself—"a source of wit in others." '[19]

Notes

Introduction
(pp. 1–21)

1. Robert Scholes and Richard M. Kane, *The Workshop of Dedalus: James Joyce and the Materials for 'A Portrait of the Artist as a Young Man'* (Evanston: Northwestern Univ. Press 1965), 98.
2. Seumas O'Sullivan, untitled manuscript, 34 lines of verse, fol. 1–2, Gogarty Collection, Bertrand Library, Bucknell University. See also the revised version of these lines, Part II, 'Letters to a Poet Friend' in *Retrospect: The Work of Seumas O'Sullivan, 1879–1958, and Estella F. Solomons, 1882–1968* (Dublin: Dolmen Press 1973), 78.
3. Lord Dunsany, *My Ireland* (London: Jarrolds 1937), 41.
4. Mark Amory, *Biography of Lord Dunsany* (London: Collins 1972), 194.
5. Sir William Rothenstein, *Since Fifty* (London: Faber & Faber 1939), 260.
6. Hilary Pyle, *James Stephens, His Work and An Account of His Life* (London: Routledge & Kegan Paul 1965), 145.
7. Darcy O'Brien, *W. R. Rodgers* (Lewisburg, Penna.: Bucknell Univ. Press 1970), 86ff.
8. Lennox Robinson, ed., *Lady Gregory's Journals, 1916–1930* (New York: Macmillan 1947), 49.
9. W. B. Yeats, *Letters*, ed. Allan Wade (New York: Macmillan 1955), 627.
10. W. B. Yeats, *Letters on Poetry from W. B. Yeats to Dorothy Wellesley*, ed. Dorothy Wellesley (London: Oxford Univ. Press 1964), 117, 137.
11. James Joyce, *Ulysses* (New York: Random House 1961), 17.
12. Oliver St John Gogarty, *Many Lines to Thee: Letters to G. K. A. Bell from the Martello Tower at Sandycove, Rutland Square and Trinity College Dublin 1904–07* (Dublin: Dolmen Press 1971), 94–5.
13. Ulick O'Connor, *Oliver St John Gogarty: A Poet and His Times* (London: Jonathan Cape 1964), 1ff.

14. *Many Lines to Thee*, 148.
15. *Ibid.*, 149.
16. Oliver Gogarty, 'A Word on Criticism and "Broken Soil"'. *The United Irishman*, 19 Dec. 1903, 6.
17. *Many Lines to Thee*, 18.
18. Stanislaus Joyce, *My Brother's Keeper: James Joyce's Early Years* (New York: Viking Press 1958), 245.
19. Augustus John, *Chiaroscuro: Fragments of Autobiography* (London: Jonathan Cape 1952), 96.
20. Horace Reynolds, typescript note on Oliver St John Gogarty, Oct. 1941, Papers of Horace Reynolds, Houghton Library, Harvard University, 65m–211 (595).
21. W. R. Rodgers, 'Oliver St John Gogarty', in *Irish Literary Portraits* (London: British Broadcasting Corporation 1972), 149.
22. This anecdote was related to me by James A. Healy, the late New York financier and bibliophile.
23. Oliver St John Gogarty, Letter to Mary Owings Miller, 18 Nov. 1941, Gogarty Collection.
24. Oliver St John Gogarty, Letter to Mary Owings Miller, 9 July 1954, Gogarty Collection.
25. George Moore, *Salve*, Vol. II of *Hail and Farewell* (London: Heinemann 1947), 133.
26. Oliver St John Gogarty, unpaginated manuscript notebook, n.d., Gogarty Collection.
27. W. B. Yeats, 'High Talk', from the *Collected Poems of W. B. Yeats*; reprinted with permission of the Macmillan Co. of London and Basingstoke, and The Macmillan Publishing Co. Inc. of New York. Copyright 1940 by Georgie Yeats, renewed 1968 by Bertha Georgie Yeats, Michael Butler Yeats and Anne Yeats.
28. O'Connor, *Gogarty*, pp. 194–7, 219–21.
29. William Dawson, 'Ballad of Oliver Gogarty', typescript, Gogarty Collection.
30. Richard Ellmann, *James Joyce* (New York: Oxford Univ. Press 1959), 212ff.
31. Horace Reynolds, typescript notes on Gogarty talk and lecture, 13 March 1933, Papers of Horace Reynolds.
32. Richard Ellmann, 'What'll We Make of You, Bucko?' *New York Herald Tribune Book Week*, 12 Apr. 1964, 5–6.
33. Oliver St John Gogarty, *Plays* (Newark, Del.: Proscenium Press 1972), 54–5.
34. Ellmann, 'Bucko', *Ibid.*
35. O'Connor, *Gogarty*, 281ff.
36. According to a letter from Gogarty to William York Tindall (8

Jan. 1953, Gogarty Collection), the maternal grandfather of Joyce's grandson threatened to sue Gogarty, columnist Sterling North, and the New York *World-Telegram.* A Sterling North column, 'Joyce, Pound and Insanity', *World Telegram,* 13 Jan. 1950, 30, quoted Gogarty on Joyce and, in the same context, made an erroneous statement, neither attributed nor attributable to Gogarty.

37. Conor Cruise O'Brien, Introduction to *Irish Literary Portraits,* viii.
38. Frank O'Connor, *My Father's Son,* (New York: Knopf 1969), 110–11.
39. Gogarty employed this cognomen for Mrs Collum extensively in correspondence with his friends.
40. Oliver St John Gogarty, Letter to William York Tindall, 8 Jan. 1953, Gogarty Collection.
41. Oliver St John Gogarty, Letter to Leonie, Lady Leslie, 28 Aug. 1927, Gogarty Collection.
42. O'Connor, *Gogarty,* 247.
43. Rodgers, *Literary Portraits,* 152.
44. Ellmann, 'Bucko', *ibid.*
45. J. M. N. Jeffries, Letter to Oliver St John Gogarty, 28 Aug. 1922, Gogarty Collection.
46. William Cosgrave, Letter to Oliver St John Gogarty, 12 Oct. 1922, Gogarty Collection.
47. Oliver St John Gogarty, Letter to Shane Leslie, n.d. [1922], Gogarty Collection. This letter, incomplete, has been pasted into Shane Leslie's copy of *Wild Apples* (1930).
48. Oliver St John Gogarty, Letter to Theodore Spicer-Simson, 31 Aug. 1922, Spicer-Simson Collection, Univ. of Miami Library.
49. *Irish Literary Portraits,* 153.
50. Oliver St John Gogarty, undated fragmentary Letter to Shane Leslie, Gogarty Collection, pasted into *Wild Apples* (1930).
51. *Irish Literary Portraits,* 154.
52. *Ibid.*
53. Ellmann, *James Joyce,* 390.
54. Hélène Cixous, *L'exil de James Joyce* (Paris: B. Grasset 1968) 280.
55. Hélène Cixous, *The Exile of James Joyce,* trans. Sally A. J. Purcell (New York: D. Lewis 1977), 224.
56. C. E. F. Trench, 'Dermot Chenevix Trench and Haines of Ulysses', *James Joyce Quarterly,* 13, No. 1 (1975), 42–3.
57. *Ibid.,* 42.
58. Oliver St John Gogarty, 'James Joyce: A Portrait of the Artist', *Mourning Becomes Mrs Spendlove and Other Portraits, Grave and Gay* (New York: Creative Age 1948), 57.

59. Oliver St John Gogarty, *It Isn't This Time of Year at All!* (London: Macgibbon & Kee, 1954), 72ff.
60. Trench, 46f.
61. Pamela (P. L.) Travers, letter to Oliver St John Gogarty, n.d., Papers of Horace Reynolds.
62. Robert Boyle, S. J., Review of *James Joyce: The Critical Heritage*, ed. Robert H. Deming, *James Joyce Quarterly*, 8, No. 3 (1971), 271.
63. Sean O'Faolain, *Vive Moi!* (Boston: Little Brown 1964), 353f.

Chapter One
(pp. 22–39)

1. Oliver St John Gogarty, 'To Stella,' *Dana* 5 (Sept. 1904), 144.
2. Oliver St John Gogarty, Review of *New Songs: A Lyric Selection made by A. E. from Poems by Padraic Colum et. al.*, *Dana* 1 (May 1904), 32.
3. Oliver St John Gogarty, 'Two Songs', in *The Venture*, ed. Laurence Housman and W. Somerset Maugham (London: John Baillie, n.d. [1904]), 38.
4. O'Connor, *Gogarty*, 64, 79.
5. Oliver St John Gogarty, 'Song', 'On The Death of a Favourite Race Horse', *Ireland*, Sept. 1904, 303, 311. Two other poems in this issue, 'The Horse Show', p. 280, and 'Welcome to the Fleet', p. 283, may have been Gogarty's.
6. Oliver St John Gogarty, Letter to Mary Owings Miller, 18 Feb. 1944, Gogarty Collection.
7. Oliver St John Gogarty, 'The Death of Diogenes, The Doctor's Dog', *T.C.D.: A College Miscellany*, 14 Feb. 1903, 16–17. This poem also appeared in the *United Irishman*, 24 Dec. 1904.
8. Oliver St John Gogarty, 'On First Looking into Kraft-Ebbing's *Psychopathia Sexualis*', in *The Merry Muses of Hibernia*, master-copy typescript, 10, Papers of Horace Reynolds.
9. Oliver St John Gogarty, *It Isn't This Time of Year at All!* (London: Macgibbon & Kee 1954), 63.
10. See Stanislaus Joyce, *My Brother's Keeper*, reprinted by permission of Faber and Faber Ltd, London, and Viking Press, New York.
11. Oliver St John Gogarty, Letter to Horace Reynolds, 20 Sept. 1952, Papers of Horace Reynolds.
12. *Merry Muses of Hibernia*, 9, Papers of Horace Reynolds.
13. Oliver St John Gogarty, Letter to Horace Reynolds, 8 Aug. 1952, Papers of Horace Reynolds.
14. Oliver St John Gogarty, *Tumbling in the Hay* (London: Constable, 1939), 230.

15. Oliver St John Gogarty, Letter to Horace Reynolds, 12 Nov. 1953, Papers of Horace Reynolds.
16. Oliver St John Gogarty, Letter to Horace Reynolds, 19 Nov. 1953, Papers of Horace Reynolds.
17. Gogarty, 'A Word on "Broken Soil" ', *ibid.*
18. Ellmann, *Joyce*, 213–14.
19. See Gogarty, Letter to Horace Reynolds, 6 Sept. 1934, Papers of Horace Reynolds.
20. A typescript of 'The Hay Hotel' in the James A. Healy Collection, Colby College Library, contains the envoi and the additional two stanzas, one bearing the designation 'Apocrypha'. The version found in 'Merry Muses of Hibernia', pp. 6–7, Papers of Horace Reynolds, contains none of these three additional verses.
21. Letter to Horace Reynolds, 24 Nov. 1943.
22. *Merry Muses of Hibernia*, 4, Papers of Horace Reynolds.
23. Oliver St John Gogarty, Letter to Horace Reynolds, 24 Nov. 1953, Papers of Horace Reynolds.
24. *Many Lines to Thee*, 56.
25. *Ibid.*, 135.
26. Oliver St John Gogarty, Letter to Seumas O'Sullivan (James Starkey) 27 Dec. 1907, Humanities Research Center, University of Texas.
27. Oliver St John Gogarty, Letter to Dermot Freyer, 29 June 1917, privately owned.
28. L. A. G. Strong, Letter to Oliver Gogarty, 6 May 1928, Gogarty Collection.
29. This poem has been ascribed to Seumas O'Sullivan and Gogarty by Alan Denson, on the basis of information provided by St John Irvine, in *Printed Writings of George W. Russell (AE): A Bibliography* (London : Northwestern University Press 1961), 113. But Gogarty's own copy of *Secret Springs of Dublin Song*, Gogarty Collection, ascribes the poem to Gogarty alone.

Chapter Two
(pp. 40–49)
1. Oliver Gogarty, 'The Irish Literary Revival: Present Poetry and Drama in Dublin,' *Dublin Evening Mail*, 4 Mar. 1905, 2.
2. Oliver St John Gogarty, letter to Ernest Boyd, 14 Feb. 1924, Healy Collection of Irish Literature, Special Collections, Stanford University Libraries.
3. Joseph Holloway, 'Impressions of a Dublin Playgoer', MS., National Library of Ireland.
4. Joyce, *Ulysses*, 14.

5. O'Connor, *Gogarty*, 150.
6. Oliver St John Gogarty, Letter to Seumas O'Sullivan (James Starkey), 15 Oct. 1913, O'Sullivan Collection, National Library of Ireland.
7. Joseph Holloway, 'Impressions of a Dublin Playgoer', MS., National Library of Ireland.
8. Andrew Malone, *The Irish Drama* (London: Constable 1929), 266.
9. Lady Gregory, Letter to Oliver Gogarty, 13 Nov. 1917, Gogarty Collection.
10. Lady Gregory, Letter to Oliver Gogarty, 22 Nov. 1917, Gregory Archives, Berg Collection, New York Public Library.
11. W. B. Yeats, *Letters* (New York: Macmillan 1955), ed. Allan Wade, 635.
12. Malone, *ibid.*
13. Oliver St John Gogarty, Letter to Horace Reynolds, 11 Mar. 1949, Papers of Horace Reynolds.
14. Malone, *ibid.* See also my Introduction to *The Plays of Oliver St John Gogarty* (Newark, Del.: Proscenium 1972), 11.
15. See Michael Hewson, 'Gogarty's Authorship of *Blight*', *Irish Book*, I (1959), 19–20.
16. Oliver St John Gogarty, Letter to Horace Reynolds, 9 Feb. 1956, Papers of Horace Reynolds.
17. In his 'Impressions of a Dublin Playgoer', Joseph Holloway incorporated the 20 Aug. reviews of the *Freeman* and other Dublin newspapers, following the 19 Aug. opening of *A Serious Thing*.
18. Holloway, 'Impressions'.
19. Holloway recorded his comments following the 25 Nov. opening. Lady Gregory's suggested revisions are found in her letter to Gogarty, 15 Oct. 1919, Gogarty Collection.
20. Gregory Letter, 15 Oct. 1919. Holloway incorporated the *Freeman* review of 26 Nov. in his diary.
21. Oliver St John Gogarty, Letter to Horace Reynolds, 12 Apr. 1951, Papers of Horace Reynolds.
22. 'Caerleon', typescript, Gogarty Collection.
23. Oliver St John Gogarty, Introduction to revised version of 'Wave Lengths', typescript, Gogarty Collection.
24. Oliver St John Gogarty, Letter to Seumas O'Sullivan, n.d. [*c.* 1923], Humanities Research Center.

Chapter Three
(pp. 50–67)
1. Oliver St John Gogarty, Letter to Lady Leslie, 29 Mar. 1923, Humanities Research Center.

2. Oliver St John Gogarty, Letter to Theodore Spicer-Simson, 19 May 1923, Spicer-Simson Collection.

3. Oliver St John Gogarty, Letter to Shane Leslie, 13 Oct. 1931, Gogarty Collection.

4. Oliver St John Gogarty, Letter to Judge Richard Campbell, 10 Oct. 1931, Healy Collection, Stanford.

5. *Many Lines to Thee*, 93.

6. Oliver St John Gogarty, 'Hear the Voice', typescript, J. S. Starkey Papers, National Library of Ireland, ns. 15, 572, fol. 10ff.

7. *Ibid.*, fol. 6.

8. For an early response to the dramatic revival, see Gogarty 'The Irish Literary Revival', *ibid.* See also *Many Lines to Thee*, 134–5.

9. Gogarty, Review of *New Songs, ibid.*

10. Alun R. Jones, *The Life and Opinions of T. E. Hulme* (Boston : Beacon Press), 30–3.

11. Oliver St John Gogarty, Letter to Dermot Freyer, 16 Dec. 1910, privately owned.

12. Oliver St John Gogarty, Letter to Horace Reynolds, 9 Nov. 1934, Papers of Horace Reynolds.

13. *Many Lines to Thee*, 87ff.

14. Oliver St John Gogarty, 'To George Redding', *The Irish Statesman* 2 July 1927, 398.

15. George Redding, 'To Oliver Gogarty', 23 July 1927, 469. 'A.B.' responded to both 6 Aug. 1927, 516.

16. Oliver St John Gogarty, *Start from Somewhere Else* (Garden City : Doubleday), 90.

17. W. B. Yeats, Preface to *Wild Apples* (Dublin : Cuala Press 1930).

18. Oliver D. Gogarty, 'My Brother Willie Was Your Father's Friend', *Bibliotheca Bucknellensis*, VII (1969), 13.

19. William Butler Yeats, Preface to *An Offering of Swans* (Dublin : Cuala Press 1923).

20. I am indebted to Oliver D. Gogarty for this information. Some clippings from the medical pad were preserved and may be found in the Gogarty Collection. See also Oliver St John Gogarty, *William Butler Yeats: A Memoir* (Dublin : Dolmen Press 1963), 24–5; James F. Carens, 'Gogarty and Yeats' in *Modern Irish Literature*, ed. R. J. Porter and J. D. Brophy (New York : Iona-Twayne 1972), 82ff.

21. *Many Lines to Thee*, 69–70.

22. Yeats, Preface to *Offering of Swans*.

23. *Ibid.*

24. T. R. Henn, 'The Rhetoric of Yeats' in *In Excited Reverie: A*

Centenary Tribute to William Butler Yeats, ed. Norman Jeffares and K. G. W. Cross (New York: Macmillan 1965), 116.

25. Oliver St John Gogarty, 'Literature and Life Style', *The Irish States-man*, 8 Mar. 1924, 814–15.
26. Oliver St John Gogarty, 'Poets and Little Children' in *Intimations* (New York: Abelard 1950), 147.
27. See Carens, 'Gogarty and Yeats', *ibid.*
28. Yeats, Preface to *Wild Apples*.
29. Carens, 'Gogarty and Yeats', *ibid.*
30. Georgio Melchiori, *The Whole Mystery of Art: Pattern into Poetry in the Work of W. B. Yeats* (New York: Macmillan 1961), 92–8.

Chapter Four
(pp. 68–87)

1. AE, Letter to Oliver St John Gogarty, n.d., Papers of Horace Reynolds.
2. Edward O'Shea, *Yeats as Editor* (Dublin: Dolmen Press 1975), 6.
3. See, for instance, his letter to Lady Leslie, 6 Jan. 1922, Humanities Research Center.
4. William Butler Yeats, Letter to Oliver St John Gogarty, 6 Jan. 1928, Gogarty Collection. Oxford University Press will shortly publish the *Collected Letters of W. B. Yeats*, edited by John Kelly.
5. William Butler Yeats, Letter to Oliver St John Gogarty, 5 May 1929, Gogarty Collection.
6. William Butler Yeats, Letter to Oliver St John Gogarty, 25 Oct. 1929, Gogarty Collection.
7. William Butler Yeats, Letter to Oliver St John Gogarty, 20 Feb. 1930, Gogarty Collection.
8. Yeats, Preface to *Wild Apples* (1930).
9. O'Connor, *My Father's Son*, 118.
10. Oliver St John Gogarty, Letter to Christopher Stone, n.d. [1923? 1928?] Humanities Research Center.
11. Oliver St John Gogarty, Letter to Ernest Boyd, 15 June 1923, Healy Collection, Stanford.
12. Oliver St John Gogarty, Letter to Shane Leslie, 19 March 1931, Gogarty Collection. Oliver St John Gogarty, Letter to Sir Edward Howard Marsh, 8 July 1930, Berg Collection, New York Public Library.
13. See William Butler Yeats, Letter to Oliver St John Gogarty, 24 Oct. 1935; Oliver St John Gogarty, Epilogue to Scharmel Iris, *Bread Out of Stone*, Preface by W. B. Yeats (Chicago: Regnery n.d.), 60.
14. David Clark, *Lyric Resonance: Glosses on some Poems of Yeats*,

I

Frost, Crane, Cummings and Others (Amherst: University of Mass. Press 1972), 69ff.
15. Yeats, Preface to *Wild Apples* (1930).
16. *Ibid.*
17. *Many Lines to Thee*, 93–5.
18. Melchiori, 3ff.
19. Oliver St John Gogarty, typescript with holograph revisions by W. B. Yeats and Gogarty, Lockwood Memorial Library, State University of New York at Buffalo. On the other hand a typescript of 'Farewell to the Princess', in the same collection, reveals that Gogarty accepted Yeats's cancellation of eight lines of his original, his revision of three lines, and substitutions for two more.
20. AE, Preface to *The Collected Poems of Oliver St John Gogarty* (New York: Devin-Adair 1954), xi–xii.

Chapter Five
(pp. 88–98)
1. James Stephens, Letter to Oliver St John Gogarty, 25 Dec. 1936, Gogarty Collection.
2. *Many Lines to Thee*, 142–3.
3. Frank O'Connor, 'The Old Woman of Beare' in *Kings, Lords, and Commons: An Anthology from The Irish* (London: Macmillan 1962), 34.
4. Oliver St John Gogarty, Letter to Judge Richard Campbell, 29 Jan. 1934, Healy Collection, Stanford.

Chapter Six
(pp. 99–109)
1. William Butler Yeats, 'The Statues', *Collected Poems* (New York: Macmillan 1956), 322–3.
2. Oliver St John Gogarty, Letter to Judge Richard Campbell, 14 May 1934, Healy Collection, Stanford.
3. O'Connor, *Gogarty*, 274.
4. *Ibid.*, 129.

Chapter Seven
(pp. 110–135)
1. Dale Warren, Letter to Oliver St John Gogarty, 27 June 1935, Gogarty Collection.
2. Dale Warren, Letter to Oliver St John Gogarty, 30 Sept. 1935, Gogarty Collection.
3. Yeats, *Letters on Poetry*, 137.

4. Timothy Patrick Coogan, *Ireland Since the Rising*, (London: Pall Mall Press 1966), 70.
5. *Ibid.*, 71ff.
6. Oliver St John Gogarty, Letter to Judge Richard Campbell, 14 Jan. 1932, Healy Collection, Stanford.
7. O'Connor, *Gogarty*, 247.
8. See: *Official Report Seanad Eireann* (Dublin: Thom & Co. n.d.), Vol. XV, 909ff.
9. *Official Report*, Vol. XII, 256.
10. *Official Report*, Vol. XIX, 1253.
11. Oliver St John Gogarty, Letter to James Joyce, n.d. [1902–4], Joyce Collection, Cornell University Library, #523. See Robert E. Scholes, *The Cornell Joyce Collection* (Ithaca: Cornell Univ. Press 1961), 88.
12. Oliver St John Gogarty, Letter to Lady Leslie, 23 Oct. 1918 [12 Oct. 1923?], Humanities Research Center.
13. Oliver St John Gogarty, Letter to William Butler Yeats, 13 Oct. 1929, Yeats Estate.
14. O'Connor, *Gogarty*, 97.
15. Oliver St John Gogarty, 'The Quest', holograph fragment, Notebook, Gogarty Collection.
16. Oliver St John Gogarty, Letter to Horace Reynolds, 21 Nov. 1936, Papers of Horace Reynolds.
17. Oliver St John Gogarty, Letter to Horace Reynolds, 14 Nov. 1936, Papers of Horace Reynolds.
18. *Ibid.*
19. Oliver St John Gogarty, Letter to Horace Reynolds, 22 Mar. 1937, Papers of Horace Reynolds.
20. *Ibid.* See also Oliver St John Gogarty, 'My Favorite Forgotten Book', *Tomorrow* (May 1946), 78.
21. Oliver St John Gogarty, Letter to Horace Reynolds, 4 Oct. 1936, Papers of Horace Reynolds.
22. 'Sinclair V. Gogarty: Brief . . . on Behalf of Defendant Oliver St John Gogarty', typescript, Gogarty Collection.
23. *Ibid.* The testimony of the poet F. R. Higgins was firm on this point and unshaken by the cross examination.
24. O'Connor, *Gogarty*, 226.
25. Joyce, *Letters*, II, 244.
26. Joyce, *Ulysses*, 183.
27. As early as 1899, Griffith's *United Irishman*, precursor to his *Sinn Fein* and naturally sympathetic to the Boers in their conflict with England, attacked Jewish interests in England as hostile to the Boer cause.

28. Philip Thody, *Aldous Huxley: A Biographical Introduction* (New York: Scribners 1973), 79.
29. For Gogarty's version of 'Sackville Street' see *The Merry Muses of Hibernia*, p. 1, Papers of Horace Reynolds.

Chapter Eight
(pp. 136–144)
1. A. K., Review of *I Follow Saint Patrick, The Dublin Magazine*, 13, No. 4 (1938), 74–5.
2. O'Connor, *Gogarty*, 287.
3. *Many Lines to Thee*, 92.

Chapter Nine
(pp. 145–163)
1. Ben Lucien Burman, 'Portrait of a Friend From Ireland' in Oliver St John Gogarty, *A Week End in the Middle of The Week and Other Essays on the Bias* (Garden City: Doubleday 1958), 15.
2. O'Connor, *Gogarty*, 53.
3. *It Isn't This Time of Year at All!* 79.
4. O'Connor, *Gogarty*, 115.

Chapter Ten
(pp. 164–181)
1. Oliver St John Gogarty, Letter to Mary Owings Miller, 18 Feb. 1945, Gogarty Collection.
2. Oliver St John Gogarty, Letter to Judge Richard Campbell, 23 July 1930, Healy Collection, Stanford.
3. Oliver St John Gogarty, Letter to Horace Reynolds, 28 Jan. 1941, Papers of Horace Reynolds.
4. Oliver St John Gogarty, Letter to Horace Reynolds, 5 Aug. 1941, Papers of Horace Reynolds.
5. I am indebted to Oliver D. Gogarty for this information.

Chapter Eleven
(pp. 182–195)
1. For one of Flann O'Brien's liveliest comments on de Valera, see his letter to Timothy O'Keefe, 16 Mar. 1965, Morris Library, University of Southern Illinois, Carbondale.
2. *Official Report Seanad Eireann*, Vol. XII, 297, 541.
3. The author's typescript of 'Once Only' is in the Gogarty Collection; the piece appeared in *The Atlantic Monthly*, Oct. 1948.

Chapter Twelve
(pp. 196–211)

1. Oliver St John Gogarty, Letter to Horace Reynolds, 22 Feb. 1939, Papers of Horace Reynolds.
2. Oliver D. Gogarty has described to me how often his father expressed gratefulness for the freedom of expression he found in the United States.
3. Oliver St John Gogarty, Letters to James A. Healy, 3 May 1944, 10 May 1944, 22 May 1944, Healy Collection, Stanford.
4. Oliver St John Gogarty, Letter to James A. Healy, 26 June 1944, Healy Collection, Stanford.
5. Oliver St John Gogarty, Letter to Mary Owings Miller, 11 June 1942, Gogarty Collection.
6. Oliver St John Gogarty, Letter to Horace Reynolds, 11 Mar. 1948, Papers of Horace Reynolds.
7. AE, 'Literature and Life: The Poems of Oliver Gogarty', *The Irish Statesman*, 14 Dec. 1929, 299–300.
8. Oliver St John Gogarty, Letters to Mary Owings Miller, 8 Feb. 1944, 20 Feb. 1944, 16 Aug. 1942, Gogarty Collection.
9. Oliver St John Gogarty, Letter to Horace Reynolds, 30 July 1940, Papers of Horace Reynolds.
10. Oliver St John Gogarty, Letter to Horace Reynolds, 28 Aug. 1941, Papers of Horace Reynolds.
11. Oliver St John Gogarty, Letter to Mary Owings Miller, 5 Sept. 1941, Gogarty Collection.
12. 'Yeats—by Gogarty', clipping from the London *Evening Standard*, 30 January 1939, enclosed in Letter to Horace Reynolds, 22 Feb. 1939, Papers of Horace Reynolds.
13. *Irish Literary Portraits*, 164. Oliver D. Gogarty has pointed out an error in this text: Richard Aherne, an actor and a friend of the Gogarty family, is confused with the Hollywood actor Brian Aherne.
14. Gogarty's two-page typescript schema, with holograph revisions, is in the Gogarty Collection.
15. Holograph notebook, *c.* 1903–1907, Gogarty Collection.

Chapter Thirteen
(pp. 212–225)

1. Oliver St John Gogarty, Letter to Mary Owings Miller, 22 July 1946, Gogarty Collection.
2. Oliver St John Gogarty, Letter to Mary Owings Miller, 15 Jan. 1954, Gogarty Collection.

Conclusion
(pp. 226–239)
1. O'Shea, *Yeats as Editor*, 67.
2. Oliver St John Gogarty, Letter to Horace Reynolds, 14 Nov. 1936, Papers of Horace Reynolds.
3. Jon Stallworthy, 'Yeats as Anthologist' in *In Excited Reverie*, 171–3.
4. Oliver St John Gogarty, Letter to Horace Reynolds, 23 Nov. 1936, Papers of Horace Reynolds.
5. William Butler Yeats, Letter to Oliver St John Gogarty, n.d. [Oct. 1935], Gogarty Collection.
6. William Butler Yeats, Letter to Oliver St John Gogarty, 24 Oct. 1935, Gogarty Collection.
7. Ellmann, *James Joyce*, 105–8.
8. William Butler Yeats, 'A General Introduction for My Work', *Essays and Introductions* (London: Macmillan 1961), 511.
9. Oliver St John Gogarty, Letter to William Butler Yeats, 17 June 1930, Yeats Estate.
10. Dale Warren, Letter to Oliver St John Gogarty, 27 June 1935, Gogarty Collection.
11. Oliver St John Gogarty, 'Tom Moore: A Master of Simile', Books of the Day, *The Observer*, 15 Aug. 1937, 4.
12. Oliver St John Gogarty, Letter to Judge Richard Campbell, 5 Apr. 1934, Healy Collection, Stanford.
13. Oliver St John Gogarty, Letter to Horace Reynolds, 9 Nov. 1934, Papers of Horace Reynolds.
14. Oliver St John Gogarty, 'The Changeling', author's typescript, 2 fol., Gogarty Collection.
15. Lady Gregory, Letter to Oliver St John Gogarty, 15 Apr. 1929, Gogarty Collection.
16. Yeats, Preface, *Oxford Book*, xv.
17. Horace Reynolds, Notes on Gogarty, 13 Mar. 1933, Papers of Horace Reynolds.
18. Oliver St John Gogarty, Letter to Louis LeGrand, 18 Dec. 1933, Healy Collection, Stanford.
19. *Ibid.*

Bibliography

I. *Selected chronological list of publications by Oliver St John Gogarty.**

'In Memoriam: Robert Louis Stevenson', Dublin: The Official Guide
Ltd. n.d. [1902].

'The Death of Diogenes, the Doctor's Dog', *T.C.D.: A College Miscellany*, IX (14 Feb. 1903), 16–17. See also: *T.C.D.: An Anthology*,
ed. D. A. Webb, Tralee: The Kerryman Ltd. 1945, 108–9.

'A Word on Criticism and "Broken Soil"', *The United Irishman*, 19
Dec. 1903, 6.

Review of *New Songs: A Lyric Selection by AE from Poems by
Padraic Colum et al.* in *Dana*, 1 (May 1904), 32.

'Winifred', *Dana*, 7 (Nov. 1904), 208.

'Song', 'On the Death of a Favourite Race Horse', and possibly 'The
Horse Show' and 'Welcome to the Fleet', *Ireland*, Vol. IV (Sept.
1904), 303, 311, 280, 283.

'To Stella', *Dana*, 5 (Sept. 1904), 144. Also appeared in *Ireland* as
'Song', in the same month.

'O'Connell Bridge', *Dana*, 7 (Nov. 1904), 215.

'Two Songs', ['My love is dark but she is fair', 'Gaze on me'], *The
Venture*, ed. Laurence Housman, W. Somerset Maughan, London:
John Baillie, n.d. [1904], 138.

'Molly', *Dana*, 10 (Feb. 1905), 308.

'The Irish Literary Revival: Present Poetry and Drama in Dublin',
The Dublin Evening Mail, 4 Mar. 1905, 2.

'In Haven', *The Oxford Magazine: A Weekly Newspaper and Review*,
7 Mar. 1906, 246.

'Ode on the Bicentenary of the Medical School, Trinity College', *The
Festival of the Bicentenary of the School of Physic in Ireland*, ed.
T. P. C. Kirkpatrick, Dublin: University Press 1912, 7–13.

* This list includes only major publications and certain individual items pertinent
to this study. A comprehensive bibliography of Gogarty's publications—juvenilia,
early pseudonymous, anonymous, and signed pieces, later reviews, articles,
prefaces, individual poems, and essays—beyond the scope of this present study,
must constitute a volume in itself.

Hyperthuleana, Dublin: F. J. Walker, at the Gaelic Press 1916 (25 copies), privately printed; Dermot Freyer's copy, bound by Galwey & Co., Dublin, bears a note that it is No. 5 and the '2' of the '25' is crossed out on the fly-leaf, suggesting that Gogarty distinguished the first five copies from the rest. Copy No. 2, at the National Library of Ireland, has Gogarty's holograph revisions, in it the second *e* of the title has been inked over by Gogarty with an *i*.

Alpha and Omega, *Blight: The Tragedy of Dublin: An Exposition in 3 Acts,* Dublin: Talbot Press 1917.

Secret Springs of Dublin Song, Dublin: Talbot Press 1918 (500 numbered copies of this anonymous collection printed). Preface by Susan Mitchell, contributors included Seumas O'Sullivan, AE (George W. Russell), W. Y. Tyrell, George Redding and Lord Dunsany, but Gogarty's work predominates. Gogarty's personal copy (at Bucknell University) contains his pencilled ascriptions.

The Ship and Other Poems, Dublin: Talbot Press, 1918. Five poems, with illustrations by Jack B. Yeats. (100 printed; most destroyed in the burning of Renvyle House.)

'Ouseley, Gideon', *A Serious Thing,* [Dublin] n.p. [1919] n.d.

'Ouseley, Gideon', *The Enchanted Trousers,* [Dublin] n.p. [1919] n.d.

An Offering of Swans, Dublin: Cuala Press 1923 (300 copies). Preface by W. B. Yeats, who selected the poems.

'Literature and Life Style', *The Irish Statesman,* 8 March 1924, 814–15.

An Offering of Swans and Other Poems, London: Eyre and Spottiswoode 1924, English edition of Cuala volume, 1923, with additional poems added.

Wild Apples, Dublin: Cuala Press, 1928 (50 copies), privately printed.

Wild Apples, New York: Jonathan Cape and Harrison Smith 1929. Preface by AE (George W. Russell). Not the same as either Cuala edition but a larger selection with 13 new poems that do not appear in the second Cuala edition.

Wild Apples, Dublin: Cuala Press 1930 (250 copies). Preface by W. B. Yeats, who selected the poems. Not the same as the 1928 edition but a selection from earlier volumes.

Selected Poems, New York: Macmillan 1933. Forewords by AE (George W. Russell) and Horace Reynolds.

As I Was Going Down Sackville Street, London: Rich and Cowan 1937. Reprinted April 1937.

As I Was Going Down Sackville Street, New York: Reynold & Hitchcock 1937. Second printing, April 1937. Third printing, May 1937. Differs significantly from the English edition.

'Tom Moore: A Master of Simile', *The Observer,* 15 August 1937, 4.

Others to Adorn, London: Rich and Cowan 1938. Three prefaces:

W. B. Yeats, from the Introduction to the *Oxford Book of Modern Verse*; forewords by AE and Horace Reynolds. *Selected Poems*, but with additional poems.

I Follow Saint Patrick, London: Rich and Cowan 1938. Reissued 1950.

I Follow Saint Patrick, New York: Reynold & Hitchcock 1938.

Epilogue to Scharmel, Iris, *Bread out of Stone*, Preface by W. B. Yeats, Chicago: Regnery n.d.

['Yeats'], *The Arrow*, Summer 1939, 19–20.

Tumbling in the Hay, London: Constable 1939.

Tumbling in the Hay, New York: Reynold & Hitchcock 1939.

Elbow Room, Dublin: Cuala Press 1939 (450 copies).

Going Native, New York: Duell, Sloane and Pearce 1940.

'The Joyce I Knew', *Saturday Review of Literature*, XXIII, 14 (25 Jan. 1941), 3–4, 15–16. See also *The Saturday Review Gallery*, ed. J. Beatty Jr. New York: Simon & Schuster 1959, 251–60.

Going Native, London: Constable 1941.

Mad Grandeur, Philadelphia: Lippincott 1941.

Elbow Room and Additional Poems, New York: Duell, Sloane and Pearce 1942. 75 signed copies with an etching, dry point, of the author by Gerald Leslie Brockhurst were also produced.

Mad Grandeur, London: Constable 1943.

Perennial, Baltimore, Maryland: Contemporary Poetry 1944. vol. I, Distinguished Poets Series of *Contemporary Poetry*, ed. Mary Owings Miller.

Perennial, London: Constable 1946. Same as *Perennial*, 1944, with the exception of four omitted poems.

Mr. Petunia, New York: Creative Age 1945.

Mr. Petunia, London: Constable 1946.

'My Favourite Forgotten Book', *Tomorrow*, V (May 1946), 78.

Mourning Becomes Mrs Spendlove, New York: Creative Age 1948.

Rolling Down the Lea, London: Constable 1949.

James Augustine Joyce, Dallas: *The Times Herald* 1949. Unpaginated pamphlet.

'They Think They Know Joyce', *Saturday Review of Literature*, XXXIII, 11 (18 March 1950), 8–9, 35–7. See also *The Saturday Review Gallery*, ed. J. Beatty Jr., New York: Simon & Schuster, 1959, 261–8.

Intimations, New York: Abelard Press, 1950.

Collected Poems, London: Constable 1951 (500 copies); New York: Devin-Adair 1954. Three prefaces: W. B. Yeats, from the Introduction to the *Oxford Book of Modern Verse*; forewords by AE and Horace Reynolds, all as in *Others to Adorn*.

Unselected Poems, Baltimore Maryland: Contemporary Poetry

1954, vol. X, Distinguished Poets Series, ed. Mary Owings Miller.

It Isn't This Time of Year at All! (An Unpremeditated Autobiography), Garden City, New York: Doubleday 1954.

It Isn't This Time of Year at All! (An Unpremeditated Autobiography), London: Macgibbon & Kee 1954.

Start from Somewhere Else: An Exposition of Wit and Humor Polite and Perilous, Garden City, New York: Doubleday 1955.

A Week End in the Middle of the Week and Other Essays on the Bias, Garden City, New York: Doubleday 1958. Posthumous publication with an introductory essay, 'Portrait of a Friend from Ireland', by Ben Lucien Burman.

William Butler Yeats: A Memoir, Dublin: Dolmen, 1963. Posthumous publication with Preface by Myles Dillon.

Many Lines to Thee: Letters to G. K. A. Bell from the Martello Tower at Sandycove, Rutland Square and Trinity College Dublin, 1904–1907, Dublin: Dolmen 1971. Posthumous publication edited with a commentary by James F. Carens.

The Plays of Oliver St. John Gogarty, Newark, Delaware: Proscenium Press 1972 (500 copies). Introduction by James F. Carens.

II. *Other works consulted*

AE (George W. Russell), 'The Poems of Oliver Gogarty', *The Irish Statesman*, 14 Dec. 1929, 299–300.

A.K., Review of *I Follow Saint Patrick*, in *The Dublin Magazine*, 13, No. 4 (1938), 72–7.

Amory, Mark, *Biography of Lord Dunsany*, London: Collins 1972.

Beckett, Samuel, *Murphy*, London: Routledge 1938; New York: Grove Press 1957.

Boyle, Robert, S. J., Review of *James Joyce: The Critical Heritage*, ed. Robert H. Deming, *James Joyce Quarterly*, VIII, 3 (Spring, 1971), 270–2.

Campbell, Joseph, *The Hero with a Thousand Faces*, Princeton: University Press 1968.

Carens, James, 'Four Revival Figures: Lady Gregory, AE (George W. Russell), Oliver St John Gogarty, and James Stephens', in *Anglo-Irish Literature: A Review of Research*, ed. R. J. Finneran, New York: Modern Language Association 1976, 436–69.

Carens, James, 'Gogarty and Yeats', in *Modern Irish Literature*, ed. R. J. Porter and J. A. Brophy, New York: Iona-Twayne 1977, 67–93.

Carens, James, 'Joyce and Gogarty', in *New Light on Joyce*, ed. Fritz Senn, Bloomington: Indiana University Press 1972, 28–45.

Cixous, Hélène, *L'Exil de James Joyce; ou l'art du remplacement*, Paris : Bernard Grasset 1968.

Cixous, Hélène, *The Exile of James Joyce*, translated from the French by Sally A. J. Purcell, New York : D. Lewis 1972.

Clark, David R., *Lyric Resonance: Glosses on Some Poems of Yeats, Frost, Crane, Cummings and others*, Amherst : University of Massachusetts Press 1972.

Coogan, Timothy Patrick, *Ireland since the Rising*, London : Pall Mall Press 1966; New York : Praeger 1966.

Dunsany, Lord, *My Ireland*, London : Jarrolds 1937; New York : Funk & Wagnalls 1937.

Eliot, T. S., *Collected Poems, 1909–1935*, New York : Harcourt Brace 1946; London : Faber 1958.

Eliot, T. S., *Selected Essays*, New York : Harcourt Brace 1950; London : Faber 1951.

Ellmann, Richard, *James Joyce*, New York : Oxford University Press 1959.

Ellmann, Richard, *James Joyce's Tower*, Dun Laoghaire : Eastern Regional Tourism Organisation 1969.

Ellmann, Richard, 'What'll we Make of you, Bucko?', *New York Herald Tribune Book Week*, 12 Apr. 1964, 5, 14.

Frye, Northrop, *Anatomy of Criticism: Four Essays*, Princeton : University Press 1957.

Gibbon, Monk, *The Masterpiece and the Man: Yeats as I Knew Him*, London : Rupert Hart-Davis 1959; New York : Macmillan 1959.

Gogarty, Oliver D., 'My Brother Willie was your Father's Friend', *Bibliotheca Bucknellensis*, VII (1969), 1–13.

Henn, T. R., 'The Rhetoric of Yeats', *In Excited Reverie: A Centenary Tribute to William Butler Yeats*, ed. A. Norman Jeffares and K. G. W. Cross, New York : Macmillan 1965, 102–22.

Hewson, Michael, 'Gogarty's Authorship of *Blight*', *Irish Book*, 1 (1959), 19–20.

Holloway, Joseph, 'Impressions of a Dublin Playgoer', MS. National Library of Ireland.

Hogan, Robert and O'Neill, Michael J., eds. *Joseph Holloway's Abbey Theatre: A Selection from his Unpublished Journal 'Impressions of a Dublin Playgoer'*, Carbondale, Ill. : Southern Illinois University Press 1967.

Hogan, Robert and O'Neill, Michael J., eds., *Joseph Holloway's Irish Theatre*, 3 vols., Dixon, California : Proscenium Press 1968–70.

Holroyd, Michael, *Augustus John*, New York : Holt, Rinehart and Winston 1974, 1975.

John, Augustus, *Chiaroscuro: Fragments of Autobiography*, London:
    Jonathan Cape 1952; New York: Pellegrini & Cudahy 1952.
Jones, Alun R., *The Life and Opinions of T. E. Hulme*, Boston:
    Beacon Press 1960.
Joyce, James, *Letters*, ed. Stuart Gilbert, New York: Viking Press
    1957.
Joyce, James, *Selected Letters*, ed. Richard Ellmann, London: Faber,
    1976.
Joyce, James, *Letters*, vols II and III, ed. Richard Ellmann, New York:
    Viking Press 1966.
Joyce, James, *Ulysses*, London: The Bodley Head 1936; New York:
    Random House 1961.
Joyce, Stanislaus, *The Complete Dublin Diary*, ed. George H. Healey,
    Ithaca: Cornell University Press 1971.
Joyce, Stanislaus, *My Brother's Keeper: James Joyce's Early Years*,
    London: Faber 1958; New York: Viking 1958.
Kennedy, Sighle, *Murphy's Bed: A Study of Real Sources and Sur-Real
    Associations in Samuel Beckett's First Novel*, Lewisburg, Penna:
    Bucknell University Press 1971.
Larkin, Philip, ed., *The Oxford Book of Twentieth-Century English
    Verse*, Oxford: Clarendon Press 1973.
Leslie, Seymour, *The Jerome Connexion*, London: John Murray 1964.
Malone, Andrew, *The Irish Drama*, London: Constable 1929; New
    York: B. Blom 1965.
Melchori, Georgio, *The Whole Mystery of Art: Pattern into Poetry in
    the Work of W. B. Yeats*, London: Routledge & Kegan Paul 1950;
    New York: Macmillan 1961.
Miller, Liam, ed., *Retrospect: The Work of Seumas O'Sullivan (1879–
    1958) and Estella F. Solomons (1882–1968)*, Dublin: Dolmen Press
    1973.
Moore, George, *Hail and Farewell*, 3 vols., London: Heinemann 1947;
    2 vols. New York: Appleton 1925.
Moore, George, *The Lake*, London: Heinemann 1921; New York:
    Appleton 1926.
O'Brien, Darcy, *W. R. Rodgers*, Lewisburg, Penna: Bucknell University
    Press 1970.
O'Connor, Frank, *Kings, Lords and Commons: An Anthology from the
    Irish*, New York: Knopf 1959; London: Macmillan 1961; Dublin:
    Gill and Macmillan 1970.
O'Connor, Frank, *My Father's Son*, Dublin: Gill and Macmillan 1968;
    New York: Knopf 1967.
O'Connor, Ulick, *Oliver St John Gogarty: A Poet and His Times*,
    London: Jonathan Cape 1964.

O'Connor, Ulick, *The Times I've seen: Oliver St John Gogarty. A Biography*, New York: I. Oblensky [1964].

O'Faolain, Sean, *Vive Moi!*, Boston: Little Brown 1964.

Official Report Seanad Eireann, vols. I–XX, Dublin: Thom & Co. n.d.

O'Shea, Edward, *Yeats as Editor*, Dublin: Dolmen Press 1975.

Pyle, Hilary, *James Stephens, His Work and an Account of His Life*, London: Routledge & Kegan Paul 1965; New York: Barnes & Noble 1965.

Robinson, Lennox, ed., *Lady Gregory's Journals, 1916–1930*, London: Putnam 1946; New York: Macmillan 1947.

Rodgers, W. R., *Irish Literary Portraits*, London: British Broadcasting Corporation 1972; New York: Taplinger 1973 [1972].

Rothenstein, William, *Since Fifty* (vol. III, *Men and Memories*), London: Faber 1939; New York: Coward-McCann 1939.

Scholes, Robert and Kane, Richard M., *The Workshop of Dedalus: James Joyce and the Materials for 'A Portrait of the Artist as a Young Man'*, Evanston: Northwestern University Press 1965.

Scholes, Robert, *The Cornell Joyce Collection: A Catalogue*, Ithaca: Cornell University Press 1961.

Stallworthy, Jon, 'Yeats as Anthologist', *In Excited Reverie: A Centenary Tribute to William Butler Yeats*, ed. A. Norman Jeffares and K. G. W. Cross, New York: St Martin's Press 1965, 171–92.

Thody, Philip, *Aldous Huxley: A Biographical Introduction*, New York: Scribner's 1973.

Trench, C. E. F., 'Dermot Chenevix Trench and Haines of *Ulysses*', James Joyce Quarterly, 13, No. 1 (1975), 39–48.

Yeats, W. B., *Collected Poems*, London: Macmillan 1950, 2nd ed.; New York: Macmillan 1956.

Yeats, W. B., ed., *The Oxford Book of Modern Verse, 1892–1935*, London and New York: Oxford University Press 1936.

Yeats, W. B., *Letters*, ed. Allan Wade, London: Hart Davis 1954; New York: Macmillan 1955.

Yeats, W. B., *Letters on Poetry from W. B. Yeats to Dorothy Wellesley*, ed. Dorothy Wellesley, Introduction by Kathleen Raine, London and New York: Oxford University Press 1964.

Yeats, W. B., *Modern Poetry*, London: British Broadcasting Corporation 1936.

Index